THE CHURCH AS THE BODY OF CHRIST IN THE PAULINE CORPUS

A Re-examination

Gosnell L.O.R. Yorke

Atlantic Union College

BS
2655.
.C5
Y67
1991

UNIVERSITY
PRESS OF
AMERICA

Lanham • New York • London

University Press of America®, Inc.
4720 Boston Way
Lanham, Maryland 20706

3 Henrietta Street
London WC2E 8LU England

Library of Congress Cataloging-in-Publication Data

Yorke, Gosnell L. O. R., 1953-
The church as the body of Christ in the Pauline corpus :
a re-examination / Gosnell L.O.R. Yorke.
p.   cm.
Rev. of thesis (doctoral)—McGill University, Montreal, 1987.
Includes bibliographical references and indexes.
1. Bible.   N.T.   Epistles of Paul—Criticism, interpretation, etc.
2. Jesus Christ—Mystical body—History of doctrines—
Early church, ca. 30-600.   3. Church—Biblical teaching.
4. Soma (The Greek word)
I. Title.
BS2655.C5Y67   1991
262'.77'09015—dc20   91-7870 CIP

ISBN 0–8191–8215–X
ISBN 0–8191–8216–8 (pbk.)

 The paper used in this publication meets the minimum requirements of
American National Standard for Information Sciences—Permanence
of Paper for Printed Library Materials, ANSI Z39.48–1984.

To

Doreen, my dear wife,

whom I have been

counseled to love

as I love my own

σῶμα.

(Eph. 5:28)

TABLE OF CONTENTS

LIST OF ABBREVIATIONS

Commentaries

AB	Anchor Bible
ABC	Abingdon Bible Commentary
CBC	Cambridge Bible Commentary
EKKNT	Evangelisch-Katholische Kommentar zum Neuen Testament
Herm.	Hermeneia
HNTC	Harper's New Testament Commentary
ICC	International Critical Commentary
MNTC	Moffatt's New Testament Commentary
NCB	New Century Bible
NICNT	New International Commentary of the New Testament
OBS	Oxford Bible Series
PCB	Peake's Commentary on the Bible
TCB	The Century Bible
TNTC	Tyndale New Testament Commentary

Journals

AAR	*American Academy of Religion*
AER	*American Ecclesiastical Review*
BTB	*Biblical Theology Bulletin*
BZ	*Biblische Zeitschrift*
CBQ	*Catholic Biblical Quarterly*
CyF	*Ciencia y Fe*
E.T.	*Ecumenical Trends*
EThL	*Ephemerides Theologicae Lovanienses*
EvQ	*Evangelical Quarterly*
HTR	*Harvard Theological Review*
IER	*Irish Ecclesiastical Record*
Int.	*Interpretation*
Intn.	*Interchange*
ITQ	*Irish Theological Quarterly*
JAAR	*Journal of the American Academy of Religion*
JBL	*Journal of Biblical Literature*
JBR	*Journal of Bible and Religion*
JES	*Journal of Ecumenical Studies*
JSNT	*Journal for the Study of the New Testament*
JSOT	*Journal for the Study of the Old Testament*

JTS	*Journal of Theological Studies*
Jur.	*Jurist*
Nov. T.	*Novum Testamentum*
NTS	*New Testament Studies*
RB	*Revue Biblique*
RSR	*Recherches de Science Religieuse*
RThPh	*Revue de Théologie et de Philosophie*
SBT	*Studies in Biblical Theology*
Sc.et Ex.	*Science et Esprit*
SJT	*Scottish Journal of Theology*
SR	*Studies in Religion/Sciences Religieuses*
SVTQ	*St. Vladimir's Theological Quarterly*
TLZ	*Theologische Literaturzeitung*
TT	*Theology Today*
USQR	*Union Seminary Quarterly Review*
VC	*Verbum Caro*
V.C.	*Vigiliae Christianae*
VD	*Verbum Domini*
VT	*Vetus Testamentum*

Other Abbreviations

A (σῶμα)	The *Anthropological* use of σῶμα in the Pauline Corpus
ARC	A Newsletter published by the Faculty of Religious Studies of McGill University, its affiliated colleges (Anglican, Presbyterian and United Church) and the Montreal Institute for Ministry (Roman Catholic).
AUSDDS	Andrews University Seminary Doctoral Dissertation Series
BDF	Blass, F., Debrunner, A., and Funk, R. *A Greek Grammar of the New Testament and Other Early Christian Literature* (Chicago: Chicago University Press, 1962).
B.E.M.	Baptism, Eucharist and Ministry
Bib. Ant.	The Biblical Antiquities of Philo
C (σῶμα)	The *Christological* use of σῶμα in the Pauline Corpus
Con.	Concilium
E (σῶμα)	The *Ecclesiological* use of σῶμα in the Pauline Corpus
ET	English Translation
Exo.R.	Exodus Rabbah
HDR	Harvard Dissertations in Religion
IDB	Interpreter's Dictionary of the Bible
IDBSup.	Interpreter's Dictionary of the Bible--Supplement
LXX	Septuagint

ix

MS(S)	Manuscript(s)
M.Sanh.	Mishnah Sanhedrin
MT	Masoretic Text
NCE	New Catholic Encyclopedia
RSV	Revised Standard Version
	Scripture quotations are from the Revised Standard Version Bible, copyright 1946, 1952, 1971 by the Division of Christian Education of the National Council of the Churches of Christ in the USA. Used by permission.
SBLSP	Society of Biblical Literature Seminar Papers
SNTSMS	Society for New Testament Studies Monograph Series
TDNT	Theological Dictionary of the New Testament
Trall.	Ignatius' letter to the Trallians
W.C.C.	World Council of Churches
WD	World Development

PREFACE

This book is a revision of a doctoral thesis submitted in 1987 to, and accepted by, the Faculty of Religious Studies of McGill University, Montreal, Canada. The idea for the thesis was conceived in the Fall of 1978 while working on my first graduate research project in New Testament Ecclesiology (at McGill University) under Dr. George Johnston. When I later became his Teaching Assistant and a student in his graduate seminar, The Church in the New Testament, I became even more convinced that the idea, as conceived earlier, should not be aborted but instead, brought to full term.

This decision was rendered all the more defensible as I painstakingly made my way through the mountain of materials relevant to the investigation. I discovered that, for the most part, contradiction and confusion rather than clarity and coherence, marked and marred the discussion; and that there were no more than the scattered and undeveloped suggestions of a few scholars who seem to be nudging us in a direction somewhat compatible with the thesis to be advanced in this study, which is, that when used of the Church in the Pauline corpus, σῶμα points not to Christ's once crucified and now risen body, as an overwhelming number of scholars assume and assert, but that it (σῶμα) simply and consistently refers to the human body, any human body. This is so, it is contended, even when and where contingent mention is made of Christ as κεφαλή of the Church.

I am especially grateful to the following who were exceedingly helpful either during the long gestation period of the thesis or later, during the revision process itself:

(1) Dr. N. Thomas Wright, my supervisor, who, in his perceptive comments on, and criticisms of, earlier drafts of some chapters, forced me more than once to "think again". More than that, he was also willing, via phone and pen, to continue his supervision from a distance during the very late stages of the thesis. This was necessitated by his relocating to Worcester College, Oxford University.

(2) The librarians at the Canadian Centre for Ecumenism (Montreal); in particular, Bernice Baranowski who made it possible for me to use not only the library at the Centre but who also made arrangements so that I could have full access to the much larger library of the Roman Catholic Seminary there (i.e., Le Grand Séminaire).

(3) Atlantic Union College, especially Dr. Edward Lugenbeal, Vice President for Academic Affairs, whose office made available financial and then secretarial assistance in the person of Ellen Fisk-Biek. Had it not been for Ellen's uncanny ability to be both quick and careful, this revision would not have been given "published recognition" as quickly as it was. In this regard, grateful mention must also be made of both Prof. Jared Bruckner, who

generously made us beneficiaries of his computer literacy, and of Dr. Lethiel Parson, Director of the College Library, who carefully proofread the manuscript from beginning to end.

(4) And finally, Doreen, my most patient wife who tolerated my numerous and sometimes prolonged absences from home during both the thesis preparation and the later revision for this book. More than that, she also allowed me to use her as a "sparring partner" whenever I was around. I would throw at her one idea after another having to do with σῶμα; and I would do so in an attempt to engage her in conversation so that I might convince myself, sometimes, that what I was thinking and writing was making sense. To her, my "sparring partner" and spouse, not to mention my three children, Chrystal, Oumari and Kanyika, each of whom must now know what it means to feel like a fatherless child, I owe a great debt of gratitude.

INTRODUCTION

In recent years, and especially in ecumenical circles, much thoughtful discussion has been centering on issues pertaining to the origin, nature, purpose, polity, the so-called post-Constantinian period, the post-modern predicament, and sometimes even the death of the church.[1] In fact, Avery Dulles has reminded us in his perceptive comments on *Lumen Gentium*, Vatican II's document on the church, that the 20th century as a whole, "has often been called the century of the church."[2] Also, Eric Jay and others have long suggested that the reasons for this 20th century scholarly preoccupation with ecclesiology are many and that they are based on factors resident both within and without the church itself.

According to some, as many as ten reasons can be adduced to account for this phenomenon among which are the following: (1) the church's response to an ever-increasing scientization of the world in which the historical, natural and social sciences, in their own way, seek to foster a sceptical rationality that at times seems inhospitable to the Christian faith; (2) the 'coming of age' of many within the church who are now adamant in their insistence that all the people of God--especially ethnic minorities and women--should now be able to share, to a greater measure, in the joys and duties of the church; and (3) the dawning recognition that the church cannot be apolitical in its presence and influence in society; that if it is not to stultify its witness, the church must more and more exhibit a preferential option for the poor and the powerless; the forsaken and the forgotten.[3]

Be that as it may, most scholars who write about the church consider it self-evident that meaningful and prolonged reflection necessitates constant reference to, and engaging dialogue with, the *fons et origo* of the ecclesiological traditions enshrined in the N.T. Following the lead of Paul S. Minear and others, most of them are now convinced that within the N.T., one encounters a plurality of images or metaphors used to describe those who had come to experience the communal joy of spiritual fellowship with their risen Lord.[4]

The ecclesiological image which has been given pride of place during much of the discussion is that of the body of Christ, i.e., σῶμα Χριστοῦ. It is true that Herwi Rikhof, among others, has correctly discerned a recent tendency particularly in Roman Catholic ecclesiology since Vatican II. This tendency has to do with the attempt to demote σῶμα Χριστοῦ as the dominant ecclesiological image in favour of that of another: the λαὸς τοῦ Θεοῦ.[5] It is a tendency which is also evident in B.E.M., arguably the most ecumenically significant document ever drafted by the Faith and Order Commission of the W.C.C.[6] However, as Brown has since prophesied, it is only a matter of time before σῶμα Χριστοῦ as ecclesiological language comes into its own again.[7]

Today, there is hardly any N.T. scholar writing about the church who fails to refer to and reflect upon σῶμα Χριστοῦ.[8] And so far, there have been at least eleven σῶμα issues to which these scholars have devoted some if not most of their critical attention. Such issues include the following: (1) the relationship between Christ's crucified but now risen σῶμα and the church as σῶμα; (2) the relationship between Col./Eph. where Christ is identified as κεφαλή of the church and 1 Cor./Rom. where no such κεφαλή-Christ ecclesiological connection is made; (3) the nature, diversity and theology of the charisms; (4) the relationship of σῶμα Χριστοῦ to other ecclesiological images found both within and without the *corpus Paulinum*; (5) the source(s) from which, supposedly, the Pauline σῶμα ecclesiology was culled; (6) the multi-cultural and multi-racial relevance of σῶμα; (7) its implications for gender equality within the church; (8) its sociological significance; (9) its ecumenical ramifications; (10) its potential for an ecological theology; and (11) its socio-political possibilities.

It is because of this wealth of information on the subject that one may be tempted to think, sometimes, that there remains nothing significant to contribute to the discussion. However, such a temptation, it will be shown, must be resisted.[9] Like other issues in N.T. studies, the mere existence of an abundance of literature on the subject does not necessarily indicate issue resolution. In fact, it seems more often to indicate the reverse.[10]

With regard to σῶμα as ecclesiological language, three N.T. scholars in particular have been quite helpful in re-enforcing our conviction that "all is not well'; that a re-examination of some aspects of σῶμα is desperately needed. First, there is R. Jewett. After devoting just over 100 pages to a careful reviewing and critiquing of mainly the German contribution to the discussion throughout the first seven decades of this century, Jewett called for the immediate formulation of an hypothesis which will serve to eliminate the ecclesiological confusion that σῶμα still generates. For Jewett, this is so especially in relation to the prevailing understanding of Paul's use of the motif in 1 Cor. *vis-à-vis* Rom.[11]

Second, there is Käsemann. In spite of the fact that a plethora of Catholic, Episcopalian (Anglican) and Protestant scholars has dealt with the issue over the years, and that in 1933, he himself wrote a doctoral thesis on the subject, Käsemann, in his magisterial commentary on Rom., could still suggest, forty years later (1973), that a monograph is needed to handle adequately some yet unresolved issues. As far as Käsemann is concerned, "obscurity still surrounds the entire question."[12]

And third, there is Gundry. Writing in 1976 in the last chapter of his book and in relation to a brief discussion of the σῶμα Χριστοῦ issue, he remarked: "That concept warrants a whole book."[13] Gundry basically takes issue with others like J.A.T. Robinson whose incautious use of language would suggest that Paul is a proponent of what may generally be referred to as a brand of "transubstantiationary ecclesiology" in which the church, collectively speaking, becomes the actual body of Christ during its moments of eucharistic sharing and celebration.[14]

To date, no one (in our judgment) has been able to resolve satisfactorily one of the most basic issues pertaining to the σῶμα debate. Our conviction remains unshaken not only after having consulted Dulles' and Granfield's most informative bibliographical update on the subject but also after having perused Perriman's more recent and provocative treatment of it.[15]

The basic and unresolved issue to which we address ourselves in this study can be raised by way of a series of crucial questions. And they are: (1) Should we, and if so, how should we relate the word, σῶμα, referring to the physical body of Jesus, the already exalted Lord, to σῶμα, in referring to the church? Are these two σῶματα one and the same--perhaps in some ill-defined and "mystical" sense?[16] Or, (2) should Jesus' own physical σῶμα be used as the metaphorical backdrop against which the church as σῶμα is to be discussed? That is, are we to understand that the church is a body which is only like (and, contrary to the first question, not identical to), Jesus' physical body, namely, that crucified, earthly body which has since been raised and now glorified by God through the power of the Spirit?[17]

Those N.T. scholars who address these two questions pertaining to this σῶμα-σῶμα relationship and their implications for the larger issue regarding the relationship between Christ and the church, generally join the queue on one side or the other; and especially on the basis of 1 Cor. where σῶμα as ecclesiological language first appears. Further, an understanding of this σῶμα-σῶμα relationship based upon its assumed usage in 1 Cor. is used as the norm by which to measure its other usages scattered throughout the *corpus Paulinum* --either in terms of developments of, or deviations from it.

We consider this σῶμα-σῶμα issue crucial because it is one which is urgently in need of a resolution if we are ever to take up the challenge particularly of Jewett and Gundry. Also, we suggest that its resolution should precede any attempt to relate meaningfully σῶμα as ecclesiological language to those other images within the Pauline corpus as well as to those within the N.T. as a whole. Without a determination of what Paul wants to convey about the church as σῶμα, it is rather unlikely that we will be in a position to relate σῶμα to other ecclesiological images anywhere in the N.T.--be it by way of comparison or contrast.

In brief, and anticipating much of what is ahead of us, then, it is our contention that the two σῶμα questions abovementioned, focussed as they are on the personal body of Christ, are ill-posed; that instead, σῶμα, with regard to the church, has the human body as its metaphorical referent. Among other things, therefore, this study will be a grammatico-historical and exegetical attempt to buttress a thesis which will be at odds with any "solution" which considers the church as body and Jesus' physical body as being one and the same mystically; or any "solution" which suggests that the two σώματα are in some sort of direct metaphorical relationship with each other.

It is for this reason, therefore, that we choose to stand in solidarity with Jewett, Käsemann, Gundry and a few others who insist that the last word has not been said with regard to σῶμα as ecclesiological language within the Pauline corpus. For us, there is still at least one fundamental question to which a defensible and perhaps, a definitive answer has not yet been given, namely, the nature of the σῶμα-σῶμα relationship in particular and its implications for the larger issue regarding the church-Christ relationship in general.

Before we proceed, however, we should at least make mention of the fact that this study does not purport to be a full-blown exposition of Pauline Christology and/or ecclesiology per se. Admittedly, we do register this caveat with the consciousness that in a study such as ours, devoted as it is to a close-up and single-minded examination of just one ecclesiological "tree", our perspective can become skewed.

The risk we are taking here is that we can become so myopic that we also come across as being oblivious to, and unaffected by, the size and shape of "the larger forest." Strauss, for example, comes to mind. In commenting on his treatment of the Gospel narratives, Hawkin tells us that Strauss' treatment is so meticulous and detailed that, "often his readers could not see the forest for the trees."[18]

The possibility of this happening to us, however, will be greatly minimized (if not entirely eliminated) since we will be making periodic forays into the larger Christological and ecclesiological "forest" while at the same time keeping our eyes fixed and focussed on our "tree", that is, on the theme of σῶμα as ecclesiological language within the Pauline corpus.

ENDNOTES

Introduction

1. See R.N. Flew, ed., *The Nature of the Church* (New York: Harper & Row, 1952); K. McNamara, "The Idea of Church: Modern Developments in Ecclesiology," *ITQ* 33 (1966):99-113; K. Rahner, *The Shape of the Church to Come* (London: S.P C.K., 1974), pp. 19-28; T.G. Bissonette, "Communidades Ecclesiales de Base: Some Contemporary Attempts to Build Ecclesial *Koinonia*," *Jur.* 36 (1976): 24-58.; D.J. Hall, *Has The Church A Future?* (Philadelphia: The Westminster Press, 1980); *idem, Thinking The Faith: Christian Theology in a North American Context* (Minneapolis: Augsburg, 1989), pp. 11-14. H. Küng, *The Church Maintained in Truth: A Theological Meditation* (New York: The Seabury Press, 1980); *idem, Theology for the Third Millenium: An Ecumenical View*, trans. by Peter Heinegg (New York: Doubleday, 1988), pp. 95f.; T.C. Bruneau, "The Catholic Church and Development in Latin America: The Role of the Basic Christian Communities," *WD* 8(1980):535-544. S. Dianich, "The Current State of Ecclesiology", in *Where Does The Church Stand?* Edited by G. Alberigo *et al., Con.*, vol. 146 (New York: The Seabury Press, 1981), pp. 92-97; H. Fries and K. Rahner, *Einigung der Kirchen - reale Möglichkeit* (Freiburg: Harder, 1983); John R. Williams, ed., *Canadian Churches and Social Justice* (Toronto: Anglican Book Centre and James Lorimer, 1984); Leonardo Boff, *Ecclesiogenesis: The Base Communities Reinvent the Church* (Maryknoll, NY: Orbis Books, 1986); James Cobble, *The Church and the Powers: A Theology of Church Structure* (Peabody, MA: Hendrickson Publishers, 1988); and Frederic Burnham, ed., *Post-Modern Theology: Christian Faith in a Pluralist World* (San Francisco: Harper & Row, 1989), pp. 37-55.

2. Walter M. Abbott, ed. *The Documents of Vatican II,* (New York: Guild Press, 1966), p. 9. Actually, Dulles attributes this remark to Otto Dibelius, a Lutheran theologian. For that, see Avery Dulles and Patrick Granfield, *The Church: A Bibliography* (Delaware: Michael Glazier, 1985), pp. 9f. Küng also reminds us that, "there is much talk nowadays about the Church in the secular world." See, *The Church* (New York: Image Books, 1976), p. 11. According to Eric Jay: "Never before has such close attention been paid to the question of the nature of the Church. The number of books, major articles, and reports of conferences on the subject is immense." See, *The Church: Its Changing Image Through Twenty Centuries, vol 2--1700 To The Present Day* (London: S.P.C.K., 1978), p.79.

3. See Jay, *ibid.*; Küng, *op. cit.*, pp. 21-24; R. Aubert, ed., "Prophets in the Church," in *Theology in the Age of Renewal, Con.*, vol. 37 (New York: Paulist Press, 1968), p. 149; K. Rahner, *op. cit.*, pp. 19-28; J. Moltmann, *The Church in the Power of the Spirit: A Contribution to Messianic Ecclesiology* (New York: Harper & Row, 1977); *idem, On Human Dignity: Political Theology and Ethics*, trans. by M. Douglas Meeks. (Philadelphia: Fortress

Press, 1984), pp. 87-92; J. Miranda, *Communism in the Bible*, trans. by R. Barr (New York: Orbis Books, 1982), pp. 67f.; and Caleb Rosado, *Women•Church•God: A Socio-Biblical Study* (California: Loma Linda University Press, 1990).

4. See Theophilus M. Taylor, "Kingdom, Family, Temple, and Body: Implications from the Biblical Doctrine of the Church for the Christian Attitude Amid Cultural and Racial Tensions," *Int.* 12 (1958): 174-193; P.S. Minear, *Images of the Church in the New Testament* (Philadelphia: The Westminster Press, 1960); G. Johnston, "The Doctrine of the Church in the New Testament," in *PCB*, edited by M. Black (Edinburgh: Thomas Nelson and Sons, 1962), pp. 719-723; R.E. Brown, "The Unity and Diversity in New Testament Ecclesiology," in *New Testament Essays* (New York: Doubleday, 1965), p. 72; A. Dulles, *Models of the Church* (New York: Doubleday, 1974), pp. 17-30; R.P. Martin, *The Family and the Fellowship: New Testament Images of the Church* (Grand Rapids: Wm. B. Eerdmans Publishing Co., 1979); J.H. Elliott, *A Home for the Homeless: A Sociological Exegesis of 1 Peter - Its Situation and Strategy* (Philadelphia: Fortress Press, 1981); David Balch, *Let Wives Be Submissive: The Domestic Code in 1 Peter* (Chico: Scholars Press, 1981); Carl S. Dudley and Earle Hilgert, *New Testament Tensions and the Contemporary Church* (Philadelphia: Fortress Press, 1987); and Daniel Donovan, *The Church As Idea and Fact* (Delaware: Michael Glazier, 1988). For Donovan, "NT ecclesiology is dominated by the use of images." See p. 21.

5. Herwi Rikhof, *The Concept of Church: A Methodological Inquiry into the Use of Metaphors in Ecclesiology* (London: Sheed and Ward, 1981), pp. 11-66; Also see Edmund Clowney, "Interpreting the Biblical Models of the Church: A Hermeneutical Deepening of Ecclesiology," in *Biblical Interpretation and the Church: The Problem of Contextualization*, edited by D.A. Carson (Nashville: Thomas Nelson Publishers, 1984), pp. 64-109.

6. B.E.M. was drafted Jan., 1982, in Lima, Peru, as Paper #111 of the Faith and Order Commission of the W.C.C. For more on this, see, *inter alios, Baptism, Eucharist and Ministry* (Geneva: World Council of Churches, 1982); M. Thurian, ed., *Ecumenical Perspectives on Baptism, Eucharist and Ministry* (Geneva: World Council of Churches, 1983); J.K.S. Reid, "Article Review: Baptism, Eucharist and Ministry," *SJT* 37 (1984): 519-527; Lorna Shoemaker, "Feminist Symposium on Baptism, Eucharist, and Ministry," *E.T.* 10 (November, 1984): 155-158; the entire issue of *JES* 21 (Winter, 1984); and Melanie May, "The Ordination of Women: The Churches' Response to Baptism, Eucharist and Ministry," *JES* 26 (1989): 251-269.

7. R.E. Brown, *The Churches the Apostles Left Behind* (New York: Paulist Press, 1984), pp. 58-60. For a discussion of the relatively recent stress on People of God in N.T. Ecclesiology, see D.J. Harrington, *God's People in Christ: New Testament Perspectives on the Church and Judaism* (Philadelphia: Fortress Press, 1980). For an attempt to contrast σῶμα Χριστοῦ with λαὸς τοῦ Θεοῦ, see George S. Worgul, Jr., "People of God, Body of Christ: Pauline Ecclesiological Contrasts," *BTB* 12 (1982): 24-28. And for an attempt to articulate the

σῶμα ecclesiology within a trinitarian framework, namely, the People of *God*, the Body of *Christ* and the Incarnating of the *Spirit*, see G. Johnston, *The Doctrine of the Church in the New Testament* (Cambridge: At the University Press, 1943), pp. 76-102. Cf. Jay, *The Church*, vol. 2, p. 195; and Donovan, *The Church*, p. 54, where mention is made of the *temple* of the Spirit rather than the Incarnating of the Spirit as in Johnston, *supra*. For a recent stress on σῶμα Χριστοῦ see Helen Doohan, *Paul's Vision of Church* (Delaware: Michael Glazier, 1989).

8. See D.J. Harrington, *Light of All Nations: Essays on the Church in New Testament Research* (Delaware: Michael Glazier, 1982); and E. Earle Ellis, *Pauline Theology: Ministry and Society* (Grand Rapids: Wm.B. Eerdmans, 1989), pp. 26-52 and 87-102.

9. In his published 1978 Cambridge dissertation, Wayne Grudem, for example, has shown that σῶμα Χριστοῦ is still generating issues that are worthy of serious investigation. See, *The Gift of Prophecy in 1 Corinthians* (Washington, D.C.: University Press of America, 1982). Also see Donald G. Boyd, "Spirit and Church in 1 Corinthians 12-14 and the Acts of the Apostles," in *Spirit Within Structure: Essays in Honor of George Johnston on the Occasion of His Seventieth Birthday*, edited by E.J. Furcha (Pennsylvania: Pickwick Publications, 1983), pp. 55-66; Victor Guénel (ed.), *Le Corps et Le Corps Du Christ dans la Prémière Épître aux Corinthiens* (Paris: Cerf, 1983); R.P. Martin, *The Spirit and the Congregation: Studies in 1 Corinthians 12-15* (Grand Rapids: Wm.B. Eerdmans, 1984); Terrance Callan, "Prophecy and Ecstasy in Graeco-Roman Religion and in 1 Corinthians," *Nov. T.* 27 (1985): 125-140; and W. Richardson, "Liturgical Order and Glossalalia in 1 Corinthians 14:26c-33a" *NTS* 32 (Jan., 1986): 144-151.

10. Two examples in this regard are: (1) the apparent erosion of confidence in the Holtzmannian hypothesis regarding Markan Priority in Synoptic studies - a hypothesis to which most N.T. scholars still subscribe and one which, for some, has long become a settled issue. Today, the 2-Gospels hypothesis of the neo-Griesbachians (Matthean Priority) seems to be gaining ground. See Bruce C. Corley, ed. *Colloquy On New Testament Studies: A Time for Reappraisal and Fresh Approaches* (Georgia: Mercer University Press, 1983), pp. 29-194; and (2) the source(s) and significance of N.T. Christology. For this, see, for example, Philip G. Davis, "The Mythic Enoch: New Light on Christology," *SR* 13 (1984): 335-343; L.E. Keck, "Toward the Renewal of New Testament Christology," *NTS* 32 (1986): 362-377; and L.D. Hurst and N.T. Wright, eds. *The Glory of Christ in the New Testament: Studies in Christology in Memory of George Bradford Caird* (Oxford: Oxford University Press, 1987).

11. See R. Jewett, *Paul's Anthropological Terms: A Study of Their Use in Conflict Settings* (Leiden: E.J. Brill, 1971), pp. 203-304.

12. See his *Leib und Leib Christi* (Tübingen: Mohr, 1933); and *An Die Römer* (Tübingen: Mohr, 1973). The latter was later translated into English as *Commentary on Romans*, trans.

and edited by G. Bromiley (Grand Rapids: Wm.B. Eerdmans, 1980). See pp. 337f. in the ET for Käsemann's mention of his uneasiness with the current discussion.

13. Robert Gundry, *SŌMA in Biblical Theology: With Emphasis on Pauline Anthropology* (Cambridge: At the University Press, 1976), p. 223. As the title of Gundry's book indicates, the ecclesiological use of σῶμα was not his primary focus. He chose to give it a mere glancing treatment in the final chapter of his book. See pp. 223-244.

14. See J.A.T. Robinson, *The Body: A Study in Pauline Theology* (London: SCM, 1952), pp. 47ff.

15. Avery Dulles *et al.*, *The Church*, pp. 67f.; and Andrew Perriman, "'His Body, which is the Church...': Coming to Terms with Metaphor," *EvQ* 62 (1990): 123-142.

16. The title of Best's thesis would suggest that he has already dealt with the issue in a definitive way. However, such is not the case. Although we do agree in some cases, his published thesis reveals some ambiguities and even inconsistencies at crucial points of the discussion. One example: On p. 111, paragraph 2, he writes: "... we cannot completely identify Christ and the church." However, in paragraph 3 of the same page (111), he also writes: "The Body of Christ (i.e., the church) is in some way Christ Himself and the members of His Body are in some way His members." More on that as we go along. See his, *One Body in Christ: A Study in the Relationship of the Church to Christ in the Epistles of the Apostle Paul* (London: S.P.C.K., 1955). Also, L.S. Thornton writes: "There is only one Body of Christ. But it has different aspects. We are members of that body which was nailed to the cross, laid in the tomb and raised to life on the third day. There is only one organism of the new creation; and we are members of that one organism which is Christ." See, *The Common Life in the Body of Christ*, 2nd ed. (London: Dacre Press, 1944), p. 298. For a similar thesis, see E.L. Mascall, *Christ, the Christian, and the Church* (London: Longmans, 1946). Although Küng is uncomfortable with the word, 'mystical', in speaking about the church, a word which to him suggests a direct relationship with Christ, a unity with divinity, he is still less than clear about the issue. He does seem to endorse what he supposedly opposes. He writes: "... *it is possible for Paul to use the words, 'body of Christ' to refer* to Jesus' body hanging on the cross, as well as to the body made present in the Lord's Supper, and as well as finally *to the Church which is made a member of the crucified body.*" (Emphasis mine). See, *The Church*, pp. 295, 308.

17. Best, as we have already suggested, is less than clear about his overall position. He seems to zig-zag between yes and no throughout his discussion. See, *op. cit.*, pp. 83-114; and n. 16 *supra*.

18. David J. Hawkin, *Christ and Modernity: Christian Self-Understanding in a Technological Age* (Ontario: Wilfrid Laurier Press, 1985), p. 11.

CHAPTER ONE

THE STATE OF THE QUESTION

A.   The History of Research

Before we move forward or perhaps, in order to do so, we need to look at what others have said and done or are saying and doing. This is necessary if for no other reason than that it will facilitate a proper diagnosis of the problem so that curative exegetical treatment, wherever possible, may be applied.

In brief terms, the discussion regarding the σῶμα-σῶμα church-Christ relationship can be summarized as follows: The understanding of the relationship between the two σῶματα in particular and its implications for the church-Christ relationship in general usually influences the search for, and choice of, the source(s) from which the σῶμα concept was supposedly culled; and the provenance assumed *a priori* sometimes influences the understanding of that relationship.

It is this scholarly preoccupation with the source(s) of σῶμα which allows us to engage in a followable recital of the names of those who, in one way or another, have attempted to expound the nature of the σῶμα-σῶμα church-Christ relationship and its implications for Pauline somatic ecclesiology as a whole.

So far, a sizeable number of such sources have been proposed, nine of which may be regarded as fairly representative since the others are basically extensions of, or elaborations upon, one or more of them. These nine include five that point to extra-N.T. provenances and four that move in one N.T. direction or another. In this section, we will do no more than discuss selectively and briefly the views of those who have aligned themselves with one or more of these nine sources. That is to say, the names listed will be more illustrative than exhaustive in scope.

Our decision to be both succinct and selective is defensible on two counts: (1) Exhaustiveness will not only consume hundreds of pages but more important, it will merely duplicate the efforts of Jewett and others;[1] and (2) a particular position tends to be perpetuated in the literature by way of "scholarly in-breeding"; the tendency to adopt someone else's position as one's own.

These two points, it should be mentioned, are also applicable to the study as a whole. As we go through it, we will not attempt to do scholarly battle with every one of the numerous N.T. scholars and others who have ever said anything about σῶμα as ecclesiological language in the *corpus Paulinum*.

1

THE CHURCH AS THE BODY OF CHRIST

Markus Barth, for example, is quite right in pointing out that "during the past three or four decades an enormous amount of literature has been produced that seeks to analyze the term `body of Christ' which Paul uses to designate the church."[2]

The fact that there is much duplication of views among scholars makes an exhaustive roll call unnecessary, not to mention the false *magnum opus* appearance (size-wise) that such a study would assume. Instead, we will deal with those scholars who have either exerted or continue to exert greatest influence on others. In this way, we will be able to present and then respond to the cross-section of views which would thereby emerge.

In terms of the historical account of the research on σῶμα Χριστοῦ, our present task, the name-calling will be limited largely to the 20th century since it was not until then that the critically attuned grammatico-historical method of exegesis was deliberately applied to the motif. The one who is generally credited with this sounder exegetical approach to an interpretation of the motif is Traugott Schmidt. In 1919, he published the work, *Der Leib Christi.*[3]

1.   The Source Hypotheses: Extra-New Testament

Here is a representative sample of those who have aligned themselves with one extra-N.T. source or another and who, in so doing, have sought to clarify the nature of the σῶμα-σῶμα relationship and its ecclesiological and Christological ramifications. For the moment, we will list only the various positions and provide a brief descriptive comment after each. Judgment will be suspended until the entire list of the nine source hypotheses has been exhausted. They are:

(a)   The Hebrew Scriptures -- (E. Best, P.S. Minear, and N.T. Wright[4]). It is generally argued that the O.T. concept of corporate personality makes best sense of the Pauline data. The basic argument is that Christ or the Messiah incorporates within Himself His N.T. people as His body; that is, Christ is assigned a representative role *vis-à-vis* His people who are likened to His own body on the basis of the fact that He is identified so closely with them.

It is further argued that this is somewhat analogous to the way in which it could be said that an O.T. figure (particularly a patriarch or a king) incorporated ancient Israel within himself as their inclusive representative. The O.T. texts cited most often in this regard are: Gen. 28:12 (Jacob *vis-à-vis* the nation of Israel) and Dan. 7:13ff. (the incorporative and messianic son of man concept).[5]

(b)   Rabbinic Judaism -- (W.D. Davies and R. Jewett[6]).   The assumption here is that the Rabbinic speculation on the body of Adam is the back-drop against which the σῶμα-σῶμα, church-Christ issue is to be discussed and resolved. The general argument is that for some Rabbis, the body of Adam, the archpatriarch, was perceived in cosmic terms; so much so, that all humankind was considered incorporated in him via his own body.

Similarly (so the argument goes), Christ in an Adam-like way incorporates the church into Himself via His own body. For Davies in particular, the evidence includes the following: M. Sanh. 4,5; Gen. R. 8,1; Ex. R. 40, 3; and especially, Sifra 89.[7]

(c) Gnosticism -- (R. Bultmann and W. Schmithals[8]). The myth of an *Urmensch* functioning as the Redeemed-redeemer of his people is the basis of this hypothesis. The assumption is made by Bultmann and others that in gnostic mythology the union between the Redeemer and the redeemed in one body is affirmed; also, that the name of the Redeemer is given to the then newly reconstituted reality.

When spelled out, the myth runs as follows: a divine *Urmensch* with a gigantic body came to earth and was incarcerated in the material world. Only a part of him was able to escape this bondage so that fragments of his body remained entangled on earth. To redeem or retrieve them, this *Urmensch* returned to earth, imparted a saving, gnostic knowledge and in so doing, was able to free the body fragments so that they could be reunited with him.[9]

Similarly (such scholars have argued), Christ functions as an *Urmensch,* Redeemed-redeemer figure in relation to His church since He has been able to attach Himself somatically to His redeemed or disentangled elect. The sources that are usually ransacked to buttress this mythological model include, for the most part, the Mandaean and Manichaean materials.[10]

(d)   Graeco-Roman Philosophy -- (W.L. Knox, L. Cerfaux and G. Johnston[11]). The assumption here is that Paul may have used a Stoic commonplace, namely, the tendency to view the world as a *corpus magnum* with an earthly ruler, such as the Roman Emperor, functioning as its *caput* or head. For comparative purposes, mention is sometimes made of Philo who supposedly employed this *corpus* concept to describe his close-knit Alexandrian Jewish community.

Mention is also made of the following: Menenius Agrippa's use of a fable (Aesop's?[12]) in which he likens his Roman compatriots (plebeians and patricians) to a body whose stomach is the envy of all the other members; Epictetus' philosophical analogy of the unity between gods and human beings;

and Seneca's political and philosophical σῶμα language. However, it is usually pointed out that such Graeco-Roman analogies fall far short of Paul's usage since unlike him, who affirms that the church is in some way the actual body of Christ Himself, the tradition knows of no one who is as explicitly identified with someone else's body as was true of Christ and His church.[13]

And finally: (e) The Corinthian Asclepion -- (A. Hill and J. Murphy-O'Connor[14]). This is one of the more recent source hypotheses postulated. The hypothesis is based on the fact that recent archaeological excavations of the Corinthian Asclepion have exposed a huge number of terra-cotta representations of individual body parts such as heads, hands and feet, arms and legs, breasts and genitals, eyes and ears. It is believed that these body parts represented the afflicted members or limbs cured by Asclepius, the son of Apollo and the god of healing.[15]

This hypothesis is being pressed because, in the words of Murphy-O'Connor:

> The theme of the Body appears in 1 Cor., and the way in which Paul formulates his remarks clearly indicates that it formed part of his oral preaching in Corinth .... Sound methodology, therefore, demands that we look first to Corinth for the source of his inspiration.[16]

In addition, and as was true of those who promote the Stoic hypothesis, Murphy-O'Connor insists that Paul goes further in that in some way, he identifies the church with Christ Himself on the basis of His body.[17]

2. The Source Hypotheses: Intra-New Testament

Having surveyed briefly the five extra-N.T. provenances that N.T. scholars have proposed in their discussion of the Pauline ecclesiological handling of σῶμα, it is now appropriate that we also make a succinct statement with regard to those *intra-N.T.* sources that have been suggested as well. However, and as was true of the former list of sources (the extra-N.T. ones), we will not, at this time, engage in scholarly debate with the various proponents and their proposals.

We will simply follow the format that we have already adopted in dealing with the extra-N.T. scholars and sources since our purpose here (as was true there), is to provide a fairly representative sample of those who have aligned themselves with one intra-N.T. source or another and who, in so doing, have sought to clarify the nature of the σῶμα-σῶμα relationship and the ecclesiological and Christological implications of it. As we promised

4

earlier, we will react briefly to the hypotheses only after we have listed them all. They are:

(a) Paul's Christophanic Encounter -- (J.A.T. Robinson and S. Kim[18]). This hypothesis is predicated upon the view that Paul may have drawn the inspiration for his ecclesiological σῶμα language from his own Damascus encounter with the risen Lord (see Acts 9, 22 and 26; cf. 1 Cor. 15:1-9; Gal. 1:11-17); in particular, that the Lord's identification with His people was made abundantly clear when, according to Luke, the Lord cross-examined Paul (Saul) as to why he was persecuting him in referring to His church. That is, Robinson (in particular) views the church as identified with, and identical to, the Lord through His own body. In his words:

> There was between the two an essential identity and continuity of appearance, of body.... The appearance on which Paul's whole faith and apostleship was founded was the revelation of the resurrection body of Christ, not as an individual, but as the Christian Community.[19]

Robinson is also willing to admit that Paul's decision to use σῶμα with reference to the church may have been influenced by other factors as well, for example, Stoic philosophy, the concept of corporate personality, Gnosticism, and the Rabbinic speculations on Adam's body.[20]

Kim, too, is a bit eclectic. He makes mention of the concept of corporate personality as well as of the late first and early second century C.E. Merkabah mystical perception of the glorious body of God whose limbs were assigned secret names--names sometimes equivalent to those used by the lover in the Song of Songs.[21] However, Kim opts to give pride of place to what he refers to as the Damascus Christophany--the appearance of the risen Christ to Paul (Saul) while on his way to Damascus to harass the fledgling Christian community there. In his words:

> The remarkable conversation, 'Saul, Saul, why do you persecute me?...Who are You, Lord?...*I am Jesus whom you persecute*' must have led Paul to recognize the unity of Christ with His people: To persecute the followers of Jesus is to persecute Him.... Such an identification of Christ with His people as this is unique in the N.T. to which 1 Cor. 8:12 is the closest parallel.[22]

(b) Paul's Eucharistic Christology -- (A.E.J. Rawlinson[23]). Rawlinson proposed that the context within which Paul first introduces his discussion of

5

THE CHURCH AS THE BODY OF CHRIST

the church as Christ's body is that to which we should look as the most likely source of it; and that is, 1 Cor. 10:16f. Here, Paul presumably makes mention of both the eucharistic and ecclesiological bodies of Christ. For Rawlinson, this then makes possible the discussion of the church as σῶμα in relation to traditional transubstantiationary assumptions in which Christ's own body, in some mysterious way, is made literally available to the church via the eucharistic species of bread and wine; further, and in ways no less mysterious, that the church also becomes that body itself. In other words, this eucharistic assumption is used as the basis upon which to argue that for Paul, Christ's σῶμα and that of the church are virtually one and the same.

(c) Paul's Nuptial Theology (R. Batey[24]). The *point de départ* for Batey's source hypothesis is the pericope, 1 Cor. 6:12-20; and especially vv. 16f. where Paul is counselling the guilty Corinthians against giving vent to their misguided sexual urges. In particular, the apostle is insisting that the Corinthians cannot be permitted to engage in sexual activity with temple prostitutes since, on the basis of Gen. 2:24, such intimate enjoyments create a unity of bodies between the participants; a unity that is entirely disharmonious with that which has already been established, through the Spirit, between the Corinthians and their risen Lord.

It is this Spirit-inspired unity which prompts Batey to infer that for Paul, the description of the church as the body of Christ is his way of underscoring the profound nuptial-like relationship that exists between Christ's one body--His own physical body--and the church as body.[25] In pressing his case, Batey also lays hold both of other marital elements in the *corpus Paulinum* (e.g., 1 Cor. 7 and Eph. 5)[26] as well as Hellenistic materials which suggest that unity between gods and wo/men was predicated upon some sort of figurative sexual performance and pleasure.[27]

And finally: (d) Paul's Theology of Baptism -- (E. Käsemann[28]). Here, Käsemann disowns the Gnostic position which he promoted in his *Leib und Leib Christi* (1933). Undoubtedly, he abandoned this position in the light of the fact that subsequent research has made far less plausible the historicity and reliability of the Gnostic *Urmensch* or *Uranthropos* myth.[29]

When Käsemann later published his commentary on Romans,[30] he suggested (rather tentatively it would appear), that Paul's theology of baptism may well have been the inspiration for his σῶμα Χριστοῦ ecclesiology instead. Käsemann considers this plausible since Paul discusses the σῶμα concept within the context of baptism in 1 Cor. 12:12-27 (see v. 13) -- the pericope in which the body of Christ as ecclesiological language is dealt with most fully.[31]

It means, essentially, that for Käsemann, reference to the church as the body of Christ is ecclesiological shorthand for saying that we have all been sacramentally incorporated via baptism into Christ's own body. That is, there has been an abandonment of the fabricated gnostic myth and model in which the once-assumed Redeemed-redeemer figure regains and retains the lost parts of his cosmic body in preference for that of Pauline baptism which seemingly allows a similar argument to be made in terms of the σῶμα-σῶμα, church-Christ relationship.

B. The Problem and Two Proposals

1. The Problem

From our brief survey, the conclusion can be drawn that the σῶμα-σῶμα issue is unresolved. N.T. scholars appear to be at an impasse and because of this, the time may well have come for us to disabuse our minds of some long-cherished assumptions regarding the σῶμα-σῶμα issue in order that we may make allowance for a different and perhaps, a better set of presuppositions in our attempt to be as faithful as possible to the ecclesiological data at hand.

Like the proverbial Ariadne's thread, the fundamental assumption that runs through, and has given birth to, the aforementioned source hypotheses is that Christ through His once-broken but now glorified body and the church as body are somehow directly related; either mystically or metaphorically. Having made this hermeneutical assumption, the challenge then confronting N.T. scholars is to search for and find the source(s) (intra- or extra-N.T.) which supposedly gave birth to the idea of speaking about the relationship between Christ and the church in such somatic terms.

In addition, the tendency is to contrast σῶμα Χριστοῦ in 1 Cor./Rom. with the σῶμα ecclesiology of Col./Eph. in which Christ, on more than one occasion, is identified only as κεφαλή of the church, His σῶμα (see, e.g., Col. 1:18; 2:19; Eph. 4:16; 5:23).   The contention generally is that whereas the church is identified (either mystically or metaphorically) with Christ's body *in toto* in 1 Cor./Rom., the church, still viewed as σῶμα, is reduced to an acephalous entity in Col./Eph. where Christ alone is now regarded as κεφαλή *vis-à-vis* the church, His σῶμα. That is, as we move from 1 Cor./Rom. to Col./Eph., σῶμα as ecclesiological language seems to undergo a shift in definition suggesting some measure of anatomical reduction--from a meaning of body in its entirety in 1 Cor./Rom. to that of a headless object in Col./Eph.[32]

On the basis of 1 Cor. and Rom., Robinson, for example, regards the

7

THE CHURCH AS THE BODY OF CHRIST

church as the extension of Christ's crucified body;[33] and Brown gives us one of the more recent illustrations not only of the basic assumption regarding Christ's σῶμα vis-à-vis the church as σῶμα (based upon 1 Cor./Rom.), but he also gives us an illustration of how σῶμα in 1 Cor./Rom. is seen generally in relation to Col./Eph. where the κεφαλή concept first appears. With uncharacteristic unclarity, he avers:

> Paul had resorted to an imaginative use of Christ's "body" in his undisputed correspondence, especially in overcoming the jealousy about charisms at Corinth. He spoke of the risen body of Christ (and thus of a real body that had lived and died) of which each Christian is a member, of a human body that had feet, hands, eyes, etc.... The author of Colossians, followed by the author of Ephesians, adopts Paul's image of the body and develops it in a new way to fit a massive emphasis on the church. In his body of the flesh by his death, Christ reconciled those who were estranged (Col. 1:22), and they have been called into one body (3:15). That body is now identified as the church, and Christ is its head (Col. 1:18, 24; Eph. 1:22-23, 5:23). From Paul's reference to the Christians as members of a real body that suffered, died, and rose, the thrust of the body imagery (in Colossians/Ephesians) has moved to a corporate understanding with Christ as Lord over that body (Eph. 4:4-5).... The ecclesiology of Colossians/Ephesians...tends to make the church and Christ one.[34]

2. The Proposal Re: Σῶμα

Throughout the history of the modern discussion, there have been a few protesters from whom basically two proposals have come. First of all, there are those who have suggested that Christ's own body is not of direct relevance to the ecclesiological expression, σῶμα Χριστοῦ, at all but that instead, σῶμα points to any human body to which the church, under Christ's control, is being metaphorically compared. That is, Χριστοῦ should not be considered an explicative genitive in relation to σῶμα in σῶμα Χριστοῦ but rather, one of possession. In other words, σῶμα Χριστοῦ as ecclesiological language should be handled similarly to the way in which one would handle the agronomic expression, the church as the *field* of God (1 Cor. 3:9b) where the word, *field*, does not point to some aspect of the Divine being but rather to that to which the church, in God's continuous possession and under His ever watchful eye, is being metaphorically compared.

This "possessive genitive" proposal, however, is usually summarily dismissed as being exegetically indefensible. In 1940, for example, Deimel's suggestion that the genitive construction in the phrase, σῶμα Χριστοῦ, merely distinguishes the church as a group in society which belongs to Christ, seemed to have fallen on deaf ears.[35] In his words, σῶμα perhaps, refers to "die naturliche gesellschaftliche Anlage und Verfassung des Menschen."[36] More recently, Gundry also made a similar suggestion which places him at variance with those who tend to relate the two bodies in some direct way. In his words:

> A distinction between two bodies of Christ has to be drawn--an individual body, distinct from believers, in which he arose, ascended, and lives on high, and an ecclesiological body, consisting of believers, in which he dwells on earth through his Spirit. In one sense, the ecclesiastical Body is just as physical as the individual body of Christ, not because it consists of the individual body of Christ but because it consists of believers whose bodies (as well as spirits) belong to Christ (1 Cor. 6:15, 19-20). In a larger sense, however, the ecclesiastical body is metaphorical in that the equation of one member with the eye of the body, another member with the ear, and so on, can be understood only in a figurative way.[37]

Gundry continues in this vein:

> This is not to deny an equation between Christ and his Body (the church), but only to deny that the equation is of a physical sort. We do not establish an equation by noting that Paul says, 'You are the Body of Christ' (1 Cor. 12:27), rather than, 'You are a body in Christ', or by noting that Paul never writes of a 'a Body of Christians' but always of 'the Body of Christ'. Other things being equal, the genitive Χριστοῦ just might be taken as possessive rather than explicative.[38]

3.   The Proposal Re: Κεφαλή

Over the years, there are a few, like Ridderbos, who have also made a second proposal, namely, that κεφαλή vis-à-vis σῶμα in Col./Eph. should not be taken in a physiological sense either but that terms such as sovereign, source, Lord or leader may be more appropriate.[39] That is, the physiological reduction of σῶμα to an acephalous entity in Col./Eph. is only apparent since the κεφαλή concept, although related to σῶμα in Col./Eph., is not its physiological complement as such. The two concepts can and do stand on their own two feet, so to speak.

THE CHURCH AS THE BODY OF CHRIST

4. A Summary Statement

In this study, we will explore more fully than has been done heretofore, the possibility that Gundry, Ridderbos, and a few others may well have shown us a more excellent way; that of a truth, the human σῶμα and *not* Christ's σῶμα is used consistently as the term of comparison for the church as σῶμα and that therefore, any "solution" which implies a physiological understanding of κεφαλή in relation to Christ and the church, His σῶμα, will not do.

It should also be pointed out here--and with much haste--that contrary to the impression that is sometimes given, a summary dismissal of these two proposals (re: σῶμα and κεφαλή) is not a refutation of them per se.[40] To dismiss them with dogmatic or even evangelical fervor or merely to question rather than challenge their exegetical integrity, is not, in itself, enough to render them ineligible for serious investigation.

The corollary to this, of course, is also true; and that is, merely to propose as a possibility that Χριστοῦ in σῶμα Χριστοῦ may be a possessive genitive, as something that "just might be" the case,[41] or that κεφαλή is not physiological in function in Col./Eph. is not, in itself, sufficient either-- regardless of how sensible the proposals may sound or how tantalizing they may appear. In other words, nothing less than a sustained and systematic grammatico-historical and exegetical look at the data in the light of these two proposals can be considered acceptable; and so far, this has not really been done.

What we have had up to this point are basically two relatively tentative suggestions: (1) that the genitive in σῶμα Χριστοῦ may be possessive in nature; and (2) that κεφαλή in Col./Eph. may not be physiological in function. By not having given these two proposals the critical attention we think they deserve has also meant that in general, scholars have not benefited sufficiently from Gundry, Ridderbos, and a few others who are attempting to nudge us in new directions where σῶμα Χριστοῦ as ecclesiological language is concerned.

10

Chapter One

1. As has already been mentioned (see p. xix, n. 11), the German contribution took Jewett just over 100 pages to report and reflect on. However, he is quite right in affirming that "one would find essentially the same issues being aired in the discussion being carried on in French or English." See *Paul's Anthropological Terms*, p. 202. For a good cross-section of English and French scholars, see p. 202, n.1 of the same work.

2. M. Barth, *Ephesians*, vol. 1, in *AB* (New York: Doubleday, 1974), p. 183.

3. T. Schmidt, *Der Leib Christi: Eine Untersuchung zum Urchristlichen Gemeindegedanken* (Leipzig: 1919). For a relatively brief overview of the history of the discussion, particularly as it relates to the question of sources, see M. Barth, "A Chapter on the Church--The Body of Christ," *Int.* 12 (1958): 133-136; H. Ridderbos, *Paul: An Outline of His Theology* (Grand Rapids: Wm.B. Eerdmans, 1975), pp. 362-395; and Käsemann, *Romans*, pp. 335-338. For a helpful and much fuller bibliographical history of the modern discussion, particularly the German, see the following: Otto Michel, *Das Zeugnis des Neuen Testaments von der Gemeinde* (Göttingen: 1941), pp. 44 ff.; Theodore Soiron, *Die Kirche als der Leib Christi* (Dusseldorf: 1951), pp. 9f.; J.J. Meuzelaar, *Der Leib des Messias: Eine exegetische Studie über den Gedanken vom Leib Christi in den Paulusbriefen* (Assen: 1961); Jewett, *op. cit.*, (1971), pp. 201-304. In her important work, Bowe discusses the somatic ecclesiology of *I Clem.* (chaps. 37-44) as part of her overall thesis that the letter does not subscribe to a monepiscopal polity as many scholars assume but that it is a sustained call to communal consensus and solidarity among believers within the church at Corinth. See Barbara Ellen Bowe, *A Church in Crisis: Ecclesiology and Paraenesis in Clement of Rome*, in HDR (Minneapolis, MN: Fortress, 1988), pp. 134-144. For a fairly detailed discussion of the patristic and scholastic use of the motif, see S. Tromp, *Corpus Christi Quod Est Ecclesia*, translated by Ann Condit as, *The Body of Christ, Which is the Church* (New York: Vantage Press, 1960). Tromp basically shows that Augustine (354-430) was the dominant figure in Roman Catholic ecclesiology throughout both the patristic and medieval periods. His view of the mystical Body of Christ as applied to the eucharistic sacrament was foundational to much of the later papal pronouncements on the Roman Catholic Church as Christ's Body; for example, Pius IX at Vatican I (1869-70) and Pius XII in his encyclical, *Mystici Corporis Christi* of June 29, 1943. For a book-length discussion of *Mystici Corporis Christi* in terms of its patristic and medieval roots as well as its contribution to Roman Catholic ecclesiology as a whole, see Emile Mersch, *The Whole Christ: The Historical Development of the Doctrine of the Mystical Body* (Durham: Dobson Books, 1949); *idem, The Theology of the Mystical Body* (St. Louis: B. Herder, 1958); E. Mura, *The Mystical Body of Christ* (St. Louis: B.

Herder, 1963); Jerome Hamer, *The Church is a Communion* (London: Geoffrey Chapman, 1964), pp. 13-34; and R. H. Lesser, *The Church Indeed is His Body* (Bombay: St. Paul Publications, 1970). For a larger ecclesiological and patristic picture, see Thomas Halton, *The Church: Message of the Fathers of the Church* (Delaware: Michael Glazier, 1985). The motif was not unknown among the early Gnostics either; for example, see the Coptic-Gnostic tractate, *The Interpretation of Gnosis*, in the Nag Hammadi documents translated by J.M. Robinson *et al.* (This reference was brought to my attention by Dr. Frederik Wisse, Associate Professor of N.T. at McGill.) And finally, for a discussion of the importance of the σῶμα motif for the reformers, see P. D. Avis, *The Church in the Theology of the Reformers* (Atlanta: John Knox Press, 1981).

4. E. Best, *One Body in Christ*, p. 110; Minear, *Images,* pp. 173ff. N.T. Wright, *The Messiah and the People of God: A Study in Pauline Theology with Particular Reference to the Argument of the Epistle to the Romans* (Oxford University: Unpublished dissertation, 1980), pp. 27ff. Also see E. Percy, *Der Leib Christi in den paulinischen Homologumena und Antilogumena* (Lund: 1942), p. 41; and much more recently, E. Earle Ellis, "*Sōma* in 1 Corinthians" in *Int.* 44 (1990): 132-144.

5. Dodd explains very well what is meant by corporate personality. He states: "Jacob, as the ancestor of the nation of Israel, summarizes in his person the ideal Israel *in posse,* just as our Lord, at the other end of the line, summarizes it *in esse* as the Son of Man .... In a deeper sense, He is not only their King, He is their inclusive representative: They are in Him and He in them." See *The Interpretation of the Fourth Gospel* (Cambridge: At the University Press, 1953), p. 246. Also see Best, *One Body in Christ*, pp. 203-207.

6. W.D. Davies, *Paul and Rabbinic Judaism* (London: S.P.C.K., 1948), pp. 53-57. For a repetition of this view, see his compilation of essays, *Jewish and Pauline Studies* (Philadelphia: Fortress Press, 1984), p. 301; also see Jewett, *op. cit.,* pp. 242-245.

7. For a discussion of similar views of others like Murmelstein, Schoeps and Staerk, see Jewett, *ibid.* E. Schweizer also goes in search of Adam and builds his case on the basis of pseudepigraphical and Philonic materials, for example, Apoc. Bar. (Syr.) 78:4; Apoc. Abr. 23:8; *Vit. Mos.* II, 60-65; and *Migr. Abr.* 38-40. See, "Die Kirche als Leib Christi in den Paulinischen Homologumena" *TLZ* 86 (1961): 161-174. Also see *idem,* s.v. "*Soma*", in *TDNT*, vol. VII (Grand Rapids: Wm. B. Eerdmans, 1971), pp. 1067ff.; and *The Church as the Body of Christ* (Virginia: John Knox Press, 1964), pp. 47ff.

8. R. Bultmann, *Theology of the New Testament*, vol. 1 (New York: Scribner and Sons, 1951), p. 182; W. Schmithals, *Gnosticism in Corinth* (Nashville: Abingdon, 1971), pp. 45ff.

9. See Jewett, *op. cit.*, p. 231.

10. *Ibid.,* p. 235.

11. W.L. Knox, "Parallels to the N.T. Use of *Sōma*," *JTS* 39 (1938): 243-246; also *idem, St. Paul and the Church of the Gentiles* (Cambridge: At the University Press, 1939); L. Cerfaux, *The Church in the Theology of St. Paul* (New York: Herder and Herder, 1959), pp. 262-286; J. Culliton, "Lucien Cerfaux's Contribution Concerning 'The Body of Christ'", *CBQ* 29 (1967): 41-59; G. Johnston, *The Doctrine of the Church in the New Testament*, pp. 85-99. Later, Johnston showed signs of giving credence to other source proposals as well, for example, the mystical Adam and perhaps, even Jesus Himself. See his *Ephesians, Philippians, Colossians, and Philemon*, in *TCB* (London: Thomas Nelson and Sons, 1967), p. 18. For other Graeco-Roman precedents for the metaphorical use of σῶμα, see Best, *One Body in Christ*, pp. 221-225.

12. See R.I. Hick, "Aesop and the Organic Body: The Body Political and the Body Ecclesiastical," *JBR* 31 (1980): 29-35; and L. Cerfaux, *op. cit.*, pp. 262ff.

13. See Johnston, *The Doctrine of the Church*, pp. 87ff.; and Jewett, *op. cit.*, pp. 229f.

14. A. E. Hill, "The Temple of Asclepius: An Alternative Source for Paul's Body Theology," *JBL* 99 (1980): 297-309. Hill, however, tends to be eclectic in his choice of sources since, for him, the concept of corporate personality (supposedly found in the Hebrew Scriptures) and the σῶμα speculations of Greek philosophy may have had some influence on Paul as well; J. Murphy-O'Connor, *St. Paul's Corinth: Texts and Archaeology* (Delaware: Michael Glazier, 1983), pp. 161-167.

15. For a fairly detailed account of Asclepius and the role he played in the Greek therapeutic tradition, see Mabel Lang, *Cure and Cult in Ancient Corinth: A Guide to the Asklepieion* (New Jersey: Princeton University Press, 1977).

16. J. Murphy-O'Connor, *ibid.*, p. 165.

17. *Ibid.*; also see *idem, Becoming Human Together: The Pastoral Anthropology of St. Paul* (Delaware: Michael Glazier, 1982), pp. 183-193.

18. J.A.T. Robinson, *The Body*, pp. 52ff.; S. Kim, *The Origin of Paul's Gospel* (Tübingen: J.C.B. Mohr, 1981), pp. 252-256.

19. Robinson, *op. cit.,* p. 58. For Ellis, the Church as the body of Christ exists "as the corporate 'body' of the resurrected Christ, made up of individual believers who have become part of that new resurrection reality." See *Pauline Theology*, p. 8.

20. *Ibid.,* p. 55.

21. Kim, *op. cit.,* p. 254; also see G. Scholem, *Major Trends in Jewish Mysticism,* 3rd edn. (New York: 1954); and especially, *Jewish Gnosticism, Merkabah Mysticism and Talmudic Tradition* (New York: 1960), pp. 36-42. The view that Pauline "mysticism" may have played

a role in the Apostle's ecclesiological handling of σῶμα has been argued for on other grounds as well; particularly in relation to his ἐν Χριστῷ formula. For instance, see A. Schweitzer, *The Mysticism of Paul the Apostle* (London: A. and C. Clark, 1931), pp. 116-127. Schweitzer seems not to have considered the body of the church and that of Christ as being actually identical. However, for him, the two σῶματα were still related in some profoundly "mystical" and corporeal way. Within the Catholic tradition, however, there are those for whom there is no doubt that the two σῶματα are one and the same. See A. Wikenhauser, *Die Kirche als der mystiche Leib Christi nach dem Apostel Paulus* (Munster: 1949), pp. 92ff.; and W. Goosens *L'Église Corps Du Christ D'Après Saint Paul: Étude de Théologie Biblique* (Paris: J. Gabala, 1949), pp. 99ff.; also see discussion of Tromp's *Corpus Christi* in n.3, *supra*; the mention of Mascall on p. xix, n. 16; and E. Mersch, *Le Corps Mystique du Christ* (Louvain: Museum Lessianum, 1933).

22. Kim, *op. cit.,* p. 253 (emphasis his). *En passant,* Kim also makes mention of Wedderburn's list of possible sources (which does include the Damascus Christophany as well). For that, see A.J.M. Wedderburn, "The Body of Christ and Related Concepts in 1 Corinthians," *STJ* 24 (1971): 74-96.

23. A.E.J. Rawlinson, "Corpus Christi," in *Mysterium Christi*, edited by G.K.A. Bell and A. Deissmann (London: Longmans, 1930), pp. 225-244.

24. R. Batey, "The *MIA SARX* Union of Christ and the Church," *NTS* 13 (1966-67): 270-281; also *idem, New Testament Nuptial Imagery* (Leiden: E.J. Brill, 1971).

25. For a similar argument, see C. Chevasse, *The Bride of Christ* (London: The Religious Book Club, n.d.), pp. 70-72. In his words, the church, "is only the Body of Christ because she is primarily the mystical Bride of Christ." See p. 71.

26. Sampley also contends for a nuptial origin of the motif but on the basis of Eph. 5:21-33. See his, *'And the Two Shall Become One Flesh': A Study of Traditions in Ephesians 5:21-33* (Cambridge: At the University Press, 1971), pp. 63ff.

27. In fact, Batey spreads his net as wide as possible. He draws data from Jewish literature (Rabbinic and Philonic), Greek philosophy (Plato) and even second-century Gnostic thought (e.g., Justin, the Gnostic; Valentinus and the Apocryphal Gospels of both Thomas and Philip are considered as well). See, "The *MIA SARX*", pp. 270ff.

28. Käsemann, *Romans*, pp. 335ff.; also see R. Brown, *The Churches,* p. 49, n. 72.

29. Years later, Käsemann reiterated the Gnostic hypothesis. See, *Essays On New Testament Themes*, in *SBT* (London: SCM Press, 1964), p. 109. For a discussion of this Gnostic hypothesis which Käsemann helped to popularize (beginning in the 1930's), see the third item under Extra-N.T. sources earlier in this chapter. The two who have been most influential in rendering the Gnostic *Urmensch* hypothesis highly implausible are C. Colpe,

Die religionsgeschichtliche Schule: Darstellung und Kritik ihres Bildes vom gnostischen Erlosermythus (Göttingen: 1961), pp. 63ff.; and H.M. Schenke, *Der Gott 'Mensch' in der Gnosis: Ein religionsgeschichtlicher Beitrag zur Diskussion über die paulinische Anschauung von der kirche als Leib Christi* (Göttingen: 1962), pp. 28ff.

30. See p. xix, n. 12. Between *Leib* (1933) and *An Die Römer* (1973), Käsemann also toyed with the possibility that *religionsgeschichtliche* influences like Stoicism and corporate personality might have been responsible for the Pauline σῶμα ecclesiology. In addition, there was Paul's own Adamic Christology. See *idem, Perspectives on Paul* (Philadelphia: Fortress Press, 1971). pp. 102-121.

31. Käsemann, *Romans*, p. 337.

32. See Ridderbos, *Paul*, pp. 376-387.

33. Robinson, *The Body*, pp. 56f; also see Käsemann, *Romans*, p. 337.

34. Brown, *The Churches*, pp. 49f. and 55.

35. See Jewett, *op. cit.*, p. 204.

36. L. Deimel, *Leib Christi: Sinn und Grenzen einer Deutung des inner kirchlichen Lebens* (Frieburg: 1940), p. 54.

37. Gundry, *SŌMA*, p. 228.

38. *Ibid.*, p. 231.

39. Ridderbos, *Paul*, pp. 378ff.

40. E.g., Käsemann, *Perspectives*, pp. 102f. Later works, however, show that he himself is still unsure about the issue. See *Romans*, p. 337; and p. xix, n. 12.

41. See end of Gundry's last quote corresponding to n. 38, *supra*.

CHAPTER TWO

THE SOMATIC ECCLESIOLOGY OF THE NEW TESTAMENT

A. Introduction

Although it may well be said that there are almost as many persons as opinions where the source and significance of σῶμα are concerned, there is still some measure of consensus on one of the fundamental issues, namely, the range or extent of the ecclesiological motif within the N.T. as a whole. In spite of Agnew's reminder that "it is difficult to speak of consensus on anything in biblical studies,"[1] it is still true to say that the vast majority of those N.T. scholars who have studied the subject have long recognized that σῶμα as ecclesiological language is a distinctive Pauline contribution to N.T. ecclesiology since the concept appears nowhere else in the N.T.[2]

This scholarly *communis opinio* has prevailed in the face of a few who have tried to suggest otherwise. Examples are the following: (1) Thornton, in his suggestion that Mk. 9:33-50 *et parr.* constitute a Synoptic equivalent in which Jesus is reported to have used "body language" during his teaching and preaching ministry; in particular, His insistence that lopping off one's limbs and making it into the kingdom dismembered is preferable to continuing to hold on to one's offending member, be it eye, hand or foot, and thereby losing out on the kingdom altogether;[3] (2) Via's look at, and his discussion of, Matthean messianism which he regards as at least an ecclesiological counterpart to the Pauline σῶμα statement;[4] (3) Schweizer's equating σῶμα to Jesus' remark regarding the vine and the branches (Jn. 15);[5] and (4) Buchanan's suggestion *en passant* that Heb. 13:3 may be a non-Pauline echo as well.[6]

1. Statistical Information on Σῶμα in the Pauline Corpus

Σῶμα appears 144 times in the entire N.T. with 51 occurrences pointing to the extra-Pauline materials. Except for Heb. 13:11 and Jm. 3:3 where the term is used to designate animal's bodies and for Rev. 18:13 where the word means "slave", σῶμα refers both to wo/man's physical constitution, the body, on 29 occasions scattered among nine N.T. books as well as to Christ's, on 20 occasions found mainly within the Passion narratives of all four Gospels.[7]

It means, essentially, that σῶμα and its cognates appear 93 times in the *corpus Paulinum*--in 1 Thess., 1 and 2 Cor., Gal., Rom., Col., Phil., and Eph.[8] Except for five occurences in 1 Cor. 15:37-40 where Paul makes mention of the body of a sown seed (vv. 37f.) and of celestial and terrestrial bodies (v.

17

40), σῶμα and its remaining 88 occurrences performs three distinct functions within the Pauline corpus; they being anthropological, Christological, and ecclesiological. For the rest of this study, the sigla, A, C, and E will be used to point to these three functions: to refer to the anthropological, Christological, and ecclesiological uses of σῶμα respectively.

In 61 cases, σῶμα is used in an obviously A way; as a reference to all or part of wo/man's physical make-up. The break-down is as follows: 1 Thess. 5:23--once; 1 Cor. 5:3; 6:13,15,16,18,20; 7:34; 9:27; 12:12,14-20,22-25; 13:3; 15:35,44--33 times; 2 Cor. 4:10; 5:6,8,10; 12:2,3--ten times; Gal. 6:17--once; Rom. 1:24; 4:19; 6:6,12; 7:24; 8:10,11,13,23; 12:1,4--11 times; Col. 2:11,23--twice; Phil. 1:20; 3:21--twice; and Eph. 5:28--once.[9]

The vast majority of N.T. scholars see such texts as primarily contributive to an overall Pauline anthropological statement and thus, they have shown exegetical integrity in not building a somatic ecclesiology on them--at least, not directly.[10] In terms of the other two categories, however, namely, C and E, scholars are much less united when it comes to determining just how the remaining 27 σῶμα texts are to be classified exegetically.

This is especially true in light of the hermeneutical assumption which places Christ's personal body in some mystical or direct metaphorical relationship with the church as body. Exegetical imprecision sometimes manifests itself in that σῶμα in a particular passage is treated as C by some and as E by others. The exegetical problem is further compounded when, sometimes, the same σῶμα text is tentatively regarded as both C and E rather than as one or the other.[11]

2.   Identification of the Problematic Σῶμα Texts in the Pauline Corpus

The 27 σῶμα texts that constitute the bone of contention among scholars are as follows: 1 Cor. 6:19;[12] 10:16,17; 11:24,27,29; 12:13,27--eight times; Rom. 7:4; 12:5--twice; Col. 1:18,22,24; 2:9,17,19; 3:15--seven times; Phil. 3:21--once; and Eph. 1:23; 2:16; 3:6; 4:4,12,16 (*bis*); 5:23,29--nine times.

Although we will be scrutinizing these texts in succeeding chapters (3 - 6), it may still be helpful at this juncture to provide a reasonably reliable English translation of each.[13] For one thing, this will enable us to see at a glance, even without exegetical effort, that some σῶματα are obviously C while some others are obviously E. In addition, it will help to give us some idea of how a few of these texts seemingly defy any facile exegetical classification in terms of their being one or the other; and in some cases, perhaps, why some scholars are tempted to treat the same σῶμα as both C and E with the implication, then, that Christ's personal body and that of the church are somehow one and the same.

The 27 σῶμα texts are as follows (emphases mine):

Do you not know that your *body* is a temple of the Holy Spirit within you, which you have from God? You are not your own; you were bought with a price. (1 Cor. 6:19)

The cup of blessing which we bless, is it not a participation in the blood of Christ? The bread which we break, is it not a participation in the *body* of Christ? Because there is one bread, we who are many are one *body*, for all partake of the one bread. (1 Cor. 10:16,17)

For I received from the Lord what I also delivered to you, that the Lord Jesus on the night when he was betrayed took bread, and when he had given thanks, he broke it, and said, 'This is my *body* which is for you.... Whoever, therefore, eats the bread or drinks the cup of the Lord in an unworthy manner will be guilty of profaning the *body* of the Lord.... For any one who eats and drinks without discerning the *body* eats and drinks judgment upon himself. (1 Cor. 11:24,27,29)

For by one Spirit we were all baptized into one *body*--Jews, Greeks, slaves or free--and all were made to drink of one Spirit.... Now you are the *body* of Christ and individually members of it. (1 Cor. 12:13,27)

Likewise, my brethren, you have died to the law through the *body* of Christ, so that you may belong to another to him who has been raised from the dead in order that we may bear fruit for God. (Rom. 7:4)

For as in one body[14] we have many members, and all the members do not have the same function, so we, though many are one *body* in Christ, and individually members one of another. (Rom. 12:4,5)

He is the head of the *body*, the church, he is the beginning, the first-born from the dead, that in everything he might be pre-eminent.... And you, who once were estranged, and hostile in mind, doing evil deeds, he has now reconciled in his *body* of flesh by his death, in order to present you holy and blameless

19

and irreproachable before him.... Now I rejoice in my sufferings for your sake, and in my flesh I complete what is lacking in Christ's affliction for the sake of his *body*, that is, the church. (Col. 1:18,21,22,24)

For in him the whole fulness of deity dwells *bodily*,[15] and you have come to fulness of life in him, who is the head of all rule and authority.... These are only a shadow of what is to come; but the substance[16] belongs to Christ. Let no one disqualify you, insisting on self-abasement and worship of angels, taking his stand on visions, puffed up without reason by his sensuous mind, and not holding fast to the Head, from whom the whole *body*, nourished and knit together through its joints and ligaments, grows with a growth that is from God. (Col. 2:9,10,17-19).

Let the peace of Christ rule in your hearts, to which indeed you were called in one *body*. And be thankful. (Col. 3:15)

Our commonwealth is in heaven, and from it we await a Savior, the Lord Jesus Christ, who will change our lowly body[17] to be like his glorious *body*, by the power which enables him even to subject all things to himself. (Phil. 3:20,21).

He (God) has put all things under his (Christ's) feet and has made him the head over all things for the church, which is his *body*, the fulness of him who fills all in all. (Eph. 1:23)

For he is our peace, who has made us both one...by abolishing in his flesh the law of commandments and ordinances, that he might create in himself one new man in place of the two, so making peace, and might reconcile us both to God in one *body* through the cross, thereby bringing the hostility to an end. (Eph. 2:14a,15,16)

When you read this, you can perceive my insight into the mystery of Christ...that is, how the Gentiles are fellow heirs, members of the same *body,* and partakers of the promise in Christ Jesus through the gospel. (Eph. 3:4,6)

There is one *body* and one Spirit, just as you were called to the one hope that belongs to your call, one Lord, one faith, one baptism, one God and Father of us all.... His gifts were that some should be apostles, some prophets, some evangelists, some pastors and teachers, to equip the saints for the work of ministry, for building up the *body* of Christ.... Speaking the truth in love, we are to grow up in every way into him who is the head, into Christ, from whom the whole *body*, joined and knit together by every joint with which it is supplied, when each part is working properly, makes *bodily* growth and upbuilds itself in love. (Eph. 4:4,5,6a,11,12,15,16).

For the husband is head of the wife as Christ is head of the church his *body*, and is himself its Saviour.... For no man ever hates his own flesh, but nourishes and cherishes it, as Christ does the church, because we are members of his *body*. (Eph. 5:23,29)

B.   The Method of Approach

In our judgment, the exegetical imprecision to which we referred earlier is partially responsible for much of the problem that still bedevils scholars as they seek to come to grips with σῶμα as an eccelesiological concept within the Pauline corpus.   It is our conviction that generally speaking, a methodological *faux pas* has marked and marred much of the discussion; and it is this: a sufficiently clear distinction between σῶμα as referring to the church and σῶμα as referring to Christ himself has not been made and maintained.

Consequently, this has given way to the tendency to squeeze a somatic ecclesiology out of texts which, it will be argued, have Christ himself and not the church as referent; the inclination to build the church on almost every body, so to speak. This should become increasingly apparent as the discussion unfolds throughout the four immediately succeeding chapters.[18]

For some, the tendency has been to draw rather convoluted and triumphalistic sounding inferences in terms of what the Pauline σῶμα motif intends to suggest regarding the *fons et origo*, nature and function of the church. As we have already pointed out, it is not unusual, for example, to hear the church defined and described as "the extension of the incarnation," "the extension of Christ's crucified body," or in some such glowing phraseologies.[19]

It is precisely because of this tendency to blur the distinctions between the C and E σῶματα, to make a categorical mistake, as it were, and with potentially far-reaching Christological and ecclesiological implications to boot, that our suggestion regarding method is most appropriate. In our view, a systematic grammatico-historical and exegetical attempt to differentiate clearly between the C and E σώματα in the Pauline corpus is methodologically mandatory and it is one which should accompany any meaningful discussion of the ecclesiological import of σῶμα, beginning with 1 Cor.[20]

We begin with 1 Cor., of course, because it is practically universally accepted by N.T. scholars that 1 Cor. antedates the three other Pauline epistles in which σῶμα Χριστοῦ as ecclesiological language also appears, namely, Rom., Col., and Eph.[21] Also, we will not only make some attempt to determine on grammatico-historical and exegetical grounds what the ecclesiological significance of σῶμα is in these four Pauline epistles but we will also attempt to do so by looking at them separately.[22]

In our closing chapter, by way of summary and conclusion, we will do the following: (1) highlight the general trends and themes as well as the developments and/or deviations (if any) as they would have emerged throughout our discussion of σῶμα[23]; (2) provide a brief statement in terms of the implications of the study for Pauline ecclesiology as a whole; and (3) return briefly to the whole question of the source hypotheses. This "return to the sources" approach seems most appropriate since, in our view, an attempt should first be made to ascertain what σῶμα Χριστοῦ means in the Pauline corpus itself before a decision is made to launch out into the deep in search of the possible source(s) of it.

C. Rationale for the Approach

Behind our decision to look at σῶμα Χριστοῦ in the four epistles separately is our desire to trace chronologically and geographically the σῶμα Χριστοῦ motif in the Pauline corpus and in so doing, to determine, as best we can, what the different church communities were told and taught about being the body of Christ in Corinth, Rome, Colossae, and perhaps Ephesus and elsewhere.[24] In addition, separate treatment will allow us to plot possible developments of, and/or deviations from, earlier usages of the motif.

Also embedded in this "un-harmonizing approach" to the four Pauline epistles is the assumption which Anderson, among others, rightly regards as legitimate. For him, an author should be allowed to interpret himself or herself within the context of the document in which s/he chooses to express himself or herself. In this regard, mention should be made of Brooks as well. In discussing the concept of baptism in Gal. (based on 3:28), he has this to say, for example:

THE SOMATIC ECCLESIOLOGY OF THE NEW TESTAMENT

It is the temptation of modern interpreters to give numerous cross-references to Paul's other writings in explaining a single text.... It must be remembered that the Galatian readers did not have this privilege. They depended solely on this epistle and their prior understanding of the Christian message as delivered by Paul.[25]

In our case, the documents to be examined are 1 Cor., Rom., Col., and Eph.; and our authors are the apostle Paul and perhaps, others.[26]

One possible objection to our approach that might be raised is that, overall, we seem to be guilty of unduly elevating one ecclesiological image at the expense of the many others which we encounter in the Pauline corpus; such as field (1 Cor. 3), olive tree (Rom. 11) or membership in the household of God (Eph. 3; cf. the Pastorals[27]). From Sanders, for example, comes the reminder that, "entering the body of Christ, important as it is for Paul, is not the whole of his thought.[28]

Our response both to that possible objection and to Sanders' observation, however, is this: of all the Pauline ecclesiological images that scholars have studied, $\sigma\tilde{\omega}\mu\alpha$ by far has been both the most prominent and the most problematic. It means, essentially, that our according it such a high profile is nothing new (it has always been most prominent);[29] and also, that the need has already been felt to say something "new" about it (it still is the most problematic).[30]

ENDNOTES

Chapter Two

1. Francis H. Agnew, "The Origin of the N.T. Apostle Concept: A Review of Research," *JBL* 105 (1986): 96.

2. See Ridderbos, *Paul*, p. 362. And for Johnston: "Paul's supreme contribution to the idea of the church is that of the Body of Christ." See, "The Doctrine of the Church in the New Testament," in *PCB*, p. 722.

3. L.S. Thornton, "The Body of Christ," in *The Apostolic Ministry,* edited by K.E. Kirk (London: Hodder and Stoughton, 1946), pp. 55f. Also see *idem, The Common Life in the Body of Christ* (London: Dacre Press, 1944).

4. See D.O. Via, Jr., "The Church as the Body of Christ in the Gospel of Matthew," *SJT* 11 (1958): 271-286.

5. Schweizer, *The Church*, p. 48. Schweizer suggests that this vine/branch tradition can be traced both to the Hebrew Scriptures (e.g., Ps. 80) where Israel is described as the vine of God and to Pseudo-Philo (in *Bib. Ant.*) where, in Schweizer's words: "Israel appears as the cosmic vine of God whose roots reach down into hell and whose branches reach up into heaven. The people of God is something like the giant body of a vine permeating the whole cosmos stretching from hell to heaven," pp. 47f. Schweizer first advanced this unconvincing argument in 1961 in his, "Die Kirche als Leib Christi," pp. 168ff.

6. See his *Hebrews,* in *AB* (New York: Doubleday, 1976), *ad loc.*

7. The break-down is as follows: Matt. 5:29,30; 6:22,23,25; 10:28; 26:12,26; 27:52,58,59--14 times; Mk. 5:29; 14:8,22; 15:43--4 times; Lk. 11:34,36; 12:4,22,23: 17:37; 22:19; 23:52,55; 24:3,23--13 times; Jn. 2:21; 19:31,38,40; 20:12--six times; Acts 9:40--once; Heb. 10:5,10,22; 13:3,11--five times; Jm. 2:16,26; 3:2,3,6--five times; 1 Pet. 2:24--once; Jude 9--once; Rev. 18:13--once. For a reference to Rev. 18:13 as the only place within the N.T. where σῶμα is to be translated "slave", see W. Bauer, W.F. Arndt, and F.W. Gingrich, *A Greek-English Lexicon of the New Testament and other Early Christian Literature* (Chicago: 1959), p. 807.

8. Statistically speaking, σῶμα ranks among the first dozen of the most frequently employed nouns in the Pauline corpus. The ranking is as follows: Θεός *(548);* Χριστός *(379);* Κύριος *(275);* Ἰησοῦς *(213);* Πνεῦμα *(146);* πίστις *(142);* ἀδελφός *(133);* ἄνθρωπος *(126);* νόμος *(119);* χάρις *(100);* σῶμα *(93);* and σάρξ *(91).* See Robert Morgenthaler,

Statistik Des Neutestamentlichen Wortschatzes (Zurich: 1958), *ad loc.*

9. We know of no reputable N.T. scholar who disagrees with this break-down. Also, Gundry has provided us with a rather revisionist and therefore, provocative treatment of Paul's somatic anthropology in his *SŌMA in Biblical Theology.* He is particularly opposed to Bultmann's existentialist anthropology in which σῶμα is interpreted primarily as the authentic expression of one's personality *coram Deo* and not as a direct reference to one's physicality as such.

10. Schweizer is among the minority of those who seek to determine Paul's somatic anthropology first and then proceed to his σῶμα ecclesiology. This is done on the basis of the assumption that an understanding of Paul's theology of wo/man as σῶμα is a *conditio sine qua non* for a discussion of the apostle's concept of the church as σῶμα. This assumption will later be shown to be implausible--beginning with Chapter Three; see, *The Church*, pp. 23-40; also see Gundry, *SŌMA*, p. 223 for an example of this assumption being raised, rather uncritically, to the level of an assertion.

11. Details with examples of scholars who equivocate here and there re: these σῶμα texts will be provided in Chapters Three to Six.

12. The exegetical problem that I Cor. 6:19 poses really has to do with whether σῶμα there is A or E, and not whether it is C or E. This σῶμα text will be discussed in Chapter Three. It is included here only because it too, suffers from the exegetical imprecision to which we have just referred.

13. All translations are based on the *RSV.* It should also be pointed out that we will be relying on E. and A. Nestle, *et al.* eds., *Novum Testamentum Graece*, 26th edn., revised (Stuttgart: 1981), as the Greek edition throughout this study. In addition, no text-critical treatment will be given to these σῶμα texts per se unless it is really warranted and contributive to the overall ecclesiological discussion. We are aware that H. Koester, among others, has some misgivings about the text-critical integrity of Nestle-Aland based on an analysis of 1 Thess. This was the essence of Koester's presentation to us on March 22, 1985 at Andover Newton Theological School --Meeting of the New England Region of *AAR/SBL.* Koester's views have since been published as one of the Essays in *The Living Text: Essays in Honor of Ernest W. Saunders* (Washington, D.C.: University Press of America, 1985). However, Nestle-Aland is not so unhelpful where the σῶμα texts are concerned as to render it unacceptable for our present purposes.

14. "Body", here, is not emphasized since it has already been placed in the anthropological category. It is given only to complete the sense of the second, *body*, which is the one to be discussed later.

15. Σωματικῶς, the adverbial form, is used only twice more in the N.T.--1 Tim. 4:8 and Lk. 3:22. See discussion later in Chapter Five.

16. The word translated, "substance", here, is σῶμα in the Greek. See discussion later in Chapter Five.

17. See no. 14 *supra.*

18. Robinson is but one example of many others whose names will appear in subsequent chapters. For now, see *The Body,* pp. 34ff. Also see T. Soiron, *Die Kirche als der Leib Christi,* pp. 9ff.

19. Again, see Robinson, *op. cit.,* pp. 45ff. Warner Traynham also writes: "One central image of the Church is that of the body of Christ. The fundamental implication of this is the Old Anglican [Episcopalian] formula that the Church is ʻthe extension of the Incarnation'". See, *Christian Faith in Black and White: A Primer in Theology from the Black Perspective* (Massachusetts: Parameter Press, 1973), p. 55; also see pp. xixf., n. 16 again; Johnston, *The Doctrine of the Church,* p. 92; and lastly, cf. Best, *One Body,* pp. 194ff. Best expresses his discomfort with such views as just mentioned.

20. This was the essence of a paper I read on March 22, 1985 at Andover Newton Theological School for the New England Regional Meetings of *SBL.* The title of the paper: "The Ecclesiological Handling of Σῶμα in 1 Corinthians: The Problem and A Proposal".

21. We will address ourselves briefly to the relevant higher critical issues in subsequent chapters (3-6) when we come to discuss the σῶμα ecclesiology in the epistles themselves. Also, we register our disagreement with Ahern who builds a somatic ecclesiology on the basis of Galatians 3:27f. as well. The one occurrence of σῶμα in 6:17 which is unambiguously A does not justify it. See B.M. Ahern, "The Christian's Union with the Body of Christ in Corinthians, Galatians, and Romans," *CBQ* 23 (1961): 199-209.

22. It should now be apparent that Phil. will not engage us in any major way. This is because the three σῶματα that appear in the epistle are either unambiguously A or unambiguously C. That is, σῶμα as ecclesiological language does not appear there. (See Phil. 1:20; and 3:21 (*bis*)). It should also be pointed out that methodologicallly, we will not engage in an exhaustive exploration of the literary conventions of the first century C.E. Graeco-Roman world in an attempt to find one parallel or another. An intra-corpus (Pauline) investigation is what is really needed to get us beyond the hermeneutical impasse as our subsequent discussion will seek to demonstrate.

23. Our method here seems entirely congruent with the spirit of Wright's sound counsel. He writes: "We must inquire into the purpose, flow of thought, and inner coherence (or lack of it) of each letter. We must examine the relationship between the different letters, not least between apparently similar or parallel passages in different letters. And we must examine the meaning, and the mutual integration, of themes and ideas in the corpus as a whole." See *ARC,* vol. XII, No. 1. (Autumn, 1984), p. 31. John Meier makes a similar methodological observation regarding our study of the Pastorals in *The Mission of Christ and*

His Church: Studies in Christology and Ecclesiology (Delaware: Michael Glazier, 1990), p. 241, n. 36.

24. Col., for example, was addressed not only to the church at Colossae but to that at Laodicea as well (see Col. 4:16). Also, early textual evidence suggests that Eph. may well have been an encyclical sent to Laodicea, Ephesus and perhaps, other cities in Asia Minor. For more on this, see Introduction to both Col. and Eph. in Chapters Five and Six.

25. Oscar Brooks, "A Contextual Interpretation of Galatians 3:27," in *Studia Biblica 1978: Papers on Paul and Other New Testament Authors* (Sixth International Congress on Biblical Studies, Oxford 3-7, April 1978), edited by E.A. Livingstone (Sheffield: JSOT Press, 1980), p. 54. Also see Norman Anderson, *A Lawyer Among the Theologians* (London: Hodder and Stoughton, 1973), pp. 16-24.

26. See n. 21 *supra*, in this regard.

27. For a very informative discussion of the household of God motif, see David C. Verner, *The Household of God: The Social World of the Pastoral Epistles* (Chico: Scholars Press, 1981); also see, Stephen C. Barton, "Paul's Sense of Place: An Anthropological Approach to Community Formation in Corinth," *NTS* 105 (1986): 225-246.

28. E.P. Sanders, *Paul, The Law, and the Jewish People* (Philadelphia: Fortress Press, 1983), p. 5. However, for the view that σῶμα is "the central and all-important conception" of the church in Paul, see T.F. Torrance, *Royal Priesthood (Edinburgh: T. and T. Clark, 1955), p. 29.*

29. M. Barth, for example, writes: "...the discussion of the 'body of Christ' has been given preference over research into about a hundred other N.T. designations for the church." See, *Ephesians*, p. 183.

30. See Introduction, nn. 11-13 again.

CHAPTER THREE

THE SOMATIC ECCLESIOLOGY OF 1 CORINTHIANS

A. Introduction

Before we examine the σῶμα ecclesiology of 1 Cor., let us (as was promised) devote some time to a discussion of some introductory issues such as the integrity and chronology of the epistle.[1] However, since these higher critical questions pose problems that are not particularly bothersome, we can afford to be relatively brief. In addition, we will provide but a cursory description of the state and situation of the Corinthian church at the time the epistle was written.

After this, and in keeping with our methodological conviction, we will attempt to isolate exegetically those σῶμα texts that are ecclesiologically relevant from those that are not. In this way, we will not only avert the danger of building the church on the wrong σῶματα but we should also be able to determine whether or not, on the basis of 1 Cor. at least, the church as σῶμα is to be considered metaphorically related to, or mystically identified with, Christ's own human but now glorified σῶμα.

1. Integrity of 1 Corinthians

There is less than scholarly solidarity on the issue of the integrity of the epistle. Over the years, considerable amounts of energy have been expended in an attempt to promote one particular partition theory or another. This is done in order to solve the problem of what some perceive as redactional "breaks and joins"[2] within the epistle. For some, 1 Cor. is really a collage of literary exchanges between Paul and the Christians at Corinth; that is, the epistle, as is, is not regarded as having been sent to Corinth all at once.

Héring, for example, is a major proponent of such a view. He suggests that there is some tension between 4:19 where Paul expresses his intention to come to Corinth soon and 16:5-9 where he says that his coming will be delayed; also, he argues that Paul's rigorous attitude toward pagan sacrificial food à la 10:1-22 seems to be at odds with 8:1-13 and 10:23-11:1 where the issue is ethically handled and reduced to a level of mere charitable tolerance of the weak and conscience-stricken. To ease the tension, as he perceives it, Héring dissects the epistle by carving it up into two sizeable portions, namely, 1:1 - 8:12; 10:23 - 11:1; and 16:1-4,10-14 on the one hand, and 9:1 - 10:22; 11:2 - 15:58; and 16:5-9,15-24 on the other.[3]

J. Weiss, another major literary critic of the epistle, hypothesizes rather elaborately that the text should be broken up as follows: 6:12-20; 10:1-13; 11:2-34; 16:8f. (perhaps with vv. 7 and 20f. added) as Paul's first letter to the Corinthians with his second and third being chapters 7-9; 10:24 - 11:1; 12:1 - 16:6 (perhaps with vv. 7, 15-19 added); and, chapters 1:1 - 6:11, and 16:10-14 (perhaps with vv. 22ff. added).[4]

Such reconstructive efforts, however, seem more credible when considered *in vacuo*. Barrett has astutely observed that when Héring's and Weiss's literary 'solutions' are juxtaposed and compared, they tend to neutralize the effects of each other. For Barrett, "they cannot both be right...and the sense that both make, must be due to the scholar making the reconstruction.[5]

It seems to us, therefore, that the integrity of the epistle should be guarded and that other explanations should be advanced to account for a seemingly incoherent text. The length of it, the possibility that the busy apostle may not have written it in one sitting, and the fact that his agenda was dictated by both the reports (1:11; 5:1; 16:17f.) and the requests he received from Corinth (7:1,25; 8:1; 12:1; 16:1) are all factors upon which a literary defense may be built. Also, as Barrett and others have long demonstrated, the epistle, as is, is quite interpretable.[6] It means, then, that we will not be following the lead of Jewett[7] and others (like Weiss and Héring) in their "scissors and paste" approach to 1 Cor. in discussing the ecclesiological significance of σῶμα in the epistle.

2. Chronology of 1 Corinthians

Generally, scholars agree on the approximate date for the writing of the epistle. There is a narrow range of approximately one to two years, extending from about late 53 C.E. to early 55. Robertson and Plummer, for example, place the epistle "in the earlier months of the year 55",[8] while Barrett locates it, "in the early months of 54, or possibly towards the end of 53."[9] Greater chronological precision than this seems impossible and perhaps, even unnecessary. That scholars are comfortable with the early-to-mid-50's for the dating of 1 Cor. is more than sufficient for our present purposes.[10]

B.   The Church in 1 Corinthians: A General Description

Perhaps in language that is a trifle too colourful and severe, Murphy-O'Connor writes:

Conceited, stubborn, over-sensitive, argumentative, infantile, pushy. All these adjectives have their place in a description of the Corinthian Christians for whom Paul was responsible. They were the most exasperating community that he had to deal with, for they displayed a positive genius for misunderstanding him. Virtually every statement he made took root in their minds in a slightly distorted form, and from this defective seed came some of the most weird and wonderful ideas ever to dismay a preacher.... Who were these people who, if they tried Paul's patience to the utmost, also forced him to clarify the ideas which have become part of the foundations of Christian theology?[11]

Most likely, the Corinthian community[12] was comprised not only of the enslaved and the free (1 Cor. 7:17-24), of male and female (1 Cor. 11:2-16), but more basically, of both Jews and Gentiles (e.g., 1 Cor. 10:1-13; 12:13). This biculturalism, for example, seems to lie hidden behind Paul's discussion of the food problem and the disagreement between the strong and weak in chapters 8-10 where, perhaps, the weak and conscience-stricken point mainly to the Jewish Christians whereas the strong and stubborn, to Gentile converts.[13]

In terms of social classes, some of Paul's colleagues and converts were quite well-to-do; for example, Sosthenes (1 Cor. 1:1; cf. Acts 18:17) and Crispus (1 Cor. 1:14; cf. Acts, 18:8) were rulers of synagogues; Erastus (Rom. 16:23; cf. 2 Tim. 4:20) was treasurer of the city of Corinth and Gaius had a home large enough to accommodate the whole church (Rom. 16:23). In addition, Aquila and Prisca travelled from Rome to Corinth as refugees but had sufficient wherewithal to travel to Ephesus later where they were able to host the community (1 Cor. 16:19); and once back in Rome, they hosted the community there as well (Rom. 16:3).[14] From the epistle, we can also surmise that some Corinthians had enough money to indulge in legal proceedings (1 Cor. 6:1-8; cf. Jm. 2:5f.) as well as to contribute financially to the needs of the saints in Jerusalem (1 Cor. 16:1-4; 2 Cor. 8f; cf. 1 Cor. 9).

In spite of this, however, it seems more likely that the majority were drawn from among the 'have-nots'. In Paul's own words, not many of them were wise according to worldly standards, not many were powerful, and not many were high-born. Instead, God chose the foolish, the weak and the despised in the eyes of the world so that they might come to fullness of life in Christ and in so doing, acquire a status which places them even above those who are the worldly wise, the proud and the powerful (1 Cor. 1:26-29).[15]

Founded or fathered by the apostle (1 Cor. 3), the Corinthian

31

THE CHURCH AS THE BODY OF CHRIST

community also comes across as one which was beset with both theological and ethical difficulties. These include: The person of Christ (1 Cor. 12:3), the relationship between belief and behavior (1 Cor. 7 and 15), and what it means to be the church of God (1 Cor. 1:10-13; and chapter 14).

It is precisely this community to which Paul first makes mention of the church as the σῶμα of Christ. And to determine what he may have meant by it, we now turn to a discussion of σῶμα as ecclesiological language within the epistle as a whole.

C.   Σῶμα as E in 1 Corinthians

In all, σῶμα occurs forty-six (46) times in 1 Cor.[16] In forty-one (41) such cases, it is used in one of three ways, namely, A (in relation to a wo/man's physical make-up), C (referring to Christ himself) and E (with reference to the church). The other five (5) occurrences of σῶμα, all clustered in 15:37-40, are not relevant for our present purposes since there, Paul makes passing reference to botanical, astronomical and animals' bodies. In addition, thirty-three (33) other appearances of σῶμα in 1 Cor. should not detain us either since on those occasions Paul uses the term in an unambiguously A way. The thirty-three (33) occurrences again are as follows: 1 Cor. 5:3; 6:13,15,16,18,20; 7:34; 9:27; 12:12,14-25 *(passim)*; 13:3; and 15:35,44.[17]

The remaining eight (8) occurrences of σῶμα are those that have posed greatest problems for exegetes as they have sought to place the word in its proper category. The eight are: 6:19; 10:16,17; 11:24,27,29; 12:13,17.[18]

Rather than discuss these texts all at once and in so doing, give short shrift to the context of each, we will scrutinize them separately and in relation to our basic objective. This will help us to determine if credence should be given to our thesis that the once broken but now glorified body of Jesus is neither to be mystically collapsed into, nor metaphorically related to, the church as body but that instead, any human body should be considered the metaphorical referent of the church as body--at least on the basis of 1 Cor.

Along the way, an attempt will be made to draw out the ecclesiological implications of σῶμα wherever σῶμα as E is found; and at the end, a summary statement will be provided. Special emphasis is being placed upon the C and E σῶμα texts in 1 Cor. since it is here that exegetical imprecision seems most evident and the potential for misunderstanding the Pauline somatic ecclesiology is greatest.

1. 1 Cor. 6:19 -- οὐκ οἴδατε ὅτι τὸ σῶμα ὑμῶν ναὸς τοῦ
ἐν ὑμῖν ἁγίου πνεύματός ἐστιν, οὗ ἔχετε ἀπὸ Θεοῦ,

καὶ οὐκ ἐστὲ ἑαυτῶν;

Do you not know that *your body* is the temple of the Holy Spirit [which is] in you, which you have from God, and you are not your own? (Translation and emphasis mine)

This first text really does not belong to our C and E discussion at all. Most N.T. scholars correctly classify it as an A. However, there are a few for whom it is an E and fewer yet, for whom it is both A and E. Illustrative of this split of opinion are the following: Barrett--A; Best--A; Bruce--A; Conzelmann--A; Fee--A; Grosheide--A and E; Gundry--A; Héring--A; Johnston--A; Küng--A; Longenecker--A; Minear--A; Orr and Walther--E; Ridderbos--?; Robertson and Plummer--A; Robinson--E.[19]

The reasons for such a preponderance of 'A's over both 'E's and A/E combinations stem from the fact that those N.T. scholars who choose A treat v. 19 as part of the pericope incorporating vv. 12-20 in which Paul addresses himself to the problem posed by the temple prostitutes at Corinth. Also (and rightly so), these scholars resist the temptation to equate vv. 19f. with 3:16f. where the apostle likens the Corinthian Christian community as a whole to a temple indwelt by the Spirit;[20] and, unlike Robinson and a few others, scholars do not allow the ecclesiological handling of σῶμα elsewhere to determine the exegesis of the text. Instead, they insist that throughout the pericope, Paul's attention is glued to the individual and his σῶμα although the terms, μέλος (member or limb), σῶμα and Χριστός appear in the same pericope (cf. v. 15).[21]

Contra Orr and Walther, for example, the ecclesiological interpretation should not be pressed solely on the basis of the fact that Paul writes τὸ σῶμα ὑμῶν in v. 19 rather than τὰ σώματα ὑμῶν as in v. 15. Rather than taking σῶμα in v. 19 as a collective singular referring to the church, it is more plausible to take the expression *ad sensum*. What Paul is in fact saying here to the promiscuous Corinthian believers is that "their bodies are the temples of His (Christ's) Spirit."[22]

It is instructive to note that in Phil. 3:21 in which an obvious A σῶμα text appears,[23] Paul also employs the singular, τὸ σῶμα, but then qualifies it with ἡμῶν in speaking about "our...body" which one day will be changed and made to be like Christ's glorious body. Gundry also draws our attention to other Pauline examples which serve to illustrate that such constructions are not entirely unusual. For instance, he points to Rom. 1:21 (ἡ ασύνετος αὐτῶν καρδία -- their senseless heart), and 8:23 (τὴν ἀπολύτρωσιν τοῦ σώματος ἡμῶν -- the redemption of our body).[24]

In light of all this, then, we do consider it certain that in the pericope,

THE CHURCH AS THE BODY OF CHRIST

6:12-20, Paul shows no overt interest in the ecclesiological significance of the word, σῶμα. Rather, he is counselling the guilty Corinthians to refrain from satisfying their misguided sexual urges by way of temple prostitution. For the apostle, the Corinthians' bodies are now embraced by, and included in, Christ's "redemptive purchase"[25] and therefore, are under God's total control through the Spirit.

It means therefore, that we have to go further into the epistle before we encounter a C or E text. In doing so, we need to by-pass Paul's discussion of spouses' conjugal rights in relation to each other's body (chap. 7) and also his deployment of the Stoic ἀγων motif as reflected in 9:24-27 where, essentially, he tells us that he has chosen to pommel and subdue his body lest, after having preached to others, he himself be disqualified from the eschatological race.[26] In short, it is not until we reach chapter 10 that we find σῶμα used in a manner that makes it relevant to us.

> 2. *1 Cor. 10:16* -- τὸ ποτήριον τῆς εὐλογίας ὁ
> εὐλογοῦμεν, οὐχὶ κοινωνία ἐστὶν τοῦ αἵματος τοῦ
> Χριστοῦ; τὸν ἄρτον ὃν κλῶμεν, οὐχὶ κοινωνία τοῦ
> σώματος τοῦ χριστοῦ ἐστιν;
>
> The cup of blessing which we bless, is it not fellowship with the blood of Christ? The bread which we break, is it not fellowship with *the body of Christ*? (Translation and emphasis mine)

Unlike 6:19, N.T. scholars have little or no reason to equivocate here. In this case, it is reasonably clear that Paul is using σῶμα with reference to the once broken and self-donated body of Christ itself; that is, he is using the word in a C way.

Barrett, adopting a minority position, argues rather unconvincingly for E on the basis of the assumption that Paul would have used σάρξ (flesh) had he meant the personal body of Christ. This argument fails to carry conviction not only because of the overall eucharistic tone and tenor of the verse (v. 16) with its mention of cup (ποτήριον) and bread (ἄρτος), but more so because of the paratactic juxtaposition of blood (αἵμα) and body (σῶμα) in the said verse. Also to be added here is the fact that in a later pericope, 11:23-34, where Paul also comments on the eucharistic significance of the body of Christ, he again uses σῶμα (v. 24 -- and this Barrett concedes) without showing any predilection for the word, σάρξ, at all.[27]

In 10:16, the apostle is focussing on the blood (τὸ αἵμα) and the body of the Lord as emblems of fellowship (κοινωνία) and he is stressing their centrality in the eucharistic liturgy. Paul considers such a stress necessary because apparently, some of the Corinthians were undermining that fellowship which they should have had with their risen Lord. They were exhibiting idolatrous tendencies by ingesting food offered to idols (chap. 8); and they were doing so in spite of the conscientious objections of others (10:14,23).[28]

These "strong saints," insensitive to the weakness of those for whom Christ died (8:11) and unsolicitous about the good of their neighbour (10:24), had to be reminded that they could neither be allowed to drink the cup ($\tau\grave{o}$ $\pi o\tau\acute{\eta}\rho\iota o\nu$) of demons and that of the Lord nor partake of the table ($\acute{\eta}$ $\tau\rho\alpha\pi\acute{\epsilon}\zeta\alpha$) of the one and that of the other (vv. 19-21). They could not be allowed to offend others in the church by callously displaying their superior knowledge and their freedom. For the apostle, such behaviour is entirely disharmonious with eucharistic fellowship with the risen Christ whose body and blood were to be symbolically made available to the Corinthians through the Spirit. In addition, such disruptive behaviour is entirely out of step with Paul's concept of the church as an integrated whole; as one which, according to v. 17 (to be discussed next), has, at least, the human body as its role model.

3. *1 Cor. 10:17* -- $\acute{o}\tau\iota$ $\epsilon\acute{\iota}\varsigma$ $\acute{\alpha}\rho\tau o\varsigma$, $\grave{\epsilon}\nu$ $\sigma\grave{\omega}\mu\alpha$ $o\acute{\iota}$ $\pi o\lambda\lambda o\acute{\iota}$ $\grave{\epsilon}\sigma\mu\epsilon\nu$, $o\acute{\iota}$ $\gamma\grave{\alpha}\rho$ $\pi\acute{\alpha}\nu\tau\epsilon\varsigma$ $\grave{\epsilon}\kappa$ $\tauo\grave{\upsilon}$ $\grave{\epsilon}\nu\grave{o}\varsigma$ $\acute{\alpha}\rho\tauo\upsilon$ $\mu\epsilon\tau\acute{\epsilon}\chi o\mu\epsilon\nu$.

Because there is one bread, we who are many are *one body*, since we all partake of the one bread. (Translation and emphasis mine)

Coming right on the heel of Paul's eucharistic reference to the blood and body of the Lord (v. 16; cf. *supra*) is this elliptical verse. As a *crux interpretum*, it has generated conflicting views among exegetes. This is especially true in terms of their treatment and translation of the phrase, $\acute{o}\tau\iota$ $\epsilon\acute{\iota}\varsigma$ $\acute{\alpha}\rho\tau o\varsigma$, $\grave{\epsilon}\nu$ $\sigma\grave{\omega}\mu\alpha$ $o\acute{\iota}$ $\pi o\lambda\lambda o\acute{\iota}$ $\grave{\epsilon}\sigma\mu\epsilon\nu$ (v. 17a).

The problem is basically this: On the one hand, $\acute{o}\tau\iota$ may be taken causally with $\epsilon\acute{\iota}\varsigma$ $\acute{\alpha}\rho\tau o\varsigma$ made a part of the protasis and $\grave{\epsilon}\nu$ $\sigma\grave{\omega}\mu\alpha$ placed in the apodosis (according to my translation, for example[29]); on the other hand, both $\epsilon\acute{\iota}\varsigma$ $\acute{\alpha}\rho\tau o\varsigma$ and $\grave{\epsilon}\nu$ $\sigma\grave{\omega}\mu\alpha$ may be regarded as complements of $o\acute{\iota}$ $\pi o\lambda\lambda o\acute{\iota}$ $\grave{\epsilon}\sigma\mu\epsilon\nu$, producing a translation like, "the many (of us) are one bread (and) one body."[30]

In commenting on the problem, Robertson and Plummer exemplify both the conflict and the competing translations. According to them:

It is not easy to decide how they (the words, $\acute{o}\tau\iota...\grave{\epsilon}\sigma\mu\epsilon\nu$) should be translated.... The $\acute{o}\tau\iota$ may = 'because' and introduce the protasis, of which $\grave{\epsilon}\nu$ $\sigma\grave{\omega}\mu\alpha...\grave{\epsilon}\sigma\mu\epsilon\nu$ is the apodosis); 'Because there is one bread, one body are we the many'....The awkwardness of this is that there is no particle to connect the statement with what precedes.... Or (better) ὅτι may = 'for' or 'seeing that' and be the connecting particle that is required; 'Seeing that we who are many, are one bread, one body.'[31]

The immediate context (vv. 14-33) appears to be of little help here. It does not seem to prepare us for an announcement of that which Paul and the Corinthians become in partaking ἐκ τοῦ ἑνὸς ἄρτου (v. 17b) -- be it ἓν σῶμα alone or both εἰς ἄρτος and ἓν σῶμα. Rather, the emphasis of the discussion seems to be placed upon that with which one should or should not have κοινωνία -- fellowship (vv. 16, 18, 20).[32]

Using as an analogy the sacrificial system of Israel κατὰ σάρκα (v. 18), Paul apprises the Corinthians that eucharistic celebration makes possible spiritual fellowship with the blood and body of the Lord (v. 16) just as the partaking of the sacrifices by Israel (κατὰ σάρκα) made possible fellowship with the altar (v. 18). For this reason, the apostle goes on to counsel the guilty Corinthians that they cannot be allowed to have fellowship with demons by partaking of food and drink sacrificed to them (vv. 14, 20, 22).

In light of this interpretation, it is therefore possible, perhaps, to translate this elliptical verse in a third way and in so doing, eliminate it entirely from the E discussion. In such a case, ὅτι may be treated epexegetically with οἱ πολλοί ἐσμεν taken concessively. The verse, when unravelled, would read something like: "That is to say, there is one bread, pointing to the one body, the Lord's physical body, even though we are many, since we all partake of the one bread."[33]

Here, Paul would be insisting that the Corinthians' plurality does not jeopardize the oneness of the Lord's body celebrated in the eucharist (v. 16b) but that instead, their plurality is subsumed under the one body represented by the one bread from which they all share (v. 17b). Such a translation would also seem to cohere with Paul's typological affirmation that during the sojourn in the wilderness, all Israel (κατὰ σάρκα), in spite of their plurality, ate and drank from the same or one spiritual food and drink, Jesus Christ, likened to the Rock (vv. 3ff.).[34] That is to say, just as Israel in her plurality (v. 8) had fellowship with the one Rock, so are the Corinthians in theirs made to have fellowship, through the Spirit, with the one body -- Christ's personal body -- the focus of the eucharistic meal.

Interesting as this may sound, however, it seems that such a translation of the verse must be considered tentative at best in view of the fact that at least three arguments can be marshalled against it. First, the translation (or better, paraphrase) appears forced and is made to depend on too many extra words; in addition, the whole argument concerning the oneness of Christ's σῶμα taking precedence over the plurality of the Corinthians can be sustained without it. In v. 16, the apostle had already declared that the one bread made possible eucharistic κοινωνία with Christ's one body; and in v. 17, he now declares that all the Corinthians, including himself, do or should partake of that one σῶμα-symbol, namely, the one bread. Second, it is somewhat treacherous to infer that Paul must have used σῶμα in both verses (16f.) in the same way -- the C way; that he must 'stick to the subject' without any apparent digressions, as it were. In 12:27 - 13:3, for example, he switches from an obvious E σῶμα text in 12:27 (you are the *body* of Christ)[35] to an obvious A in 13:3 (if I give my *body* to be burned)[36]; and third, a comparison with Rom. 12:5a confirms that σῶμα should in fact be taken as complement of ἐσμεν in 1 Cor. 10:17a. In the former verse (Rom 12:5a), Paul unequivocally affirms that, "we who are many are one body"; and this ecclesiological affirmation, with minor literary variations, is but a carbon copy of that which we have in 1 Cor. 10:17a. When juxtaposed, the appropriate sections of the two verses read as follows: οἱ πολλοὶ ἓν σῶμα ἐσμεν (Rom. 12:5a) and, ἓν σῶμα οἱ πολλοί ἐσμεν (1 Cor. 10:17a).[37]

Still to be determined, however, is whether ἓν σῶμα alone or both it and εἰς ἄρτος are complements of ἐσμεν. In opting for the former, Käsemann, for one, suggests that Paul in 1 Cor. 10:16 chooses to reverse the traditional eucharistic sequence of bread and wine (cf. 1 Cor. 11:23-26; Mk. 14:22-25 *et parr.*) in order to make a smooth transition from the C σῶμα of v. 16b to the E σῶμα as sole complement of v. 17a.[38]

Syntactically speaking, this seems reasonable but, on its own, it is incapable of carrying the argument. It seems to be reinforced, however, when we consider Paul's ecclesiology as a whole. Nowhere else, for example, does he liken the church to the eucharistic loaf.[39] Without professing to be an expert at reading the mind of Paul, it does seem highly unlikely that the apostle would have formulated such a potentially profound "bread ecclesiology" so ambiguously in 10:17 but then chose not to redeploy and perhaps, even clarify it when the occasion made it possible.[40]

In 1 Cor. 11:17-34, the pericope to be discussed next, Paul again discourses on the need for proper comportment at both the communal meal (vv. 17-22) and the eucharistic meal (vv. 23-34) without giving the slightest indication in the latter that he considers the bread even as much as an ecclesiological leitmotif. This is even more surprising in view of the fact that like 10:14-33 (v. 32), Paul makes mention of the church, ἡ ἐκκλησία, but this time on two occasions (11:18, 22). In the former (10:14-33), he admonishes the Corinthian individualists not to give offence to Jews, to Greeks or to *the church of God*. In the latter (11:17-34), he reprimands the

THE CHURCH AS THE BODY OF CHRIST

Corinthian 'haves' who, in assembling as *a church* (v. 18) to celebrate the Lord's supper (v. 20), despise *the church of God* (v. 22) in not waiting for, and sharing with, the 'have-nots' so that all may eat and drink and do so together.

For these reasons therefore, it seems best to concur with the majority opinion. We should in fact translate 10:17, the *crux interpretum*, as we have already done, namely, "Because there is one bread, we who are many are one body, since we all partake of the one bread."

For most N.T. exegetes, then, σῶμα in this verse comes as, at least, a clear reference to E; to that which we (Paul and the Corinthians) are as symbolized by the partaking of the one bread. Conzelmann, however, rightly refuses to go along with Cerfaux who wants us to hold on to C for v. 16b and C and E for v. 17a. By arguing for C and E for v. 17a, Cerfaux interprets Paul as having mystically collapsed Christ and the church into one.[41]

Cerfaux's C/E position for v. 17a seems clearly inadmissible since Paul simply says that 'we are one body' and not 'we are the one body of Christ', referring to the C σῶμα of v. 16b. The two σῶματα here are different. In our view, v. 17a admits of neither a mystical nor a metaphorical relationship between the σῶμα of Christ (v. 16b) and that of the church (v. 17a). The personal and now glorified body of Christ which was given in death for our liberation and which, at Corinth, was or should have been at the center of the eucharistic liturgy is not in fact (mystically) or like (metaphorically) the body which is the church.

It is instructive to note in this regard that Paul actually uses the bread (ἄρτος) and not σῶμα (referring to the personal body of Christ) as the basis upon which to build his σῶμα ecclesiology in v. 17. He affirms that it is in their common partaking of that *one bread* that the Corinthians are to be made mindful of who they really are -- like *one body;* one *human* body.

The apostle does not compare, much less identify, the church as body with Christ's own body; that body which, having been raised by the power of God, now sits exalted in heavenly places. In the words of Gundry: "This is Paul's golden opportunity to equate the 'one body' of believers with the physical body of Christ just mentioned [in v. 16b]. He does not."[42]

In our view, then, the transubstantiationary assumptions that have long been associated with v. 16 and other eucharistic texts must not be allowed to cloud or colour the discussion of what it means for the Corinthians to be like a human body (v. 17a).[43] Of all the ecclesiological metaphors that Paul had at his disposal, such as field (3:5-15) and family (8:11-13), perhaps he chose σῶμα in 10:17a not only because it may have been triggered by the C σῶμα issue of the preceding verse (16b), but more so because it was considered the most appropriate metaphor for the issue at hand.

In addition to arguing for the non-identity of the σῶματα of 10:16b and v. 17a, and for the ʿany human bodyʾ interpretation of σῶμα in the latter, Best also tries to account for Paul's decision to use σῶμα so differently and in such close proximity to each other. He writes: "It was only natural that he should link it (body of Christ) up with the other way in which he uses the phrase, especially as the eucharist was a fellowship meal as well."[44]

Further, it seems evident to us that Paul's choice of σῶμα in v. 17a was motivated by his desire to highlight the concepts of inter-dependence among the Corinthians' weak and strong, mutual care and concern for each other and a commonness and coordination of purpose. Also, he may well have had in mind his up-coming use of σῶμα (in later chapters yet to be discussed) where he is to handle, at least in principle, issues similar to those in 10:14-33, namely, the enthusiasm, schismatic tendencies and cliquishness of those Corinthians whose interpersonal skills left much to be desired.[45]

With that having been said, then, let us now turn our attention to that to which we have already alluded: 1 Cor. 11 where σῶμα, as the object of our pursuit, also appears.

4. *1 Cor. 11:24ab, 27* -- καὶ εὐχαριστήσας ἔκλασεν καὶ εἶπεν Τοῦτό μού ἐστιν τό σῶμα τὸ ὑπὲρ ὑμῶν[46]...."Ωστε ὃς ἂν ἐσθίῃ τὸν ἄρτον ἢ πίνῃ τὸ ποτήριον τοῦ κυρίου ἀναξίως, ἔνοχος ἔσται τοῦ σώματος καὶ τοῦ αἵματος τοῦ κυρίου.

And having given thanks, he broke (the bread) and said: This is *my body* (broken) for you.... Whosoever eats the bread or drinks the cup of the Lord unworthily is guilty of profaning *the body* and the blood of the Lord. (Translation and emphasis mine)

Here, we have chosen to divert slightly from our format by not discussing these two σῶμα texts separately. We can afford to do so because the texts speak with one voice and they do so unambiguously. In them, and like 10:16, Paul makes mention of the physical body and blood of the Lord within the context of the Lord's Supper (v. 20).

For our present purposes, it is also unnecessary to allow ourselves to be drawn into the *traditionsgeschichtlich* controversy with regard to Paul's version of the eucharistic tradition as compared with the Synoptics.[47] Instead, it seems rather appropriate at this point that we avoid undue prolongation of the discussion and in so doing, simply allow Jewett to speak for us. In his view, "it is clear that the word σῶμα in 1 Cor. 11:24 and 27 refers to the traditional belief of Christ's actual presence in the sacrament and

THE CHURCH AS THE BODY OF CHRIST

not to the ecclesiological σῶμα Χριστοῦ."[48]

Such confidence, however, should not be expressed in relation to v. 29 which some scholars regard as another C σῶμα while for others, it is an E. Because of this divergence of opinion, we have decided to resort to our former format, namely, to deal with the verse separately.

> 5. *1 Cor. 11:29* -- ὁ γὰρ ἐσθίων καὶ πίνων[49] κρίμα ἑαυτῷ ἐσθίει καὶ πίνει μὴ διακίνων τὸ σῶμα.[50]

> For he who eats and drinks, not discerning *the body*, eats and drinks judgment upon himself.   (Translation and emphasis mine)

Exhibitive of those who take σῶμα here as C and those who see it as E are the following: Banks--E?; Best--E?; Barrett--C? Bruce--E; Fee--E; Grosheide--C; Héring--C; Jewett--C; Johnston--E; Käsemann--C; Küng--C; Murphy-O'Connor--E; Robertson and Plummer--C; and Robinson--E.[51]

From this sampling of N.T. scholars and commentators, it can be deduced that this verse seems to defy any facile classification in terms of σῶμα being either C or E. In fact, Barrett arrives at his tentative C conclusion only after having toyed with all three possibilities -- A, C, and E.[52] Those who commit themselves to one or the other, however, tend to do so in favour of C. Generally, they insist that the immediately preceding verses (vv. 27f.) seem to demand it since Paul is commenting on the Lord's own body and blood eucharistically symbolized by the eaten bread and the drunk cup. The apostle, they point out, begins v. 29 with the language of eating and drinking and although he makes mention of σῶμα alone instead of that and αἷμα (blood) to correspond with the two eucharistic acts as he had already done in vv. 27f., he is still to be understood as referring to the Lord's personal body in the verse (v. 29). That is, σῶμα in vv. 27-29 is taken as C throughout with τὸ αἷμα perhaps omitted rather inadvertently in v. 29.

Those who take the text as E tend to do so basically for two reasons. One is based on the omission of τὸ αἷμα discussed above, and the other, on the similarity between this verse and 1 Cor. 10:17 where we were already informed that eucharistic sharing should have made the Corinthians mindful of who they were --ἓν σῶμα.[53] Suggesting that many simply have not noticed the possibility that σῶμα can be taken as a reference to the church, Johnston, in addition, affirms that such an interpretation seems justified not only by the use of ἓν σῶμα in 1 Cor. 10:17 but more so, "by the whole tenor of Chapters 10-12."[54]

Of the two options before us, namely C and E, the E interpretation seems the better -- and for the following reasons: First of all, it is far more likely that Paul's omission of τὸ αἷμα in v. 29 was intentional. It is entirely unconvincing to suggest, for example, that Paul's mere eucharistic reference to the Lord's body and blood in vv. 24,27 necessarily demands an understanding of τὸ σῶμα as a reference to the Lord's personal body in v. 29 as well. We have already seen that Paul is able to switch, almost without warning, from C to E as in the case of 10:16f. where he makes passing reference to the ecclesiological usefulness of σῶμα in v. 17 just after having made mention of its eucharistic significance in v. 16.

In the pericope now under consideration (11:17-34), Paul makes mention of 'coming together' (vv. 17, 33f.), 'assembling as a church' (v. 18), 'despising the church' (v. 22), and 'waiting for one another' (v. 33), all of which indicate that here, too, he could well be thinking of both C and E under the rubric of σῶμα. For Paul, σῶμα sometimes points to Christ whose body is the cynosure of the eucharistic liturgy (10:16; 11:23-27) -- that is, C; as well as to the human body with which the Corinthian community is metaphorically associated (10:17; 11:29) -- that is, E.

Because the issue in both contexts (10:14-33 and 11:17-34) is so similar, having to do with a callous, self-righteous, un-Christian disregard of those with troubled consciences in the former and those with empty stomachs in the latter, it is quite understandable why Paul would elect to redeploy σῶμα in an E way in 11:29. For the opulent Corinthians to recline on the cushion of their socio-economic privileges at the expense of their more indigent Christian brothers and sisters in the Church is to make a mockery of the Lord's Supper (τὸ κυριακὸν δεῖπον -- 11:20) and also to be guilty of not discerning the body (μὴ διακρίνων τὸ σῶμα -- v. 29), that is, the church.[55]

Also, and in keeping with our thesis contention, it seems clear here that Paul is simply using the human body, any human body, as a metaphorical signifier of the church. If he had Christ's personal body in view, he could have expressed himself much more clearly -- especially in view of the fact that he makes explicit reference to the two eucharistic acts of eating and drinking both immediately before and immediately after his use of σῶμα as E in v. 29. In the preceding vv. (24,27), he refers to the actual body of the Lord in discussing its eucharistic significance but then simply uses τὸ σῶμα and not τὸ σῶμα αὐτοῦ (v. 24) or τὸ σῶμα κυρίου (v. 27) in referring to the church at Corinth (v. 29). This is essentially what he had just done in 10:16f.-- refer to the eucharistic significance of the body of Christ in v. 16 and then refer to the Corinthians simply as one body, ἐν σῶμα, in v. 17.

With this in view, then, let us now turn our attention to the last chapter in which our problematic σῶμα texts appear in the epistle, namely, chapter 12.

THE CHURCH AS THE BODY OF CHRIST

6. *1 Cor.* 12:13 -- καὶ γὰρ ἐν ἑνὶ πνεύματι ἡμεῖς πάντες εἰς ἓν σῶμα ἐβαπτίσθημεν, εἴτε Ἰουδαῖοι εἴτε Ἕλληνες, εἴτε δοῦλοι εἴτε ἐλεύθεροι, καὶ πάντες ἓν πνεῦμα ἐποτίσθημεν.

For by one Spirit we were all baptized into *one body*, whether Jews or Greeks, slaves or free, and we were all watered by the one Spirit. (Translation and emphasis mine)[56]

Σῶμα in this verse has been taken in one of three ways. For some, it is E; for others, it is C; and for still others, it is both.

Barrett, for example, is perhaps the best contemporary illustration of the E view. Following J. Weiss, he suggests that εἰς should be taken telically rather than locally since for him, the first part of the verse should be translated as follows: "In one Spirit we were all baptized *so as to become* one body."[57] This view is also consistent with Dunn's observation that, "in Paul it (εἰς) has the basic sense of 'motion towards or into' some goal."[58]

For Conzelmann, on the other hand, σῶμα is also E but he takes εἰς locally. Influenced by Gnostic prepossessions, this allows him to raise the church to a pre-existent and supra-mundane plane; the sort of thing that Gundry finds exegetically indefensible and ecclesiologically questionable. In Conzelmann's words:

> (This) is an indication in favour of the interpretation that the body of Christ is pre-existent in relation to the "parts". Incorporation into it takes place through baptism. The latter brings about the eschatological abrogation of human differences: In Christ, they no longer exist -- that is to say, in His body, the Church.[59]

According to M. Barth and L. Ramoroson,[60] εἰς should also be considered local. However, they further insist that σῶμα here is strictly C pointing to Christ Himself into whose body we are all spiritually incorporated via baptism. Their insistence is grounded in the conviction that Paul's baptismal theology articulated elsewhere (e.g., Rom. 6:3ff.; Gal. 3:27f.) is entirely consonant with a local understanding of εἰς and a C interpretation of σῶμα in 1 Cor. 12:13. For them, Paul nowhere suggests that baptism is εἰς the church. In addition, and still in their view, the close proximity of Χριστός in v. 12 to σῶμα in v. 13 makes a C interpretation of the latter contextually binding.[61]

And finally, there are those who avoid the either-or construct altogether and instead, opt for both C and E. Cerfaux, for instance, takes the position that Paul has mystically identified Christ's own body with the church as body.[62] For Schnackenburg, this identification is with Christ's earthly body[63] whereas for Käsemann, it points to the body of the exalted Lord, the Spirit-giving One.[64]

The basic assumption underlying the C/E combination is that baptism into Christ means incorporation into Himself, into His body, which, in some way, is also the church. The scholars who favour some version of the C/E view contend that Paul could not have had C or E alone in mind in v. 13. This is so because, after using the human body as an analogy in v. 12a and in so doing, underscoring the notion of unity in diversity, the apostle applies the analogy not to the Corinthian church as one would have expected but to Christ Himself. That is, Paul does not say at the end of the analogy in v. 12c, "so also is the Corinthian Church," but "so also is Christ" (οὕτως καὶ ὁ Χριστός).[65] Küng, for instance, equates 'so also is Christ' with 'so also are the faithful in Christ',[66] and for Johnston, "Christ and the Church are *practically identified.*"[67]

In summarizing the competing views that have arisen on the basis of v. 13a, then, we are left with the following: (1) σῶμα is E because εἰς is either local or telic; (2) σῶμα must be considered C in view of Paul's theology of baptism articulated elsewhere in which εἰς constitutes part of his baptismal formula (e.g., Gal. 3:27f.; Rom. 6:3f.); and (3) σῶμα must be considered both C and E especially on the basis of the assumption that Paul practically identifies Christ and the church in his mention of Χριστός at the end of v. 12 when presumably, what he also meant was the church.

Further, it should be pointed out that the vast majority of N.T. scholars seem to align themselves with the third position -- the C/E view. Because of this and its implications for Pauline ecclesiology insofar as the church-Christ relationship is concerned, let us look at it more closely. The other two positions (C and E) will be discussed in relation to it.

First of all, let us take a second look at the immediate context of v. 13a. In doing so, we need to lay hold of v. 12 in which the apostle introduces his σῶμα analogy. There he says:

Καθάπερ γὰρ τὸ σῶμα ἕν ἐστιν καὶ μέλη πολλὰ ἔχει,
πάντα δὲ τὰ μέλη τοῦ σώματος πολλὰ ὄντα ἕν ἐστιν
σῶμα, οὕτως καὶ ὁ Χριστός·

For just as the body is one and has many members, and all the members of the body, being many, are *one body*, so it is with Christ. (Translation and emphasis mine)

THE CHURCH AS THE BODY OF CHRIST

To begin, Paul makes two points about the human body. First, he makes mention of the unity of the body; a unity which is preserved in spite of the body's many limbs or members. And second, he follows with the assertion that all the many limbs or members of the body go together to form one body.

It means, therefore, that in our attempt to understand the use of the analogy later on (vv. 13-27), we need to keep both aspects of it in mind: (1) the unity of the human body in spite of its plurality of limbs (v. 12a); and (2) the many limbs going together to form one human body (v. 12b). It is this two-pronged approach which allows us to follow Paul more easily and straightforwardly. The appendage, v. 12c, "so also is Christ," is entirely meaningful since it is consonant with the two points the apostle has just made on the basis of the analogy in v. 12ab and which he is about to spell out in vv. 13-27; that is, Christ, like the human body (any human body), maintains His unity or integrity under all circumstances; and as is true of the human body that all its limbs go together to comprise it, so it can be said of Christ that in some way, all His limbs or Spirit-baptized Corinthians go together to form one body, the church (v. 13); a church that belongs to Him (v. 27).

In other words, Paul says, "so also is Christ" (v. 12c), because he wants to say, "so also is Christ," and not, "so also is the church."[68] To see the church here in this appendage is to leap ahead of the apostle slightly. It is to miss the crucial Christological point that the plurality of the Corinthians is subsumed under, and made subservient to, the unity of Christ (cf. 1:10-12). Like the human body of v. 12a which enjoys its oneness or unity in the face of its many members, Christ, too, preserves His oneness or integrity in the face of the Corinthians who now belong to Him. He does so through the Spirit and in spite of the ethnocultural and especially charismatic diversity (cf. vv. 4-11) of all the Corinthian Christians.

The case for C/E in the following verse (v. 13) stems, perhaps, from a failure to see that Paul, within the context of his $\sigma\tilde{\omega}\mu\alpha$ language in v. 13, is laying hold of the second part of the analogy (v. 12b), namely, that through the Spirit, all the Corinthians go together to form one body, one human body -- be they Jew or Greek, slave or free; and also, that it is in v. 27 that the apostle seeks to make even more meaningful the compact and enigmatic appendage of v. 12c: "so it is with Christ". Ziesler's observation is quite germane here. He writes:

> As for the body of Christ, it is in no way equivalent to Christ as a person, but is the community of those who live by and under the divine power.... In 1 Cor. 12:12-31... the apparent equation of the church with Christ in v. 12 must be understood in the

light of the whole argument, which is that the church is the body empowered and controlled and defined by the Spirit (see especially vv. 13 and 1-11). 'So also is Christ' in v. 12 is thus a condensed expression for this view, which is more fully set out in v. 27, 'Now you are the body of Christ and individually members of it,' and which rests on the understanding of the church as the community of the Spirit.[69]

Of equal importance (and as we have already suggested), Paul in this whole passage (vv. 12-27) is choosing to ground his discussion of the church in the Christological affirmation that diversity and in particular, charismatic and ethnocultural diversity (cf. vv. 4-11, 13-26), does not play havoc with Christ's unity or integrity. For him, unity in Christ is the given whereas for the Corinthians, the diversity of grace-gifts proved to be problematic. It was problematic for them because, evidently, some πνευατικοί (v. 1), some of the "gifted" Corinthians, were prioritizing the charisms in the church on the basis of the assumption that some of these gifts were better than and, perhaps, even normative for all others (12:31).[70] In addition to uplifting love as the greatest of all gifts and that which through grace has been granted to all, the apostle appeals to the Corinthians to manifest a sober recognition of, and a mature adherence to, the whole concept of their diversity of gifts made possible by the one and the self-same Spirit; the One who comes as both baptizer and bestower (cf. vv. 4,11,13).

In short, Paul's pastoral appeal in the entire pericope (vv. 12-27) is for diversity in the church within the context and conviction of the oneness of Christ; and this is in contradistinction to the crippling and confining uniformity for which some of the "gifted" Corinthians were agitating (cf. 1:10-13); those Corinthians who themselves, with their diverse gifts, were to function like a multi-membered but well-coordinated human body under the controlling power of Christ through the Spirit. It is for this reason, then, that we consider the decision to regard σῶμα of v. 13 as E alone to be most plausible, compatible as it is with one of the points of the analogy, namely, the second one: that indeed, all the many Spirit-baptized Corinthians go together to form the local church likened to a human body. Also, the suggestion of Barrett and others who take εἰς telically is entirely compatible with it and should, therefore, be given some credence.

With this understanding of the verse (v. 13) before us, then, let us now turn to our last "problem" σῶμα in the epistle; a σῶμα to which we have already alluded.

7. *1 Cor. 12:27* -- Ὑμεῖς δέ ἐστε σῶμα Χριστοῦ καὶ μέλη

THE CHURCH AS THE BODY OF CHRIST

ἐκ μέρους.

Now you are *the body of Christ* and individually, members. (Translation and emphasis mine)

For most N.T. exegetes, σῶμα here is taken articularly although it appears anarthrous in the verse. The correct grammatical assumption is that the proper name, Χριστοῦ, in the expression, σῶμα Χριστοῦ, exerts an articular influence on σῶμα and therefore, makes the translation legitimate.[71] In a more tentative fashion, Schweizer also suggests that "the omission of the article may be due to its (σῶμα) status as predicate," although he adds that "the articles are not impossible if the uniqueness of the predicate should be stressed."[72]

More important, however, is the common assumption that since Paul has virtually employed Χριστός as a synonym for the church in v. 12c, he is to be interpreted as saying that in some profound and inexplicable way, the Corinthians are in fact the body of Christ; that "real body' which in the words of Brown, "suffered, died, and rose."[73] In a more cautious but somewhat nebulous manner, Best avers:

> In ... 1 Cor. 12:12, we seem to find the church called 'Christ'; yet that expression is later reduced (v. 27) to 'Body of Christ' .... Perhaps we may say that in these tentative approaches to calling the church 'Christ' Paul is feeling after terminology which will permit him to express the unity which he knows to exist between Christ and his church.[74]

Contrary to this prevailing position is Barrett's. For him: "The genitive (Χριστοῦ) is not of identity but of possession and authority; not, the body which is Christ, of which Christ consists, but the body that belongs to Christ, and over which he rules."[75]

Gundry, as we pointed out earlier, also disagrees with those for whom Χριστοῦ in v. 27 is an explicative genitive or one of identity. In his words, it "just might be taken as possessive."[76]

From this discussion so far, then, we can at least make one observation, namely, that the problem cannot be solved conclusively by simply arguing on grammatical grounds. Instead, we need to look elsewhere for our bearings. We need to look at the flow of Paul's discussion going back to v. 12 and moving forward to v. 27. We need to do so because it is in v. 12 that the σῶμα-Χριστός analogy first appears whereas it is at v. 27 that the apostle "sums up."[77]

46

THE SOMATIC ECCLESIOLOGY OF 1 CORINTHIANS

We need to remind ourselves that in v. 12, Paul does not in fact employ Χριστός as a synonym or as scholarly shorthand for the church. It means, then, that one cannot validly argue that Christ and the church in v. 27 are somehow identified via His σῶμα on the basis of the assumption that the apostle had earlier identified the two in v. 12 for there, he had not. In his fourteen (14) uses of σῶμα between vv. 13-26 inclusive, Paul seeks to show that proper human bodily function presupposes the presence, plurality and performance of all the limbs or members such as hand and foot (vv. 15,21), eye (vv. 16f.,21), ear (vv. 16f.), and head (v. 21).

The apostle stresses the presence, plurality and performance of these limbs because his eyes are focussed on the many charisms in the Corinthian community some of which included prophecy (vv. 28f.), teaching (vv. 28f.), healing (vv. 9,28,20), speaking in various kinds of tongues (vv. 10,28,30), and the ability to interpret them.[78] Because a discussion of these charisms will at best be of subsidiary relevance to our main purpose, however, we will not be deterred by them here. Instead, we need say only that Paul is attempting to avert both division (σχίσμα -- v. 25) and disorder (14:40) in Corinth. He is employing his analogy, his σῶμα language, at length (vv. 13-26) so as to prepare for his ecclesiological statement in vv. 27-31 and beyond where he contends that diversity and not uniformity of charisms is the norm; that co-ordination of effort and commonness of purpose, the goal; and that the building up of the Corinthian church as the body of Christ is made possible by what they do, by what they say, and most important, by how they love. (cf. Chapters 13f.)

At the very heart of this conviction, however, is the assertion in 12:27 that the Corinthians themselves are the body of Christ and individually, members. That is, the Corinthians are not like a human body in some vague sense but, rather, they belong to Him who stands and reigns as Lord over them (cf. v. 3). By using Χριστοῦ as a possessive genitive (à la Gundry, e.g.), Paul is neither identifying the Corinthian church as a body with the body of Christ, His personal body, nor is He likening the one to the other. Instead, He is simply likening the cantankerous Corinthians to any human σῶμα.

In addition to the point already made, that a close relationship between the two bodies should not be argued for in v. 27 on the basis of a supposed identity in v. 12, four other arguments can be advanced to buttress our position regarding our possessive genitive interpretation of v. 27. They are as follows:

(1) In vv. 12f., Paul pauses long enough to strike two notes with the use of σῶμα -- one Christological and the other, ecclesiological; first, that Christ's unity is maintained amidst His many Spirit-baptized Corinthian

members; and second (and by inference), that all such members go together to form one body, His church. However, Paul nowhere makes mention of Christ's personal body; not in v. 13 and certainly not in vv. 14-26 either. In fact, his σῶμα language in vv. 14-26 is completely devoid of Christological content and this is rather strange, to say the least, if Paul were really on his way to announcing that metaphorically or mystically the Corinthians are the personal body of Christ Himself (v. 27). In other words, v. 27 as summary statement only summarizes what Paul actually says analogically about the Corinthians on the basis of σῶμα in vv. 12-26 -- nothing more and nothing less.

(2) Having looked back at vv. 14-26 in particular, we can now look forward at v. 28 and on up to chapter 14 as well since chapters 12-14 as a whole, in which Paul discusses the issue of the charisms, constitute one of the literary blocs of the epistle. In doing so, we discover that nowhere does the apostle even remotely suggest, much less elaborate upon, the closeness of relationship supposedly between Christ Himself via His own body and the Corinthians as body. Again, this would be most surprising if in fact, and according to Murphy-O'Connor, "the name 'Christ' is given to the community."[79] Actually, the words σῶμα and Χριστός do not appear at all in this whole section, namely, 12:28 - 14:40, except as an A σῶμα in 13:3 where Paul uses a rather illuminating hyperbole in speaking about himself; in declaring that pure and patient love for others is eminently superior to, and far more commendable than giving his body to be burned.

In expressing his surprise, Küng exemplifies the problem that many scholars (including himself) seem to have who assume that Paul, in some way, has brought the two σῶματα together in 12:12-27. He writes: "It is striking that Paul's remarks about the community as the body of Christ never appear in the context of Christology or soteriology or even of an explicitly theoretical ecclesiology. The context is rather that of an admonition, a paranesis."[80]

This point should be stressed since seemingly, there is no plausible explanation (at least, none is ever given) as to why the apostle would choose to relate Christ and the church as intimately as he supposedly does on the basis of σῶμα in 12:27 and then completely ignore it in his further discussion of the charisms issue which supposedly gave birth to this identity and intimacy in the first place. It seems highly unlikely that such a profound and provocative "Christological ecclesiology" would have been given such a glancing treatment throughout the entire discussion (chapters 12-14).

Also of note is the fact that Paul in v. 28 simply uses ἐκκλησία, the usual word for the church, and he uses it as an equivalent to σῶμα in v. 27.[81] For the rest of the discussion, ending at 14:40, he again chooses to use ἐκκλησία and he does so, twice (14:19,28) without once referring to σῶμα

THE SOMATIC ECCLESIOLOGY OF 1 CORINTHIANS

again. This, at least, suggests that the apostle is not investing the word, σῶμα (v. 27), with that much importance per se. What is important is the ecclesiological statement that is being made, namely, there being diversity of charisms for the good of all.

(3) If the apostle is in fact relating Christ and the church as closely as he is understood to be doing in v. 27, he would, in a way, be giving credence and credibility to the Corinthians in their excessive self-confidence and enthusiasm. Such a potentially profound ecclesiology would be at odds with the immaturity (3:1; 14:20) and moral substandardness that characterised the community such as in-fighting (chapter 1), incestuous living (chapter 5), fornicating with temple prostitutes (chapter 6) and litigious wrangling (chapter 6).

And finally: (4) A survey of Paul's use of Christological titles in the rest of 1 Cor. shows that at no other time does he indicate that Christ and the Corinthians are to be so closely related as the prevailing interpretation of v. 27 would suggest. We are therefore left to wonder openly as to why Paul would make mention of such a profound concept *en passant* (and in a paranaetic pericope at that) when he neither prepared us for it ahead of time nor explains what he may have meant by it in later sections of the epistle.

Of the 115 times that the apostle uses Christological titles in the epistle, Χριστός appears alone on 45 occasions. It also appears in combinations such as Χριστός with κύριος and/or Ἰησοῦς 19 times while the other 51 occurrences make mention only of κύριος and/or Ἰησοῦς.[82] For Paul, the Corinthians are as babes in Christ (ὡς νηπίοις ἐν Χριστῷ - - 3:1); they are like His servants (ὡς ὑπηρέτας Χριστοῦ-- 4:1), they now belong to Him (ὑμεῖς δὲ Χριστοῦ -- 3:23), and if faithful, they will be seen by all to be His when He comes (οἱ τοῦ Χριστοῦ ἐν τῇ παρουσίᾳ αὐτοῦ-- 15:23). In a word, the One who died (1:17,23; 5:7; 8:11; 15:1), was raised (15:13ff.), is now preached (1:6,17,23; 15:12), and is coming again (1:7f.; 15:23) is none other than the Christ who though one in the Spirit with the Corinthians (cf. 6:15-17) is not to be identified with them but instead, stands and reigns as Lord over them (1:2; 7:17,32,35; 8:6; 9:1; 10:22; 11:32; 12:3; 15:27; 16:22).

D. Summary

In Paul's first epistle to the Corinthians, it seems clear that Christ and the church are not so intimately related as to allow us to consider His own σῶμα, that which was once dead but now alive and exalted, as that very σῶμα with which the church is mystically identified or that very σῶμα with which the church is metaphorically associated.

THE CHURCH AS THE BODY OF CHRIST

Paul is able to make different ecclesiological statements on the basis of σῶμα but in doing so, he consistently likens the church to a human body. That is, Christ's σῶμα itself is not of direct relevance to Paul's ecclesiological σῶμα language per se. It is relevant only in the larger sense that had it not been for Christ's self-donation on the cross via His body, that body which is now made eucharistically relevant (1 Cor. 10:16; 11:24,27), the church at Corinth would not have existed at all and Paul would not have been able to compare the Corinthians to anything; be it body, building, or babes (see 1 Cor. 3).

It is true that, at times, a discussion of the personal body of Christ appears alongside that of the church. In two of the three contexts in which Paul discusses the church as σῶμα in 1 Cor., he also makes mention of Christ's personal σῶμα, namely, 10:16f. and 11:24-29. However, this must not be used as *prima facie* evidence to neutralize our conclusion since the apostle has shown himself capable of using σῶμα in obviously A, C, and E ways and at times, in close proximity to each other. It means, therefore, that nothing but a close-up exegetical look at the problematic σῶμα texts in 1 Cor. is admissible -- precisely what we have sought to do in this chapter. It is on the basis of this exegetical effort that we are led to the conclusion that in 1 Cor., the human σῶμα, any human σῶμα, and not Christ's own personal σῶμα, is in fact the *tertium comparationis* for the church as σῶμα.

ENDNOTES

Chapter Three

1. See p. 26, n. 21. Scattered references will be made to the text-critical status of the epistle in so far as such references are of direct relevance to the v.(v) being examined. In terms of Pauline authorship and the authenticity of 1 Cor., we need only consult the early literary evidence such as *1 Clem.* 35:5f.; 37:5; 47:1-3; 49:5; Ignatius' *Eph.* 16:1; *Rom.* 4:3; *Trall.* 12:3; *Phil. 3:3*; and P^{46} *(ca.200 C.E.)*.

2. Conzelmann, *A Commentary on the First Epistle to the Corinthians*, in *Herm.*, trans. by J. Leitch (Philadelphia: Fortress Press, 1975), p. 2.

3. See J. Héring, *1 Corinthians*, ET (London: The Epworth Press, 1962), *ad loc.* Héring considers chapter 13 a separate piece as well.

4. See J. Weiss, *Der Erste Körintherbrief*, (Göttingen: 1897), *ad loc.* For examples of other fairly extensive reconstructive efforts, see Kümmel, *op. cit.*, pp. 202-205. A more recent illustration of the lingering influence of partition theories, at least on the basis of chapters 8-10, is: Donna Bosworth, "1 Corinthians 8-10", a paper read at the Pacific Northwest Region Annual Meeting of *AAR/SBL*. May 2nd, 1985 (University of Calgary, Alberta, Canada).

5. See Barrett, *op. cit.,* p. 14; also see Conzelmann, *op. cit.,* p. 4.

6. *Ibid,;* also see, J. Brunt, "Rejected, Ignored or Misunderstood? The Fate of Paul's Approach to the Problem of Food Offered to Idols in Early Christianity," *NTS* 31 (1985): 113-124, esp. nn. 2f., p. 122; and J.W. Welch, "Chiasmus in the New Testament," in *Chiasmus in Antiquity,* edited by J.W. Welch (Hildesheim: Gerstenberg, 1981), pp. 211-249. Welch basically argues that 1 Cor., among others, is an integrated and chiastic whole. See esp. pp. 216f.; also, Charles Talbert, *Reading Corinthians: A Literary and Theological Commentary on 1 and 2 Corinthians* (New York: Crossroad, 1989), p. xix.

7. Mainly under the influence of J. Weiss, Jewett suggests that 1 Cor. is comprised of letters A, B, C, and D with $\sigma\hat{\omega}\mu\alpha$ as E appearing in all but A. See *Paul's Anthropological Terms*, pp. 254-304.

8. A. Robertson and A. Plummer, *A Critical and Exegetical Commentary on the First Epistle of St. Paul to the Corinthians*, in *ICC* (Edinburgh: T. and T. Clark, 1967), p. xxxi.

9. Barrett, *op. cit.*, p. 5.

51

10. For a recent and detailed account (based upon both internal and external evidence) of when Paul may have visited Corinth for the first time, and by inference, when he may have written 1 Cor., see J. Murphy-O'Connor, *St. Paul's Corinth*, pp. 129-152.

11. J. Murphy-O'Connor, *1 Corinthians* (Delaware: Michael Glazier, 1979), p. ix. Neyrey is not much more charitable in his description of the community. He states: "The most important piece of information about the Pauline church at Corinth is its factionalism." See J.H. Neyrey, *Christ is Community: The Christologies of the New Testament* (Delaware: Michael Glazier, 1985), p. 200; for the same view, see C.K. Barrett, *Essays on Paul* (Philadelphia: The Westminster Press, 1982), p. 22.

12. Elsewhere, Murphy-O'Connor, among others, hazards the view that there may well have been a number of house churches in Corinth. He bases this assumption mainly on the fact that Paul makes mention of "the whole church" that met in Gaius' house (1 Cor. 14:23; Rom. 16:23), and of the church coming together to eat a communal meal and to celebrate the Lord's supper (11:17-34). Murphy-O'Connor draws the inference that these "coming togethers" were periodic in nature and that one of such "get togethers" may also have been occasioned by 1 Cor. itself. That is, the entire church in Corinth may have gathered to hear the epistle read; to hear the apostle's responses to the reports and requests that were sent his way (see 1 Cor. 1:10; 7:1ff.; 8:1ff.; 12:1ff.; 16:1ff.). Overall, this proposal seems both creative and cogent. For one thing, a typical well-to-do Corinthian such as Gaius would probably have had a home that could accommodate a maximum of no more than 50 people. Be that as it may, neither ecclesiastical scenario (house churches or one congregation) would affect our exegetical examination of $\sigma\hat{\omega}\mu\alpha$ in 1 Cor. See J. Murphy-O'Connor, *St. Paul's Corinth*, pp. 155-159. Other examples of those who argue for house churches at Corinth and elsewhere are: F.V. Filson, "The Significance of Early House Churches", *JBL* 58 (1939): 105-112; R. Banks, *Paul's Idea of Community* (Exeter: Paternoster Press, 1981), pp. 38f; A.J. Malherbe, "House Churches and Their Problems," in his *Social Aspects of Early Christianity* (Baton Rouge: Louisiana State University Press, 1977); and E.A. Judge, *The Social Pattern of Christian Groups in the First Century* (London: Tyndale, 1960). In his recently published dissertation, Yarbrough simply takes it as a given that there were house churches at Corinth and elsewhere. See O.L. Yarbrough, *Not Like the Gentiles: Marriage Rules in the Letters of Paul* (Atlanta, GA: Scholars Press, 1985), p. 123; and even more recently, see the compelling case made by Branick, *The House Church in the Writings of Paul*, pp. 101-114.

13. Minear is of a similar conviction. See, *Obedience of Faith: The Purposes of Paul in the Epistle to the Romans* (London: SCM Press Ltd., 1971), pp. 29f.

14. In the succeeding chapter, we will discuss briefly this problematic chapter in our attempt to determine what the state and situation of the Roman church was like when the epistle was written.

15. Gerd Thiessen is a pioneer among those who are attempting to analyze the early church(es) along social scientific and socio-economic lines. In terms of the Corinthian community, he is particularly interested in the eating habits of the Corinthians as reflected in 1 Cor. 11:17-34. He sees there, a clear demarcation between the 'haves' and the 'have-nots' with the possibility (probability) that, in keeping with regular Graeco-Roman culinary customs, the richer Christians were accustomed to partake of the more expensive "ticket items" such as meats, whereas the poorer saints had to settle for lesser things like, perhaps, "hogs' funguses". See, *The Social Setting of Pauline Christianity: Essays on Corinth,* ed. and trans. with intro. by J. Schutz (Philadelphia: Fortress Press, 1982). For a recent suggestion that not that many Corinthians were as poverty-stricken as is generally assumed, see Gail O'Day, "Jeremiah 9:22-23 and 1 Corinthians 1:26-31: A Study in Intertextuality," *JBL* 109 (1990): 259-267.

16. For a full statistical break-down of all forty-six (46) occurrences of σῶμα in 1 Cor., see pp. 17f.

17. See p. 18 again for earlier listing with reference also made to the solid scholarly consensus that now exists re: the classification of these σῶματα as A.

18. For the *RSV* translations of these verses, see pp. 19-21.

19. C.K. Barrett, *op. cit., ad loc.;* E. Best, *One Body in Christ,* pp. 74ff.; F.F. Bruce, *1 and 2 Corinthians,* in *NCBC* (London: Oliphants, 1971), *ad loc.;* H. Conzelmann, *op. cit., ad loc.;* Gordon Fee, *The First Epistle to the Corinthians* in *NICNT* (Grand Rapids: Wm.B. Eerdmans, 1953), *ad loc.;* R.H. Gundry, *SŌMA in Biblical Theology,* pp. 220, 228; J. Héring, *op. cit., ad loc.;* Johnston, *The Doctrine of the Church,* p. 100; H. Küng, *The Church,* p. 224; R.N. Longenecker, *Paul: Apostle of Liberty,* (New York: Harper & Row, 1964), p. 53; P.S. Minear, *Images,* p. 97; W.F. Orr and J.A. Walther, *1 Cor.,* in *AB, ad loc;* H.N. Ridderbos, *Paul,* pp. 372f. Ridderbos discusses the pericope, 6:12-20, as a whole and in relation to the ecclesiological use of σῶμα drawn mainly from other sections of 1 Cor. such as chapter 12, as well as from Rom. Hence, we found it virtually impossible to ascertain how he understood v. 19 itself; Robertson and Plummer, *op. cit., ad loc.;* J.A.T. Robinson, *The Body,* pp. 76f.

20. E.g., Küng, *ibid,* pp. 224, 248.

21. See Jewett, *Paul's Anthropological Terms,* p. 302.

22. Johnston, *op. cit.,* p. 220.

23. A dissenting view, here, has not been found.

24. Gundry, *op. cit.,* p. 90.

25. For a brief discussion of the imagery of slavery which undergirds v. 20 and hence, the justification for the use of the neologistic expression, 'redemptive purchase', see J.P. Sampley, *Pauline Partnership in Christ: Christian Community and Commitment in Light of Roman Law* (Philadelphia: Fortress Press, 1980), p. 2; and Fee, *First Corinthians*, pp. 264f.; Orr *et al.* tentatively and rather unconvincingly suggest that v. 20 is a veiled reference to the prostitution price.

26. Pfitzner has provided us with a detailed discussion of these verses. He argues that Paul is not arguing for a form of legalistic 'works' righteousness but instead, is using the Stoic commonplace to underscore the fervour and seriousness with which he has chosen to undertake his kerygmatic commission. Cf. V.C. Pfitzner, *Paul and the Agōn Motif* (Leiden: E.J. Brill, 1967); cf. A.J. Malherbe, *Paul and the Popular Philosophers* (Minneapolis: Fortress Press, 1989), pp. 88, 119.

27. C.K. Barrett, *op. cit., ad loc.*

28. For a detailed discussion (published thesis) of all 13 occurrences of κοινωνία in Paul, see G. Panikulam, *Koinōnia in the New Testament* (Rome: Biblical Institute, 1979). Panikulam argues that the 13 uses of κοινωνία in Paul do not point to the mysterious and mystical relationship between God and us. Instead, it points to a spiritual relationship that operates both vertically and inter-personally. Also see B.P. Prusak, "Hospitality Extended or Denied: *Koinōnia* Incarnate from Jesus to Augustine," *Jur.* 36 (1976): 89-126.

29. See discussion of text to follow.

30. See the *KJV* for a similar translation. We found it rather interesting that this version of 1 Cor. 10:17 forms the basis of an ecclesiological doctrine for the United Society of Believers in Christ's Second Coming (the Shakers). According to them: "To constitute a true faith of Christ, there must necessarily be union of faith, of motives, and of interest, in all the members who compose it. There must be 'one body and one bread' and nothing short of this union in all things, both spiritual and temporal, can constitute a true church, which is the body of Christ." See M. Emory *et al.*, "The Tax Exempt Status of Communitarian Religious Organizations: An Unnecessary Controversy?" in *Cults, Culture and the Law: Perspectives on New Religious Movements*, edited by T. Robbins *et al.* (Chico, California: Scholars Press, 1985), p. 178.

31. Robertson *et al., op. cit., ad loc.* Another example of this can be found in the recent ecclesiological study: Richard J. Stevens, *Community Beyond Division: Christian Life Under South Africa's Apartheid System* (New York: Vantage Press, 1984), p. 108. Granted, Stevens is not a N.T. scholar. However, his work is still helpful in giving us some idea of how 1 Cor. 10:17 is sometimes understood in less specialized circles.

32. Robertson *ibid.;* also see Panikulam, *op. cit.*, pp. 17ff.

33. Héring also mentions this possibility *en passant*. His suggested translation is somewhat different from the one proposed here but at least they amount to the same thing, namely, the removal of σῶμα from the E category in preference for C. However, he finally opts for both ἄρτος and σῶμα as complements of ἐσμεν. See *op. cit., ad loc.*

34. The fact that αὐτό (same) appears in vv. 3f. and ἕν (one) appears in v. 18 should not be pressed as *prima facie* evidence against linking the two passages. Paul seems to be using the two words interchangeably. In 12:8-11, especially v. 11, for example, he discusses the Spirit's apportionment of the grace-gifts and in doing so, seems to employ a hendiadys. He says, ' πάντα δὲ ταῦτα τὸ ἓν καὶ τὸ αὐτό πνεῦμα '. For an insightful analysis of Paul's Christocentric (better yet, ecclesiocentric) reinterpretation of the Hebrew Scriptures, see Richard Hays, *Echoes of Scripture in the Letters of Paul* (New Haven: Yale University Press, 1989). An earlier work, though somewhat rather rambling in style, can also be consulted with profit. See Richard M. Davidson, *Typology in Scripture: A Study of Hermeneutical τ ύπο ς Structures* in *AUSDDS* (Michigan: Andrews University Press, 1981).

35. More on this text later in the chapter.

36. There is solid scholarly consensus on this point. We know of no dissenting view.

37. Jewett also makes the same observation in opting for σῶμα as complement of ἐσμεν in 1 Cor. 10:17a; cf. *Paul's Anthropological Terms*, p. 304.

38. Käsemann, *Essays on New Testament Themes*, pp. 109f. Schweizer considers this suggestion plausible. See, "*Sōma*" in *TDNT*, vol. VII, p. 1070, n. 436; and so does Panikulam; *op. cit.*, pp. 18f.

39. Minear, for example, could find no other text which explicitly supports a 'bread' ecclesiology although he tries to build an ecclesiology on what appears to be the minutest detail; cf. *Images*, pp. 36f. Also, Héring's citing of 1 Cor. 5 is indefensible since the church is not being likened to bread there. Rather, Paul makes mention of "the unleavened bread of sincerity and truth" in contradistinction to the immoral Christian actions and attitudes of some within the church. See Héring, *op. cit., ad loc.*

40. Robertson and Plummer seem to favour taking both εἰς ἄρτος and ἓν σῶμα as complements of ἐσμεν. Their reason for doing so, however, is not very persuasive. It is not clear why taking ὅτι causally leaves us with no connections with v. 16. It must be admitted, however, that the double complement idea long antedates the contemporary discussion. Cf. *Didachē* 9:4.

41. Cf. Conzelmann, *op. cit., ad loc.;* and Cerfaux, *The Church*, p. 265. Also see p. 14, n. 23, where reference was made to Rawlinson.

42. Gundry, *SŌMA*, p. 238.

55

43. *Ibid.*, p. 236.

44. Best, *One Body*, p. 91.

45. For a detailed discussion of the larger ethical, exegetical and socio-ecclesiological issues arising out of chapters 8-10, see Lorenzo De Lorenzi, ed. *Freedom and Love: The Guide for Christian Life (1 Cor. 8-10; Rom. 14-15)* (Rome: St. Paul's Abbey, 1981). Also see Wendell L. Lewis, *Idol Meat in Corinth: The Pauline Argument in 1 Corinthians 8 and 10* (Chico, California: Scholars Press, 1985); and Dennis Smith, *Social Obligation in the Context of Communal Meals: A Study of the Christian Meal in 1 Corinthians in Comparison with Graeco-Roman Meals* (Unpublished Th.D. Thesis, Harvard University, 1980).

46. Some MSS have the interpretative participle, κλώμενον (broken), here. This appears, for example, in corrected versions of א and D (Claromontanus). A text-critical judgment is not that crucial, however, since the addition or omission of κλώμενον has little or no effect on our understanding of the function of σῶμα in the verse.

47. For a still fairly useful historical review of the discussion (up to the mid 70's), see H. Kiesler, *Origin of the Christian Eucharist* (Unpublished Ph.D. thesis, McGill University, 1975); also useful is G.D. Kilpatrick, *The Eucharist in Bible and Liturgy: The Moorhouse Lectures 1975* (Cambridge: At the University Press, 1983).

48. Jewett, *op. cit.* p. 264. Conzelmann unsuccessfully tried to affix an ecclesiological interpretation to v. 27. See *op. cit., ad loc.*

49. D and corrected versions of א, for example, add ἀναξίως. This scribal and interpretative addition seems to have been made under the influence of v. 27.

50. Like ἀναξίως above, the words τοῦ κυρίου appear here as an epexegetic addition in some MSS like D and corrected versions of א. Most likely, this scribal addition was influenced by v. 27 as well. See *KJV, ad loc.*, e.g., for the incorporation of τοῦ κυρίου.

51. Banks observes that, "although this has been generally interpreted as a reference to Christ's crucified body, the community itself is almost certainly in view as well, if not exclusively." See *Paul's Idea of Community*, p. 63; Best points out that Paul first uses the σῶμα motif (as E) in 1 Cor. at 10:17 and then, "probably also a second time (11:29)." See, *One Body in Christ*, p. 84; Barrett, although tentatively opting for C himself, confuses us a little in suggesting that, "it may be that the Corinthians took the word *body* in a sacramental, Paul, in a 'fellowship' sense." See *op cit., ad loc;* Bruce, *op. cit., ad loc;* Fee, *op. cit., ad loc;* Grosheide, *1 Cor., ad loc.;* Héring, *op. cit., ad loc.;* Jewett, *Paul's Anthropological Terms*, p. 300; Johnston, *Doctrine of the Church*, p. 90; Käsemann observes that: "Es scheint mir nicht möglich *to sōma* auf etwas sonst ausser dem Abendmahlselement zu beziehen." See, *Exegetische Versüche und Besinnungen* (Göttingen: 1960), p. 26; Küng, *The Church*, p. 289; Murphy-O'Connor, *Becoming Human Together*, p. 192; Orr and Walther,

representing a very small minority, make the assumption that there is identity of bodies here. See *op. cit., ad loc.*; Ridderbos, *Paul*, p. 426; Robinson, *The Body*, p. 47.

52. See, op. cit., ad loc.

53. E.g., Murphy-O'Connor, *ibid.*, p. 192.

54. Johnston, *op. cit.*, p. 90. Gibbs also agrees. See J. G. Gibbs, *Creation and Redemption: A Study in Pauline Theology* (Leiden: E.J. Brill, 1971), p. 147. For Fee, "all the evidence points in this direction [E]." See *op. cit.*, p. 563.

55. For a discussion of the places of entertainment (triclinium and atrium) within a typical first-century home of a Corinthian well-to-do and the social snobbishness that was sometimes fostered, see J. Murphy-O'Connor, *St. Paul's Corinth*, pp. 155ff.

56. Most scholars seem to translate the verse (καὶ πάντες ἐν πνεῦμα εποτίσθημεν) as follows: "And we were all made to drink of the one Spirit." (See *RSV*, e.g.). However, the straightforward aorist passive rendition of εποτίσθημεν seems consistent with ἐβαπτίσθησαν earlier in the verse as Dunn suggests. Neither translation, however, is determinative of how σῶμα is used in the verse. See J.D.G. Dunn, *Baptism in the Holy Spirit: A Re-examination of the New Testament Teaching on the Gift of the Spirit in Relation to Pentecostalism Today*, in *SBT* (London: SCM Press, 1970), pp. 130f; Branick, *The House Church in the Writings of Paul*, p. 33; and G.J. Cuming, "Epotisthemen (1 Corinthians)," *NTS* 27 (1981):283-285.

57. Emphasis mine. See Barrett, *op. cit., ad loc.* For a similar argument, also see F. Mussner, *Christus des All und die Kirche im Epheserbrief* (Trier: Paulinus, 1955), pp. 276f.

58. Dunn, *ibid.*, pp. 130ff.

59. Conzelmann, *op. cit., ad loc.* Against this supra-mundane view, see Gundry, *SŌMA*, pp. 223. Gundry is in fact disagreeing with Bultmann who held a similar view.

60. See M. Barth, "The Church As Body", *SJT* 58, pp. 131ff.; and repeated in *IBD Sup.*, 1976; L. Ramoroson, "L'Église, Corps Du Christ dans les Écrits Pauliniens: Simples Esquisses," *Sc. et Es.* 30 (1978): 129ff.

61. Bultmann, for example, discusses Paul's view of the rite of baptism as 'into Christ' but makes no mention of the church as body in relation to 1 Cor. 12:13. On three of the four occasions when he cites this verse in one of his major works, he uses the following combinations: (i) Rom. 6:3; 1 Cor. 12:13 -- p. 39; (ii) 1 Cor. 12:13; Gal. 3:27f. -- p. 141; (iii) Gal. 3:27; Rom. 6:3; 1 Cor. 12:13 -- p. 142. See Bultmann, *Theology of the New Testament*, vol. 1. Betz sounds a cautionary note here. He points out that Paul does have "quite a variety of interpretations of the preposition εἰς" with respect to baptism. He lists

Rom. 6:3f.; 1 Cor. 1:13-17; 10:2 (εἰς τὸν Μωῦσῆν ἐβαπτίσθησαν); and 12:13. His listing of 1 Cor. 15:29 and Col. 2:12 is not very useful, however, since εἰς is not mentioned in either one. It is true that instead of ἐν τῷ βαπτισμῷ (Col. 2:12a), Ps - Athanasius has βαπτίσματι εἰς τὸν ᾅδην (in the baptism into hades -- the world of the dead). However, we doubt very much that Betz ever had this in mind. See H.D. Betz, *Galatians: A Commentary on Paul's Letter to the Churches in Galatia*, in *Herm.* (Philadelphia: Fortress Press, 1979), *ad loc.*

62. L. Cerfaux, *The Church*, pp. 270ff. Norman Petersen also moves us in this direction without actually using the language of mysticism. Based on 1 Cor. 12:12-13,27, he declares that believers are baptized "into one body which is Christ." See *Rediscovering Paul: Philemon and the Sociology of Paul's Narrative World* (Philadelphia: Fortress Press, 1985), p. 243.

63. R. Schnackenburg, *The Church in the New Testament*, pp. 174-176.

64. E. Käsemann, *Perspectives on Paul*, pp. 111f.

65. For a relatively recent illustration of this argument, see John Ziesler, *Pauline Christianity*, in *OBS* (Oxford: Oxford University Press, 1983), p. 56.

66. Küng, *The Church*, pp. 292ff.

67. Emphasis mine. Such a statement seems to be quite typical of those who exhibit subtly the discomfort which this view generates. The language tends to be guardedly used (e.g., practically) while the hermeneutical model based upon it (the C/E view) is treated as sure-footed. See Johnston, *The Doctrine of the Church*, p. 90.

68. Best also follows those who tend to equate Christ and the church on the basis of 12:12. See, *One Body in Christ*, p. 81.

69. J. Ziesler, *op. cit.*, p. 62.

70. More will be said about v. 27 shortly. Also, it makes better sense to take v. 31 indicatively rather than imperatively; that is, Paul is not admonishing the Corinthians to seek the better or even the best gifts. That would run counter to all he has just said in vv. 14-30: that there is no such thing since all the gifts are important, to be appreciated, and to be employed for the common good. Instead, he is, in fact, telling the Corinthians that they are aspiring after, or perhaps coveting, what they perceive as the higher gifts. For a similar argument, see Murphy-O'Connor, *1 Cor.*, p. 122; and Talbert, *Reading Corinthians, ad loc.* Also, see Barrett and Conzelmann for two representative treatments of the problem of disorderly worship in Corinth created by a glaring lack of understanding and appreciation of the grace-gifts within the Christian community. An even more recent discussion is Martin's (see p. xix, n. 9).

71. See *BDF*, pp. 253ff. However, Moule is still willing to toy with the possibility that σῶμα may be better handled anarthrously -- thus yielding the translation, "...a body of Christ...." See *Origin*, pp. 71f.; also Küng, *The Church*, p. 297.

72. E. Schweizer, *The Church*, p. 41.

73. Brown, *The Churches*, p. 50.

74. Best, *One Body*, p. 82.

75. Barrett, *op. cit., ad loc.*

76. Gundry, *SŌMA*, p. 228 (again see p. 15, n. 38 of this study and accompanying text). Furnish shows no discomfort in holding on to the metaphor of σῶμα as E (and that alone) throughout 1 Cor. 12 and earlier back in 10:17 and 11:29. See Victor P. Furnish, "Belonging to Christ: A Paradigm for Ethics in First Corinthians," *Int.* 44 (1990): 145-156.

77. Conzelmann, *op. cit., ad loc.*

78. That Paul is not providing us here with an exhaustive list of charisms seems clear. Instead, he is giving us a representative sample. In vv. 8-10, for example, he lists 9 charisms; in v. 28, he lists 8, all of which do not appear in vv. 8-10 and vice versa; and in vv. 29f., the 7 mentioned are a shortened but conflated version of the two previous lists. In addition, the list of 7 that appear later in Rom. 12:6-8 is both similar to, and different from, what we have in 1 Cor. 12. See J. Murphy-O'Connor, *1 Cor.*, p. 118, for a similar observation. A relatively recent and fairly useful study of the charisms is Siegfried S. Schatzmann, *A Pauline Theology of Charismata* (Peabody, MA: Hendrickson Publishers, 1987).

79. Murphy-O'Connor, *Becoming Human Together*, p. 183. Also see Peterson, *Rediscovering Paul*, p. 174, n. 14.

80. Küng, *The Church*, p. 296. Also see Käsemann, *Romans*, p. 338. Another important point that should be made here is that Paul does not base his σῶμα ecclesiology on his anthropological theology either. The pericope, 12:12-27, is not a conveyor of such concepts as flesh, faith, life, and death as one would have expected had the apostle been thinking of wo/man *vis-à-vis* Christ and the law (e.g., Rom. 7f.). The same is true of 10:16f. and 11:24-29. Instead, the apostle discusses σῶμα in a rather general and anatomical sense so as to underscore the whole notion of diversity in unity. It means, essentially, that *contra* Gundry *et al.*, we do not have to ascertain Paul's anthropological theology first before proceeding to his σῶμα ecclesiology -- at least not on the basis of 1 Cor. See Gundry, *SŌMA*, pp. 228ff., and pp. 17f. of this study. Also see Ziesler, *op. cit.* pp. 54f; and Ellis, "*Sōma* in First Corinthians".

81. Purdy is wrong in saying that ἐκκλησία does not appear anywhere in 1 Cor. 12:12-30. Evidently, he overlooked v. 28. See, A.C. Purdy, "Paul the Apostle," in *IDB*, edited by G.A. Buttrick *et al.* (New York: Abingdon, 1962), p. 699.

82. The passages are: 1: 1, 2, 3, 4, 5, 6, 7, 8, 9, 10, 12, 13, 17, 23, 24, 30, 31;   2: 2, 8, 16; 3:1, 5, 11, 23;   4: 1, 4, 5, 10, 15, 17, 19;   5: 3, 4, 7;   6: 11, 13, 14, 15, 17;   7: 10, 12, 17, 22, 25, 32, 33, 35, 39;   8: 6, 11, 12;   9: 1, 2, 5, 12, 14, 21;   10: 4, 9, 16, 21, 22, 26;   11: 1, 3, 11, 20, 23, 26, 27, 32;   12: 3, 5, 12, 27;   14:37;   15: 3, 12, 13, 14, 15, 16, 17, 18, 19, 20, 22, 23, 31, 57, 58;   16: 7, 10, 19, 21, 22, 23, 24.

CHAPTER FOUR

THE SOMATIC ECCLESIOLOGY OF ROMANS

A. Introduction

Having determined, as best we can, that the apostle Paul in writing to the Corinthians back in the mid-fifties of the first century C.E. neither mystically identified nor metaphorically associated the σῶμα of Christ with that of the church, it is now appropriate that we turn our critical attention to the next epistle in which σῶμα as E is thought to exist, namely, the epistle to the Romans. In doing so, we will attempt to ascertain whether mystical identification or metaphorical association of the two σῶματα does in fact occur there.

However, before we engage in such a discussion, we will devote some attention, though briefly, to a few critical introductory issues which are of some relevance to us. In addition, we will provide a cursory description of the state and situation of the Roman church at the time the epistle was written.

1. Integrity of Romans

Some scholars have questioned the integrity of the epistle.[1] Based upon arguments arising out of what they perceive as significant differences throughout the epistle in terms of both theme and theology, such scholars, in general, have suggested that Romans is comprised of four distinct and self-contained units: chapters 1-4; 5-8; 9-11 and 12-16.[2] That this is the case, however, seems very doubtful especially in light of Wright's compelling arguments against it and his plausible defense of the thesis that the epistle stands before us as a unified product; as a well integrated text in which its parts, however delineated, cohere with and contribute to the whole.[3]

2. Chronology of Romans

Very few, if any, would challenge the view that Paul wrote Romans after 1 Corinthians. In some ways, Gerd Lüdemann is representative in his affirmation that 1 Cor. has "chronological priority" over Gal. and that Gal. was written shortly before Romans.[4] In terms of a specific date, however, we are less sure although Robinson's contention that the "early months of A.D. 57 (is) the most likely date of composition," seems to us to be as good as any.[5]

What is of importance to us, of course, is that Rom. follows 1 Cor. in time of writing and therefore justifies our reversing the canonical sequence insofar as these two epistles are concerned.[6] Even more important is the fact that a study of Rom. will enable us to ascertain whether or not σῶμα there shows such ecclesiological developments of, or deviations from, that which we have already encountered in 1 Cor. as to force us to abandon our contention that σῶμα as ecclesiological language in the *corpus Paulinum* has the human body, any human body, as its metaphorical referent. But before that, let us (as promised) look briefly at the church community in Rome as a whole.

B. The Church in Romans: A General Description

Unlike what he said about the Corinthians, Paul could not claim to be father and founder of the Christian community at Rome (see 1 Cor. 3 and 4; cf. Rom. 1:8-15; 15:14-33). Because the apostle had not yet visited the imperial capital, some scholars assume that he could not be as intimately acquainted with the many persons and problems that we seem to encounter in the epistle itself (e.g., chapters 14-16[7]). This then leads them to the assumption that the epistle does not reflect the specific situation in the Roman church per se but instead, picks up faint echoes from, and mirrors some of the problems of, Paul's own churches such as those at Corinth, Thessalonica and Galatia. Dodd, for example, is a proponent of such a view.[8] And so is Leenhardt who writes:

> Paul is not really addressing a particular group of people, whose concrete circumstances he is considering while pointing out their errors.... In spite of certain appearances, Paul is not here concerned to remonstrate with Christians at Rome, whom he does not know any more than he knows their special problems.... The problem which the apostle is treating...is a practical problem which he is treating theoretically and abstractly.[9]

Minear and others have correctly warned us against unduly limiting Paul's network of relationships that he may well have established with many transient Christians throughout the Graeco-Roman world including the imperial capital itself. According to Minear, Paul was most likely in touch with former co-workers such as Prisca (Priscilla in Acts) and Aquila who, at the time the epistle was written from Corinth, were already back in Rome (16:3-5b).[10] News and names could, and most likely would, have flowed freely between the apostle and his colleagues and converts. In Minear's words:

THE SOMATIC ECCLESIOLOGY OF ROMANS

For a long while the apostle had been planning a trip to Rome and Spain (15:22-33). Such a trip required preparation well in advance. It is altogether likely, therefore, that he would have solicited every bit of information he could secure about conditions in Rome. We know that communication was very frequent between Paul and many other cities -- in Galatia, Macedonia, Achaea, and Judea -- communication both by person and letter. Why should Rome be excluded from the list? There is no good reason.[11]

If Paul is more than noddingly acquainted with the Roman church, as we have suggested, it means, then, that in fact he is indulging in more than vague generalizations and abstractions (à la Leenhardt, for example). Instead, the apostle does give us some insight into the actual state and situation of the church.

From the epistle, one can at least infer that the church was bi-cultural, comprised of both Jews and Gentiles (e.g., chapters 1-3 and 9-11). In addition, some conflict may have arisen between these two groups on the basis of their theological understanding of the gospel or Christ-event and the ethical ramifications arising therefrom (e.g., chapters 14 and 15). Commenting on the problem that is addressed in 14:1 - 15:13, for example, Robinson observes:

> This tension between those who observed food-laws and sabbath-days and those who didn't was only, as Paul has hitherto tactfully refrained from rubbing in, the old antagonism of Jew and Gentile. For Paul, the Jew is also the weaker brother, as in the closely parallel discussion in 1 Cor. 8-10.[12] And it was precisely in the breaking down of this barrier once for all that for him the gospel consisted: 'Accept one another as Christ has accepted us (both Jew and Gentile), to the glory of God' (verse 7).... The whole drift of Rom. 1-11 has been to show that Christ made himself *both* the 'servant of the Jewish people to maintain the truth of God by making good his promises to the patriarchs *and* at the same time the bringer of God's 'mercy' to the Gentiles (verses 8-9).[13]

To go beyond this basic Jew/Gentile distinction in a discussion of the church at Rome, one would have to "read between the lines" and in so doing, engage in speculations which, although thoughtful and thought-provoking in and of themselves, are unsubstantiatable speculations nonetheless. Minear is perhaps the best known scholar in this regard. On the basis of chapters 14-16

63

THE CHURCH AS THE BODY OF CHRIST

in particular, he argues for the existence of at least five different groups of Roman Christians all of whom may have worshipped separately. He carves up the community into: (1) the intolerant Jewish weak; (2) the intolerant Gentile strong; (3) the Jewish doubters; (4) the tolerant Jewish weak; and (5) the tolerant Gentile strong.

This thesis has not found much favour among scholars, based as it is on numerous unsupportable suggestions which are strewn along the way. Far more promising, however, is the suggestion that there may well have been a number of house churches, each of which was a *corpus mixtum*, socioculturally speaking.[14]

That the epistle was addressed to such a culturally mixed Christian community perhaps scattered among different house churches in the capital seems to us to be the most plausible position overall. That is, we opt to go along with Patterson, Banks, Malherbe and others.[15]

Having said that, it now becomes necessary to re-focus our attention on the σῶμα issue; to determine, as best we can, what the apostle sought to tell and teach the Roman Jews and Gentiles about the church as the body of Christ; in particular, to ascertain if, unlike in 1 Cor., Paul identifies or likens Christ's own personal σῶμα with, or to, that of the church.

C. Σῶμα as E in Romans

Paul uses σῶμα 13 times in the epistle and on 11 occasions, he uses it in an unambiguously A way; sometimes pointing solely to one's physical constitution and at other times, to one's physicality used as a synecdochic representation of the total being.[16] He speaks about God having given up wicked and ungodly people to the lusts of their hearts leading to the dishonouring of their bodies (1:24); of Abraham, the paragon of faith, whose impotent, pre-Isaac body was as good as dead (4:19); and of any human body which functions only because of the presence, plurality and performance of its limbs (12:4). In addition, Paul informs the Romans that, among other things, baptism in Christ means spiritual death to their sinful bodies (6:1-6); that although their bodies are now dead to sin, life is being given to them through the life-giving Spirit (8:10f.); and that the eschatological wait is now on for the complete redemption of their bodies when at the *parousia* the first-fruits of the Spirit will then give way to the fullness of the harvest (8:22f.).

In the epistle, we also find some ethical monitions involving σῶμα. The Romans are admonished not to let sin reign in their mortal bodies (6:12); to put to death the deeds of the body (8:13); and to present their bodies as living sacrifices or in priestly service to the world (12:1). Finally, and not to be overlooked, is the cry of both anguish and anticipation we pick up in 7:24.

There, Paul seemingly speaks as a representative of Israel in the flesh.[17] He wonders and worries about who is able to bring deliverance from the body which has been sold and subjected to both sin and death. Having looked rather briefly at these 11 unambiguous A σῶμα texts, let us now consider the last 2 of the 13 occurrences of σῶμα in Rom. (7:4 and 12:5). These are especially important for our present purposes since in one of them (12:5), we find an obvious ecclesiological use of the term while in the other (7:4), perhaps. It is for this reason that we have chosen to isolate and exegete them separately. In doing so, we will not only be reproducing the format which we have already followed in dealing with 1 Cor. but more important, we will be able to ascertain whether or not credence should still be given to our thesis that in Rom., like in 1 Cor., Paul uses the human body as the metaphorical backdrop for the church as body instead of mystically collapsing Christ's personal body into that of the church as is the habit of some scholars, or even metaphorically relating the one to the other as is true of most.

After our exegetical effort, we will provide a summary statement in which we will pull together the preceding discussion as well as briefly compare and contrast σῶμα as ecclesiological language in Rom. with that in 1 Cor.

1.   Rom. 7:4 -- ὥστε, ἀδελφοί μου, καὶ ὑμεῖς ἐθανατώθητε τῷ νόμῳ διὰ τοῦ σώματος τοῦ Χριστοῦ, εἰς τὸ γενέσθαι ὑμᾶς ἑτέρῳ, τῷ ἐκ νεκρῶν ἐγερθέντι, ἵνα καρποφορήσωμεν τῷ θεῷ.

Likewise, my brethren, you too have died to the law through *the body of Christ*, so as to belong to another, to him who was raised from the dead, in order that we may bear fruit for God. (Translation and emphasis mine)

Actually, most scholars regard σῶμα in this verse as strictly C. However, there are a few for whom it is both C and E. Exhibitive of this split of opinion are the following: Best -- C and E?; Black -- C and E; Bultmann -- C; Cranfield -- C; Dodd -- C and E; Dunn -- C; Gundry -- C; Käsemann -- C; Kim -- C; Minear -- C and E; Ridderbos -- C; Robinson -- C and E; Schweizer -- C; Wilckens -- C; and Wright -- C and E.[18]

A question mark appears beside Best because he seems to have become somewhat ambiguous over the years. In *One Body In Christ* (1955), he declares: "The context (Rom. 7:1-6) does not carry any suggestion that we should expect to find a reference to the church here. Thus we consider such an application of the words, ‛the body of Christ' to the church as unnecessary and misleading."[19] However, he later expressed the view (1967) that Paul may have chosen the expression, τοῦ σώματος τοῦ Χριστοῦ, in 7:4a because of its E associations in 12:5 and in order to underscore the Roman's solidarity and togetherness with Christ.[20]

This notion of σῶμα underscoring solidarity and togetherness may have been influenced by Robinson and others for whom σῶμα in Paul is shorthand for, and summary of, what it means to be in authentic relationship with God and others. However, Gundry has since provided us with a solid refutation of such a view and instead, has demonstrated exegetically that sometimes in Paul, σῶμα merely points to one's physical constitution, including Christ's, and at other times, to one's physicality used *pars pro toto*.[21]

The C/E positions of Black, Dodd, Minear, and Robinson are all based on the assumption that in some mysterious and perhaps, mystical sense, the personal body of Christ and that of the church are to be identified. Black, for example, interprets διὰ τοῦ σώματος τοῦ Χριστοῦ (7:4) as reference to the death of Christ into which all Christians are baptized to become members of His personal body.[22]

Another exegetical assumption that is sometimes made regarding the C/E view here is that since Paul speaks about the church as the body of Christ in other contexts (e.g., 1 Cor. 12), he is probably referring to the church as body in this context as well. This tendency to see the church in almost every body, however, is entirely questionable for the simple reason that Paul is capable of using σῶμα τοῦ Χριστοῦ in a strictly C way as well (e.g., 1 Cor. 11:24,27).[23]

Drawing an inference from what appears to be an awkwardly constructed analogy found in vv. 1-3, the apostle simply affirms that a married woman is bound by law or belongs to her husband as long as he lives but that remarriage is entirely permissible in the event of his death. Similarly, he argues, the Christians at Rome have died to the law though the σῶμα of Christ and, therefore, now belong to Him who has been raised from the dead in order that fruit may be borne for God.

The apparent awkwardness of this analogy stems from the fact that Paul mentions the death of *the husband* as a precondition for remarriage (or re-belonging) by *the wife* (vv. 1-3) but then goes on to say that it is *we* (presumably referring to the Romans and himself) who have died so that *we* may 'remarry' and this time belong to Christ. As Käsemann has long pointed out, however, Paul is basically insisting that death is a dissolver of relationships and that which makes new ones both possible and permissible.[24]

In terms of the C/E issue, Wright should be mentioned as well since he, too, opts for both C and E in discussing Rom. 7:4a. However, he does so for a somewhat different reason. For him, the Hebrew concept of corporate personality best explains the relationship between Christ and the church. In arriving at this conclusion, he correctly shows that Rom. 7:4 is a tiny part of a larger whole. It is the eschatological application of a lesson that should be drawn from the analogy of vv. 1-3; and that is, Jewish Christians, once incorporated in Adam, once under the death-dealing influence of sin, and once proud possessors of the law or Torah, have now died to their former form of existence through the body rather than through the flesh of the Christ or Messiah so that now, being incorporated into the body of this Messiah, they constitute, with the Gentile Christians, the *bona fide* and end-time people of God. In terms of its larger setting, Wright also correctly situates the verse (v. 4) within the context of chapters 5-8: moving from Paul's Adamic Christology in chapter 5 to the apostle's soteriological statement about the believer's deliverance in Christ, the Messiah, in chapter 8.

We have no quarrel with Wright in terms of the larger and perhaps, more substantial features of his argument. Overall, they seem both clear and cogent. However, we do have one bone to pick with him; and it is this: apart from the fact that the concept of corporate personality (supposedly based on the Hebrew Scriptures) is nebulous at best and, perhaps, completely false at worst,[25] it is not at all clear to us why Paul's use of σῶμα and not σάρξ in 7:4a necessarily means that the apostle is referring both to the church as body and to the body of the Messiah Himself instead of referring only to the Messiah's personal body which was given in death for the liberation of the world -- Jew and Gentile alike. Sanders, among others, has reminded us that Paul sometimes uses σῶμα and σάρξ interchangeably and that the latter is not always weighted down with such negative connotations like faithlessness, sinfulness and enmity with God.[26] In addition, the apostle treats the terms synonymously within the larger context of Rom. 7:4 itself (cf. 8:9-14). And lastly, and perhaps most important, he is capable of using both with reference to the Messiah's own body; that crucified body which symbolizes God's saving power at work in both the church and world (see 1 Cor. 10:16 again; and cf. Col. 1:22).

As important as the larger context is for an understanding of σῶμα in 7:4a, however, one should not overlook the most immediate context of it, namely, 7:4b. In this verse (v. 4), Paul both reminds and reassures the Jewish Christians at Rome. He reminds them that already they have died to Torah, meaning that they have been liberated from its power through the self-given or crucified body of Christ. And because of this, Paul can also give the assurance that they now belong to Him who was raised from the dead; to Christ, the agent of God -- the One who demands and deserves both faithfulness and fruitfulness. That is, a C understanding is all that is required

THE CHURCH AS THE BODY OF CHRIST

here (v. 4a). For us, E seems entirely extraneous.

Best put it well in his *One Body In Christ*, a position which he made unnecessarily ambiguous in his later commentary on *Romans*.[27] For him, a strictly C view of σῶμα in v. 4a "is entirely in keeping with the second half of the verse which refers to His (Christ's) resurrection."[28]   In addition, Ridderbos rightly regards the C/E position as invalid while for Käsemann, "it is ... arbitrary in the context to relate σῶμα Χριστοῦ as in 12:4f., 1 Cor. 12:12ff., to the body of the risen Lord in the church."[29] Of course, we are not entirely in agreement with Käsemann in his assumption that the church is somehow "the body of the risen Lord", if by that is meant the Lord's actual body in some way. However, we do agree with him that the E discussion is out of place here. And finally, Wilckens: For him, "der Gedanke, dass sie durch die Verbindung mit Christus ein Leib als Gemeinde werden und sind, kommt im Rom. 7,4 nicht sum Tragen."[30]

This means, essentially, that we consider the majority position, the C view, the sounder of the two. Rom. 7:4 should not be considered relevant to a discussion of Paul's somatic ecclesiology as such. Instead, it should at best be allowed to play a supportive role since it makes mention not of σῶμα per se but of Χριστός -- the One to whom the church belongs. It means, also, that we should now go on to consider the last of the σῶμα texts in the epistle and to do so in light of our present objective.

Of the dozen occurrences of the term which we have discussed so far, then, we have determined that one is C (7:4) while the other eleven are A.[31] That which completes our "baker's dozen" is 12:5, a text which just about every scholar regards as clearly relevant to the E discussion. In looking at this text, we will strive to keep our eyes fixed and focussed on our main objective which, of course, is to determine whether or not σῶμα there points to any human body as the *tertium comparationis* for the church as body.

> 2. *Rom. 12:4f.* -- καθάπερ γὰρ ἐν ἑνὶ σώματι πολλὰ μέλη
> ἔχομεν, τὰ δὲ μέλη πάντα οὐ τὴν αὐτὴν ἔχει πρᾶξιν,
> οὕτως οἱ πολλοὶ ἓν σῶμά ἐσμεν ἐν Χριστῷ, τὸ δὲ καθ'
> εἷς ἀλλήλων μέλη.

> For just as in one body we have many limbs (or members), but
> all the limbs do not have the same function, so it is that the
> many of us are *one body in Christ*, and individually members
> one of another. (Translation and emphasis mine)

These two verses of chapter 12:4f. are part of the pericope incorporating vv. 1-8; and in this chapter and pericope, we are introduced to a series of ethical monitions beginning with Paul's metaphorical appeal to the Roman Christians that they present their bodies in spiritual and sacrificial service to God since such is considered reasonable, holy, unworldly, and therefore, perfectly acceptable to Him (vv. 1-3). Also falling under the rubric of practical "Christian Living"[32] in this chapter are the admonitions to let love be genuine; to hate what is evil; to hold fast to what is good; to love with sibling affection; and to outdo one another in showing honour (vv. 9f.).

The catena of admonitions continues in v. 11 and goes way beyond the end of this twelfth chapter (v. 21). Paul, through Tertius (cf. 16:22), calls upon the Roman Christians, Jew and Gentile alike (cf. chapters 14f.), to live out the didactic demands of the gospel *in concreto*. For instance, they are never to flag in zeal but instead, should ever be aglow with the Spirit (12:11a). They should serve the Lord, rejoice in hope, be patient in tribulation, be constant in prayer, be hospitable, and donate to the needs of the saints (vv. 11b-13). In addition, they should bless and not curse their persecutors (cf. Matt. 5:10-12);[33] should weep with those who weep; rejoice with those who rejoice (cf. 1 Cor. 12:26); be humble and avoid vengeance; and as far as possible, should be at peace with everyone (vv. 14-21 *passim*).

It is in the midst of these paranaetic directives that the apostle chooses to introduce his Ε σῶμα terminology in likening the Roman Christians to one body in Christ (12:5a) and each one as limbs or members of it (v. 5b). The basic exegetical problem that this verse poses for most scholars, especially those who make the hermeneutical assumption that the σῶμα of Christ and that of the church are either mystically the same or metaphorically similar is this: How does one account for the fact that supposedly, Paul employs the same human body analogy in order to inform *the Corinthians* that in some mystical way they constitute the actual body of Christ Himself (*à la* 1 Cor. 12:12-27 esp.[34]) but then chooses to tell *the Romans* that metaphorically, they are but a human body (any human body) in Christ? In other words, why were the cantankerous Corinthians told that they and Christ are "practically identified"[35] on the basis of σῶμα (taking Χριστοῦ as an explicative genitive in 1 Cor. 12:27[36]) while no such identification is made between Christ and the Romans on the basis of that same σῶμα which was once given in death but then later raised by God through the power of the divine Spirit? Jewett, perhaps, explains the problem more clearly than most. These are his words:

> In contrast to 1 Cor. 12, Rom. 12 speaks of the church as "one body in Christ" but avoids calling the church "Christ's body". Whereas the metaphor introduced by καθάπερ in 1 Cor. 12 was transformed into a realistic description of the church as Christ's actual body by the unexpected insertion of the phrase

οὕτως καὶ ὁ Χριστός, in Romans the metaphor is retained until the end with no hint that the body is anything more than a unity within the sphere of Christ. Whereas the discussion of 1 Cor. closed with the radical insistence that "you are the body of Christ and individually members of it" (1 Cor. 12:27), in Rom. 12 Paul concludes by emphasizing that they are members of one another.... There is a decisive shift in Rom. 12 away from the identification of the ecclesiastical body with Christ Himself.[37]

It is this understanding of Rom. 12:4f. *vis-à-vis* 1 Cor. 12:12-27 which prompts Jewett to call for the immediate formulation of an hypothesis which will resolve the problem as he and others perceive it.[38] Jewett rightly concedes that the formula, ἐν Χριστῷ, in Rom. 12:5a forces us to see the Romans as a body (any human body) and as standing clearly apart from Christ and His once crucified but now risen body.[39]

However ἐν Χριστῷ is understood (and much has been made of it[40]), no legitimate interpretation of ἐν σῶμα ἐν Χριστῷ can conceivably be made to yield an identification of σῶμα as C with σῶμα as E. For example, what sense would it make to say that the Romans are one body in Christ's own human body? It is little wonder, then, that the problem is not with Rom. 12:4f. insofar as our present thesis is concerned since scholars have correctly understood Paul to be using any human body as the metaphorical backdrop for the Roman church as body and as standing clearly apart from Christ's own body. Instead, the problem lies with the scholars' understanding of σῶμα as ecclesiological language within the context of 1 Cor. and especially 12:12-27.

Barrett, among others, is not very helpful at this point in his suggestion that the ἐν Χριστῷ of Rom. 12:5a is "a stage on the way to the 'body of Christ' of 1 Cor. 12:27."[41] For one thing, no explanation is ever given as to why Paul would suggest some sort of identity of bodies to the Corinthians to whom he wrote *earlier* but not to the Romans who were addressed *later* -- and from Corinth at that. That is, how can the *later* version in Rom. be considered a stage toward the *earlier* one in 1 Cor.? In addition, and perhaps more important than this basic chronological problem, Barrett himself in his earlier commentary on 1 Cor. rightly takes issue with those who argue for identity of bodies on the basis of 1 Cor. 12:12-27.[42]

Also, we do find Moule somewhat unclear and perhaps, unnecessarily 'hedgy' in his approach to the whole σῶμα-σῶμα debate in that what he gives with one hand, he seems to take away with the other.[43] However, he is still to be followed in that he refuses to see σῶμα in Rom. 12:5a as anything but

70

an ecclesiological metaphor with the human body (any human body -- cf. v. 4) standing as referent.[44]

Commenting on the verse in a manner that is both clear and cogent, Cranfield has this to say:

> What we have here (12:5) is basically a simile, in spite of the form of v. 5, and...the point which Paul is making is simply that Christians, like the various members of a single body, although they differ from one another and have various functions, are all necessary to each other and equally under an obligation to serve one another, because they all belong together in a single whole.[45]

D. Summary

Let us now provide our own summary of what we think the apostle Paul is communicating to the Roman Christians in his ecclesiological use of σῶμα. As part of this summary, we will compare and contrast briefly the ecclesiological handling of σῶμα in Rom. and 1 Cor. We will do so not because we cannot resist the urge to harmonize but more so because we will then be in a much better position to take up Jewett's challenge regarding the need to resolve the apparent tension between Rom. 12 and 1 Cor. 12 insofar as the σῶμα-σῶμα debate is concerned.[46]

To begin, let us remind ourselves that in Rom. 12:5 Paul makes use of σῶμα as E and that he does so nowhere else in the epistle.[47] In terms of the σῶμα-σῶμα relationship in Rom., the conclusion that has already been drawn regarding 1 Cor. is no different, namely, the church at Rome is being likened to a human body. It is neither being metaphorically associated with, nor being made identical to, Christ's own redemptive body. For Paul, σῶμα as E in Rom. is on no higher a plane than his "botanical ecclesiology" concerning the grafted tree which we encounter in chapter 10. Σῶμα is one ecclesiological image among many (an important one, no doubt), and on exegetical grounds, it is not really worthy of the over-elevation that is sometimes accorded it; at least, not on the basis of Rom.

It is our conviction that in both epistles (1 Cor. and Rom.), written within three years of each other, the apostle Paul seeks to tell and teach the Corinthians and Romans that, among other things, the properly functioning human body is a most appropriate image to describe those who had gone from death to life; to describe those who, be they Jew or Gentile, strong or weak, rich or poor, male or female, had come to fullness of life through the Spirit.

71

THE CHURCH AS THE BODY OF CHRIST

In particular, the Corinthians are admonished to worship the one true God (1 Cor. 10:1-15); to be sensitive to, and appreciative of, all those for whom Christ has died (10:17-33); to share and celebrate the Lord's Supper with fellow believers who are less affluent (11:17-34); and to edify each other and glorify God by engaging in a mature use of those gifts with which at baptism they were all endowed by the one and the self-same Spirit (12:12 - 14:40).

In Rom., comparatively less use is made of σῶμα as E. Appearing only in 12:5, it comes as part of Paul's paranaetic appeal to the Roman believers that they behave in a manner that is entirely consistent with their new status as saved ones. They too, are to be good and faithful stewards of the charisms that have been bequeathed to them.

For us, and *contra* Jewett,[48] the expressions σῶμα τοῦ Χριρτοῦ (1 Cor. 12:27) and σῶμα ἐν Χριστῷ (Rom. 12:5) are no different in terms of the σῶμα-σῶμα relationship. In both cases, the local churches (at Corinth and at Rome) are being likened to a human body -- a well co-ordinated human body. The personal body of Christ Himself has no direct bearing on either expression. We find it rather instructive, for example, that Clement, in writing from the Roman church to the strife-ridden Corinthians perhaps some time in the 90's C.E., shows no knowledge of Paul ever having told the Corinthians that the personal body of Christ and that of the church are somehow one and the same. Instead, Clement simply echoes Rom. 12:5 in *I Clem.* 46:7 as he urges the factious Corinthians to be as communitarian as Paul, in I Cor., had long admonished them to be.[49]

For us (and to repeat), Paul uses σῶμα Χριρτοῦ in 1 Cor. 12:27 to remind the charisms-endowed Corinthians that they, through the Spirit, are in Christ's continuous possession and that whether they be Jew or Gentile, slave or free, they now stand under His Lordship (cf. 1 Cor. 12:3). In the case of σῶμα ἐν Χριστῷ (Rom. 12:5), the Romans, be they Jew or Gentile, are also being told that they should now act like a well co-ordinated body in which each limb or member does his or her Spirit-inspired part.

ENDNOTES

Chapter Four

1. Examples include the following: Cranfield, Feuillet and Scroggs. For that, see N.T. Wright, *The Messiah and the People of God,* pp. 2-8; and B.S. Childs, *The New Testament As Canon: An Introduction* (Philadelphia: Fortress Press, 1984), pp. 251f.

2. Especially contentious is chapter 16 which some believe had Ephesus and not Rome as its original destination. For the most part, the Ephesian hypothesis rests on the assumption that Paul would not have known that many Christians whose names he lists in chapter 16 since, at the time of writing the epistle, he had not yet been to Rome.

3. Wright, *The Messiah and the People of God,* pp. 167f., 245f.

4. G. Lüdemann, *A Chronology of Paul,* in *Colloquy On New Testament Studies,* pp. 298f. There are some who place Gal. before 1 Cor. but who still accord 1 Cor. chronological priority over Rom. For example, see Peter Richardson, *Paul's Ethic of Freedom* (Philadelphia: The Westminster Press, 1979), p. 14.

5. John A.T. Robinson, *Wrestling With Romans* (Philadelphia: Westminster Press, 1979), p. 1. Robinson earlier committed himself to this date in his, *Redating The New Testament* (Philadelphia: The Westminster Press, 1976).

6. See p. 30, for a brief discussion of the chronology of 1 Cor. There, we located the epistle between late 53 and early 55 C.E.

7. For chapter 16, see n. 3 *supra,* and n. 11 to follow.

8. C.H. Dodd, *The Epistle of Paul to the Romans* in *MNTC* (London: Collins Fontana Books, 1959), p. xxviii.

9. F.J. Leenhardt, *The Epistle to the Romans: A Commentary,* ET (London: 1961), pp. 345f.

10. Minear provides us with a rather plausible defense of chapter 16 as constituting part of the original epistle. He does so in terms of its thematic continuity with chapters 1-15 in general and those of 14 and 15 in particular. See, *The Obedience of Faith,* pp. 20-35. Brown and I. Howard Marshall also consider the chapter to be a part of the original epistle. See R.E. Brown and J.P. Meier, *Antioch and Rome: New Testament Cradles of Catholic Christianity* (New York: Paulist Press, 1983); and Marshall's review of the book in *JSNT* 25 (1985): 125f. To be added also, are the following two observations: (1) in 16:3-5a, Paul speaks about Prisca and Aquila in a manner that strongly suggests that those to whom he

was writing did not know of Prisca's and Aquila's laudable work on behalf of Paul and all the churches of the grateful Gentiles. This could hardly have been the case had he been writing to Ephesus where both Paul and the couple had lived and worked for quite some time; and (2) the reference to *all* the churches of Christ from which greetings were being sent via the apostle (16:16b) make very little (if any) sense in light of the Corinth-to-Ephesus hypothesis. Writing from Corinth, Paul (or rather, Tertius -- 16:22) could hardly be sending greetings from *all* of the Gentile churches to *some* of the very churches in Ephesus which he himself had founded. To make sense, greetings from all most likely would be sent to those not included in the all. And this again points to Rome as opposed to Ephesus since the former, unlike the latter, could not be included in the company of all the grateful Gentiles from whom greetings were being sent.

11. Minear, *op. cit.,* p. 21.

12. Minear, perhaps more than any other, considers chapters 14 and 15 as the *point de départ* for a discussion of the entire epistle; and he, too, works with the equation that the weak = the Jews, and the strong = the Gentiles.

13. J.A.T. Robinson, *Wrestling*, p. 144.

14. See G. Johnston, "The Constitution of the Church in the New Testament," in *PCB*, pp. 724-727, esp. 726. Also, Minear himself is aware that insofar as splitting up the Roman church into such specific groups is concerned, he is as a lone voice crying in the wilderness, so to speak. See *op. cit.,* p. 7; J.M. Patterson, "House-Churches in Rome," *VC* 23 (1969): 264-272; and p. 52 of this study.

15. See n. 14 *supra.* For an uncompelling argument that Paul preached *only* to Gentiles and by inference, that the Roman church was entirely non-Jewish in composition, see Lloyd Gaston, *Paul and the Torah* (British Columbia: University of British Columbia Press, 1987).

16. For a sustained discussion of, and disagreement with, those who tend to deprive σῶμα of its physical connotations and instead, opt for terms like, the whole being, personality, individuality, solidarity, and human essence, see Gundry, *SŌMA*, chapters 1-16.

17. For an informative discussion of the long-standing debate surrounding the ἐγώ of Rom. 7, see Douglas J. Moo, "Israel and Paul in Romans 7:7-12," *NTS* 32 (Jan., 1986): 122-135, and the literature cited there, especially N.T. Wright, *The Messiah and the People of God*, pp. 151f.

18. E. Best, *One Body in Christ*, p. 53; cf. *idem, Romans, ad loc.,* in *CBC* (Cambridge: At the University Press, 1967); M. Black, *Romans, ad loc.,* in *NCB* (London: Thomas Nelson and Sons, 1973); R. Bultmann, *Theology of the New Testament*, vol. 1, p. 147; C.B. Cranfield, *Romans, ad loc.,* in *ICC* (Edinburgh: T. and T. Clark, 1979); C.H. Dodd, *Romans, ad loc.;* Dunn, *Baptism*, p. 146; *idem, A Commentary On Romans 1-8,* (Dallas:

74

Word, 1988), *ad loc.;* R. Gundry, *SŌMA*, pp. 239f.; E. Käsemann, *Romans, ad loc.;* S. Kim, *Origin,* p. 302; Minear, *Images,* pp. 174-178; H. Ridderbos, *Paul,* pp. 365f.; J.A.T. Robinson, *Wrestling, ad loc.;* cf. *idem, The Body,* pp. 47ff.; Schweizer, *The Church,* pp. 41f.; U. Wilckens, *Der Brief An Die Römer* (Rom. 6-11), *ad loc.,* in *EKKNT* (Zürich: Benziger Verlag, 1980); and N.T. Wright, *The Messiah and The People of God,* pp. 142-151.

19. E. Best, *One Body In Christ,* p. 53.

20. E. Best, *Romans, ad loc.*

21. See n. 16, *supra.*

22. M. Black, *op. cit., ad loc.*

23. See Jewett, *Paul's Anthropological Terms,* p. 264 and p. 39 of this study.

24. Käsemann, *Romans, ad loc.*

25. Ziesler, for example, has this to say: "It is now very doubtful whether there ever was a Hebrew idea of corporate personality which could explain Paul's language." See, John Ziesler, *Pauline Christianity,* p. 60; also see A.J.M. Wedderburn, "Some Observations on Paul's Use of The Phrases 'In Christ' and 'With Christ'," *JSNT* 25 (1985):80 and 95, n. 30. For an insightful critique of the whole concept of corporate personality which H. Wheeler Robinson *et al.* popularized in Biblical studies, see J.W. Rogerson, "The Hebrew Conception of Corporate Personality: A Re-examination," *JTS* 21 (1970): 1-16.

26. E.P. Sanders, *Paul, The Law, and the Jewish People,* p. 120, n. 52; Also helpful here with regard to Paul assigning to σάρξ, and other words like πίστις, different meanings in different contexts, is A.C. Thiselton, *The Two Horizons: New Testament Hermeneutics and Philosophical Description with Special Reference to Heidegger, Bultmann, Gadamer, and Wittgenstein* (Grand Rapids: Wm. B. Eerdmans, 1980), pp. 276-283.

27. See nn. 19f., *supra* and the accompanying text.

28. Best, *One Body,* p. 53.

29. Käsemann, *Romans, ad loc.*

30. Wilckens, *op. cit., ad loc.* Also see Cranfield, *op. cit., ad loc.*

31. See n. 16, *supra* and the accompanying text.

32. This caption appears in the *RSV* and it is used to cover the closing five chapters of Rom., i.e., chapters 12-16.

33. For a discussion of some logia of Jesus that may be lodged in Paul's epistles and with the implication that such logia most likely circulated among his churches, see David G. Dungan, *The Sayings of Jesus in the Churches of Paul* (Philadelphia: Fortress Press, 1971).

34. See previous chapter under vv. in question for our refutation of such a thesis; in particular, pp. 41-49.

35. According to Johnston, *The Church*, p. 90.

36. See n. 34, *supra*.

37. Jewett, *Paul's Anthropological Terms*, p. 303.

38. See p. xiv again where Jewett was mentioned as one of those who have expressed the need to have σῶμα as ecclesiological language re-examined.

39. Jewett, *op. cit.*, p. 304. Also see Gundry, *SŌMA*, pp. 235f., for a similar view.

40. See C.F.D. Moule, *The Origin of Christology* (Cambridge: At the University Press, 1977), pp. 54-69. More recently is A.J.M. Wedderburn, "Some Observations of Paul's Use of the Phrases 'in Christ' and 'with Christ'". (See n. 25 *supra*). The expression, ἐν Χριστῷ, appears five times in Rom., namely, 9:1; 12:5 and 16:7,9,10. In addition, there are other Christological combinations with ἐν. 'Ἐν Χριστῷ 'Ιησοῦ: six times (3:24; 6:11; 8:1,2; 15:17; 16:3); ἐν κυρίῳ 'Ιησοῦ: once (14:14); ἐν κυρίῳ: seven times (16:2,8,11,12 (*bis*), 13,22); and ἐν Χριστῷ 'Ιησοῦ τῷ κυρίῳ ἡμῶν: twice (6:23; 8:39). According to Murphy-O'Connor, ἐν Χριστῷ alone occurs over 150 times in the Pauline corpus. See, *Becoming Human Together*, p. 183. For a brief but informative discussion of those five in Rom., plus the sixteen other Christological occurrences, see Cranfield, *op. cit.*, pp. 833ff.

41. Barrett, *Romans, ad loc.*

42. See his *1 Cor., ad loc.* as well as the discussion of 1 Cor. 12:13,27 in our previous chapter. For the specific reference, see n. 34 *supra*.

43. See C.F.D. Moule, "The Corporate Christ" in his, *The Origin of Christology*, pp. 47-96. In discussing the rather nebulous concept of the corporate Christ in relation to Paul's ecclesiological use of σῶμα, Moule suggests very tentatively throughout the discussion that for Paul, Christ's own body sometimes consists of the limbs or members of Christians who, together, go to form that one body. This, he terms the corporate Christ. However, Moule concedes that 1 Cor. 12:12f. is the only place in the Pauline corpus where such a position *may* find some support although he is quick to point out that such an interpretation of the text is not as compelling as it is sometimes made out to be (see our discussion of the texts on pp. 41-49 for details). In spite of this admission, however, and the very tentative nature of the discussion throughout, Moule still concludes by insisting that the concept of the

corporate Christ (and its assumed relationship to the σῶμα-σῶμα issue) is in fact present in the Pauline corpus. For a similar argument re: this nebulous corporate Christ concept, see J. Murphy-O'Connor, *Becoming Human Together,* pp. 183ff. In spite of its title, Neyrey's book does not really address the issue of the corporate Christ; at least, not within the context of the Pauline corpus. Instead, he is endeavouring to show that the apostle consistently and creatively adapts his Christology in order to speak to the specific pastoral problems which may have sprung up in the different Christian communities; be it at Corinth, Philippi, Colossae or Ephesus. See J.H. Neyrey, *Christ is Community*, pp. 195-268.

44. Moule, *op. cit.,* p. 92.

45. Cranfield, *op. cit., ad loc.*

46. See n. 38, *supra.*

47. See earlier discussion of 7:4 and the documentation that accompanies it.

48. See n. 38, *supra.*

49. For a brief reference to Clement's somatic ecclesiology (based on Paul's in Rom. 12:5), see Barbara Bowe, *A Church in Crisis*, p. 139.

CHAPTER FIVE

THE SOMATIC ECCLESIOLOGY OF COLOSSIANS

A. INTRODUCTION

Much could be (and has been) written about Colossians. Wright, for example, reminds us that in the last twenty years or so, the study of this relatively short epistle "has moved on by leaps and bounds."[1] This being the case, we will attempt to be as faithful as possible to our present objective. We will keep our eyes fixed and focussed on the σῶμα-σῶμα issue and in so doing, seek to ascertain whether or not our thesis still has much of a leg to stand on, as it were. We will endeavor to determine if the churches in Colossae and elsewhere in Asia Minor (cf. 2:1-3; 4:15f), like those in Corinth and Rome, have the human body as metaphorical referent. This, as we have been saying all along, stands in contradistinction to, and in tension with, those scholars who would suggest that in some ill-defined mystical sense or inexplicably metaphorical way, the personal body of the crucified and risen Christ is at the very heart of σῶμα as ecclesiological language in the Pauline corpus. More than that, we will also have to come to grips with κεφαλή as a Christological concept in Colossians since there, and for scholars such as Brown, κεφαλή acts as a necessary anatomical complement to σῶμα when used ecclesiologically.[2]

In brief, then, the two basic questions that will engage us exegetically in this chapter relative to the σῶμα-σῶμα debate are: (1) Is the church at Colossae and elsewhere being made one with, or similar to, Christ's crucified but now risen σῶμα or not? And (2) how is Christ as κεφαλή related to the church as σῶμα (cf. 1:18; 2:18f.)?

Before we go looking for possible answers to these questions, however, let us (in keeping with tradition as it were),[3] devote some time, though briefly, to the "higher" critical issues such as the authorship, authenticity and chronology of Colossians, the third member of our team of four.[4] Also antecedent to our main discussion will be a brief exposé, based on the epistle itself, of the general state and situation of the churches to which the epistle was originally written.

The usefulness of this brief exercise lies in the fact that it will enable us to get σῶμα as ecclesiological language rooted and grounded in its specific historical and larger ecclesiological setting. Without them both, the discussion runs the risk of being deficient.

THE CHURCH AS THE BODY OF CHRIST

1. Authorship and Authenticity of Colossians

Unlike our two previous epistles, namely, 1 Cor. and Rom., we cannot be sure that in the case of Col., we are dealing with one of Paul's authentic epistles.[5] Brown points out that by way of broad approximation, about 60% of critical scholarship judges that the apostle did not write Col.[6] Among those falling in this category, for example, are Lohse and Schweizer.[7]

Much of the argument against Pauline authorship rests on the assumption that in terms of theology[8] and/or style, Col. stands apart from those other epistles which are indisputably Paul's. Wright comments on this and in the process exposes the basic problem with such a view. He points out that:

> Some of those who doubt Colossians' authenticity build their case on theology, saying that the style of the letter does not provide a clear enough indication. Others, happy to say that the theology of the letter is substantially Pauline, think that the style alone forces us to say that someone other than Paul wrote it. This suggests, actually, that neither the style nor the theology is as decisive in mounting an argument against authenticity as some have suggested. More recent work has shown that an excellent case for Pauline authorship can still be made out.[9]

By "more recent work", Wright is referring specifically to O'Brien's commentary on Col.[10] And like O'Brien, he places himself within the category of Brown's 40%.[11] He does so not only because the arguments of the 60% are somewhat subjective and tend to be neutralized when allowed to react and interact with each other, but more so because the counter-arguments themselves can very much hold their own; for instance, Paul's reference to himself throughout (cf. 1:1-14,24 - 2:5; 4:7-18) and the less than cogent case usually made for the pseudonymous writing of letters in the ancient church.

On balance, we consider Pauline authorship to be more defensible. For us, Col. was written (co-written -- cf. 1:1) by one who was neither responsible for establishing the Christian communities at Colossae and Laodicea in the Lycus Valley in Asia Minor nor by one who had ever visited them in person (see 1:8ff.; 2:3ff.). This being the case, we will proceed to discuss σῶμα as an ecclesiological concept which Paul himself articulates both here and elsewhere, viz., 1 Cor. and Rom.[12] In doing so, we will endeavour to determine exegetically, insofar as the σῶμα-σῶμα debate is concerned,

THE SOMATIC ECCLESIOLOGY OF COLOSSIANS

whether or not the apostle does exhibit some measure of consistency in his use of the human body as a role model for the church. However, before we do that, let us consider briefly the chronological issue as well.

2. Chronology of Colossians

Dating Col. is not easy and according to Bruce, "dogmatism is to be avoided".[13] At the moment, there are three competing time-frames each of which has Paul writing from a different place: Ephesus[14], Caesarea[15], and Rome[16], with the first pointing to the *terminus a quo* (early to mid 50's), and the third, to the *terminus ad quem* (early 60's). Of the three, the Rome hypothesis is the most dominant while that regarding Caesarea is least so.

The fundamental conviction which undergirds them all is that Paul was a prisoner when he wrote and sent the epistle via Tychicus to its addressees in Asia Minor (4:2-4,7-9,18). For the most part, Ephesian imprisonment is deduced from 1 Cor. 15:32 and 2 Cor. 1:8; the Caesarean is based on Acts 24:27; and the Roman, on Acts 28:16ff.

Without getting bogged down in the arguments *pro et contra*, we need say only that overall, we consider the majority position (Roman) the most persuasive or perhaps, better yet, the least problematic of the three: Paul's ability to change his plans; the ease with which run-away slaves and others could move about in the Graeco-Roman world; the fact that while a prisoner in Caesarea, Paul was destined for Rome and nowhere else; and the lack of "hard" evidence for an Ephesian imprisonment are all facts and factors that influence us in our decision to gravitate towards Rome. However, we are heartened by the gentle reminder that our being left "with frustrating uncertainty about 'introductory' questions of date and place may also indicate that such questions are not as central to interpretation as is sometimes imagined."[17]

Our decision to date Col. in the early 60's and to locate its origin in Rome is not motivated by any attempt to place the discussion of $\sigma\hat{\omega}\mu\alpha$ on some type of trajectory analogous to what Robinson, Koester, and others were attempting in N.T. studies some years ago.[18] Rather, we are simply opting for what appears to be the most plausible hypothesis at the present time. Also (and more important), we are seeking to determine what the apostle thought and told other Christian communities (at Colossae and Laodicea) about the church as the $\sigma\hat{\omega}\mu\alpha$ of Christ and Christ as $\kappa\epsilon\phi\alpha\lambda\dot{\eta}$ of it.

Having already followed him from Ephesus to Corinth, (the places from which 1 Cor. and Rom. were written respectively[19]), let us now ascertain, as best we can, whether or not Paul, in writing from Rome in the early 60's, deviated from his earlier metaphorical use of the human $\sigma\hat{\omega}\mu\alpha$ in speaking about the church to the Asia Minor Christians at Colossae and Laodicea (again, see 2:1-3; 4:15f.). But before doing so, we first need to paint a larger picture.

B. The Church in Colossians: A General Description

It is unclear as to whether or not the church at Colossae was predominantly Jewish or predominantly Gentile. Internal evidence would seem to suggest the latter. In his final greetings, for example, Paul identifies Aristarchus, Mark (Barnabas' cousin) and Jesus (also called Justus) as the only Jewish co-workers who were with him at the time of writing. Next, he makes mention of Epaphras, another fellow-worker (1:7f.) and evidently a Gentile, whom he identifies as one who, like Onesimus, came from the same ethnic stock as the Colossians themselves (4:7-13; also cf. 1:3-8).

Without having to settle the issue one way or the other, at least we are on fairly solid ground in our belief that both Jews and Gentiles (in whatever ratio) worshipped together. This is so because we really have no reason to assume that the church to some degree, and like those in Corinth, Rome, and elsewhere, did not reflect the bi-cultural composition of both the larger society as a whole[20] as well as those comprising Paul's own team of itinerant co-workers (see Col. 3:11; 4:10-13).

Granted, the language at points appears quite Jewish; for instance, there are echoes of the exodus event (1:11-14) and the creation account (1:15-17; 3:10). The reference to circumcision and uncircumcision (2:11; 3:11), the elemental spirits of the universe (2:8), principalities and powers (2:15), and the worship of angels (2:18) may also be relevant in this regard.[21]

Also, there are terms and themes which, for some, conjure up images of the mystery religions, Platonism, Stoicism, Pythagoreanism, or even a syncretistic *mélange* thereof.[22] Usually mentioned in these contexts are κεφαλή (1:18; 2:10,19), κόσμος (2:8), φιλοσοφία (2:8), πλήρωμα (1:19; 2:9), σοφία (1:28; 2:3,23), and σῶμα (see esp. 2:9,17).[23]

However, when the details of such arguments regarding these terms and themes are scrutinized, it becomes quite apparent that they are usually informed by *traditionsgeschichtlich* and rhetorical interests that tend to cast more shadows than sunshine on the subject; they cloud instead of clarify the data as we have it in Col. Wright, for one, has demonstrated that the language of the epistle seems to be Jewish through and through and that, therefore, one does not have to scour land and sea in search of possible non-Jewish and Graeco-Roman provenances for those terms and themes considered integral to the so-called Colossian heresy but adjudged extraneous to the religious traditions of Israel, the ancient and pre-messianic people of

THE SOMATIC ECCLESIOLOGY OF COLOSSIANS

God.[24] In our view, Col. is best understood as an example of Paul's pastoral attempt to consolidate Jewish and Gentile Christians in the community of faith and to warn them against would-be recruiters who would come to tempt them to embrace Judaism in addition to, or perhaps, instead of, remaining rooted and built up in Christ and established in the faith; that faith which Epaphras, Paul's beloved fellow servant in Christ, had handed on to them (see 1:3-8; 2:6-23).

It is within this context of consolidation and caution that we find $\sigma\hat{\omega}\mu\alpha$ employed for the third time in an E way[25]; and $\kappa\epsilon\phi\alpha\lambda\dot{\eta}$ appearing for the first time as a designation for Christ. In keeping with our basic purpose which is to determine whether or not $\sigma\hat{\omega}\mu\alpha$ as E has the human body rather than Christ's own crucially (*crux*) significant body as referent, and the role and relevance of the $\kappa\epsilon\phi\alpha\lambda\dot{\eta}$ concept in relation to it, let us now turn our exegetical attention to the data in question.

C. $\Sigma\hat{\omega}\mu\alpha$ as E in Colossians

$\Sigma\hat{\omega}\mu\alpha$ and its cognates appear nine times in the epistle and as was true of 1 Cor. and Rom., the term does perform all three theological functions there: A, C, and E[26]. A quick look at the *Critical Concordance to Colossians* reveals that $\sigma\hat{\omega}\mu\alpha$ appears in its adverbial form, once ($\sigma\omega\mu\alpha\tau\iota\kappa\hat{\omega}\varsigma$ -- 2:9); the ablative singular, also once ($\sigma\hat{\omega}\mu\alpha\tau o\varsigma$ -- 1:24); the nominative singular, twice ($\sigma\hat{\omega}\mu\alpha$ -- 2:17,19); the dative singular, also twice ($\sigma\hat{\omega}\mu\alpha\tau\iota$ -- 1:22; 3:15); and the genitive singular, thrice ($\sigma\hat{\omega}\mu\alpha\tau o\varsigma$ -- 1:18; 2:11,23).[27] Of the three functions, $\sigma\hat{\omega}\mu\alpha$ as A seems least problematic; C, more so; and E, most so.[28]

In terms of the A usage, Paul uses $\sigma\hat{\omega}\mu\alpha$ twice. First, he informs the Colossians in 2:11 that baptism is co-burial with Christ (cf. Rom. 6:1-6) which he then likens to the cutting off and casting away of the body of flesh in his (Christ's) circumcision.[29] And second, he (Paul) reminds them that pre-Christian Jewish religion, even with its rigorous ascetic ethic, only creates an appearance of wisdom and causes severity to the body. Such a lifestyle, according to him and contrary to those who were promoting it, should therefore not be regarded as a *sine qua non* for proper Christian living (2:8-23; esp. v. 23).

In turning next to $\sigma\hat{\omega}\mu\alpha$ as C in the epistle, we discover, as we have already mentioned, that this usage is a bit more difficult to understand fully. The three C's in the epistle are more easily spotted than interpreted. However, it must be acknowledged that the first (1:22) is relatively straightforward. There, Paul reminds the once estranged and hostile Colossians that in Christ's own body of flesh and by His death, they have now been reconciled to God--the One to whom Christ, the Reconciler, is now able to present them as holy, blameless, and irreproachable. But this is with the proviso that they remain stable and steadfast in the faith and not shifting from the hope of the gospel that has been preached to them and to every creature under heaven (v. 23).

Unlike 1:22, 2:9 presents us with a greater challenge. There, we encounter σωματικῶς, the adverbial form of σῶμα.[30] Paul makes mention of the fact that in Christ, the fullness of God dwells bodily and what he means by it is not entirely clear. From Moule, we learn that:

> Commentators, ancient and modern, group themselves, roughly speaking, round five interpretations: (i) 'as an organized body', i.e., the totality of the Godhead... (ii) 'expressing itself through the body of Christ', i.e., the church... (iii) 'actually' -- in concrete reality, not in mere seeming... (iv) 'in essence'... (v) 'assuming a bodily form', becoming incarnate.[31]

Moule's five positions can further be reduced to two, namely, C (#'s (i), (iii), (iv), and (v)) and E (# (ii)). Of these, Moule toys briefly with E but then correctly goes on to express his discomfort with it since σωματικῶς appears so compressed and its manner of introduction so strange and epigrammatic. Instead, he rightly opts for C (under iii and v) which, "combined, seem, on the whole, to present the fewest difficulties".[32]

In our view, Wright is also correct in juxtaposing this enigmatic C verse with 1:19. In doing so, he regards 2:9 simply as the Christological expansion of 1:19 where Paul had earlier declared that in Christ the fullness of God was pleased to dwell.[33]

Attempting to relate it directly to E, Lohse unconvincingly suggests that:

> Since the author[34] chose the word, bodily, to express this thought, a relationship to the statements about 'body' is no doubt intended.... This body of his is the church over which he already in the present exercises his universal rule.[35]

The speciousness of this argument lies in the fact that one cannot so facilely move from the particular to the universal where σῶμα is concerned. In Col., and as was true of 1 Cor. and Rom., Paul does not always use σῶμα with E in mind. As we have already seen, in 2:23 σῶμα is unambiguously A -- and that alone -- while in 1:22, it is unequivocally C -- and that alone. With regard to 2:9, we do insist that σωματικῶς is a C text and nothing more.

84

THE CHURCH AS THE BODY OF CHRIST

Christ' in the distinctive Pauline sense are unsatisfactory."[41]

It means, then, that of the nine occurrences of σῶμα in Col., we are now left with the remaining four that the vast majority of scholars rightly regard as those in which we find the church actually referred to as the σῶμα of Christ and at times, to Christ as the κεφαλή of it. The four are: 1:18,24; 2:19 and 3:15.

In contrast to what we have done previously (for 1 Cor. and Rom.), we will not be looking at these texts separately. Instead, we will use the first one (1:18) as our *point de départ* and then consider the three others alongside and in the light of it. The reason for this is that 1:18 already incorporates within itself those elements which we find in the others and which are of relevance to us in this study. In particular, its mention of both κεφαλή and σῶμα would force us to lay hold of those other texts in the epistle where one or both of these terms also appear. In addition, the epistle is much too short a work to permit total segregation of those texts in question; again: 1:18,24; 2:19; 3:15.

With this in mind, then, let us now seek to confirm or disconfirm the thesis before us, namely, that in Col. the human body and not Christ's personal body acts as the metaphorical referent for the church as body. Further, that κεφαλή, in referring to Christ and in relation to the church as σῶμα, does not mean head in a physiological sense but rather, something else.

Col. 1:18, our starting text, reads as follows:

καὶ αὐτός ἐστιν ἡ κεφαλή τοῦ σώματος τῆς ἐκκλησίας· ὅς ἐστιν ἀρχή, πρωτότοκος ἐκ τῶν νεκρῶν, ἵνα γένηται ἐν πᾶσιν αὐτὸς πρωτεύν.

And He is *the head of the body*, the church; He is the beginning, the firstborn from the dead, so that He may be first in all things. (Translation and emphasis mine.)

This verse is part of what is, perhaps, a pre-Pauline Christian hymn (vv. 15-20) which the apostle adopts and adapts for his own purpose and one which serves as a kind of prospective summary of, if not the whole epistle, then at least chapters 1-3.[42] Preceding the hymn in vv. 1-14 are Paul's (and Timothy's) greetings to the Colossians (vv. 1-2) and the mention of prayers of both thankfulness and petition (vv. 3-14). Paul is grateful to God because, through Epaphras' ministry, the gospel had borne the fruits of faith, hope and love among the Colossians. Further, the apostle assures them that he is forever asking God to strengthen them with his power and to fill them with the knowledge and understanding of His will.

This passage (vv. 15-20), of which our first E σῶμα text is but a part (v. 18), has been the subject of much scholarly debate for quite some time. Much of it has to do with the pre-Christian conceptual universe within which supposedly, the key concepts of the hymn first circulated. So far, two major hypotheses have vied for supremacy: (1) gnosticism in which, among other things, the cosmos is sometimes imaged as the σῶμα of a god who acts as κεφαλή;[43] and (2) Rabbinic speculations on the Hebrew Scriptures; in particular, the creation account of Gen. in which the Torah is imaged as God's agent of creation,[44] and the Wisdom speculations of Prov. 8. These speculations are regarded as having been transposed into a Christological key in Col. 1:15-20 with the accents placed on Christ's creative and redemptive accomplishments and, therefore, His unrivalled position of primacy vis-à-vis both the church in particular and the created order in general (cf. 1:13-20; 2:9f.).[45]

Of these two positions, the second is now generally regarded as being more plausible. For one thing, the gnostic argument tends to be anachronistic, based as it is on data drawn mainly from the second century C.E. and beyond. Further, some of the key concepts in vv. 15-20, plus those in the epistle as a whole, such as beginning (ἀρχή -- v. 18), first-born (πρωτότοκος -- v. 18), wisdom (σοφία -- 2:3), head (κεφαλή -- 1:18; 2:19), and circumcision (περιτομή -- 2:11), can all be accounted for on the basis of the Hebrew Scriptures and sometimes, the relevant Rabbinic speculations that go along with it.[46]

More important, however, is that the passage as it is in Col. seeks to portray God in Christ as both creator (vv. 15-17) and redeemer (vv. 18-20). Martin is correct in affirming that this has now become the majority view. In his words, vv. 15-20 "form a compact, self-contained hymn written in praise of the cosmic Christ, the Lord of creation and redemption".[47]

With regard to the σῶμα-σῶμα debate in particular, the problem posed by this verse (v. 18) is really two-fold: (1) Is the church as σῶμα being made one with, or being likened to, the personal body of Christ or not? And (2) What does Paul most likely mean in referring to Christ as κεφαλή of the church, His σῶμα ?

Of these two questions, the first, perhaps, is the less difficult. In affirming from the outset that Christ is κεφαλή of *the* body (τοῦ σῶματος) which is the church, and not of *His* body, namely, Christ's own body, it is rather clear that in this verse, at least, the apostle does not have Christ's personal body in view. But then, how could he? What sense would it make, for example, to say that the church is or is like Christ's personal body without a head? It is not surprising, therefore, that the real question which arises out

THE CHURCH AS THE BODY OF CHRIST

of 1:18 for most scholars is not how to relate the two σώματα per se but rather, how does Christ as κεφαλή relate to the church as σῶμα?

Before we address ourselves to this question, let us make another observation; and it is this: The fact that Paul does not refer to Christ's personal body in v. 18 (in speaking about the church) makes it rather doubtful that he does so just a few verses later in v. 24. His speaking about joyfully suffering for the sake of the church which is His (Christ's) body (τοῦ σώματος αὐτοῦ) must mean that αὐτοῦ is functioning there as a simple possessive genitive and not as one of identity -- unless we consider Paul's use of language so loose as to defy any attempt at a consistent explication of it regarding σῶμα. In our view, the *onus probandi* is on all those who would so insist.

In v. 24, and as he had already done some years earlier (cf. 1 Cor. 12:27), the apostle likens the church to a human body which he then declares to be Christ's prized and purchased possession. Christ's personal body, that body which was given in death but which has now been raised by God through the Spirit is not exegetically relevant to Paul's σῶμα ecclesiology -- at least not on the basis of Col. 1:18,24. It is relevant only in the more extended sense that had it not been for that self-donated body which was impaled on the cross, the church would not have existed and therefore, could not be likened to anything -- including the human body.

With that having been said, then, let us now turn our attention again to the κεφαλή question as it arises in 1:18. Taking the term to mean head in a physiological sense and considering it the anatomical complement to σῶμα,[48] most scholars are forced to redefine and reduce σῶμα to the state and status of an acephalous entity whereby Christ as a bodyless head and the church as a headless body go together to form the body *in toto*.[49]

Such scholars further insist that this Christ-church, κεφαλή-σῶμα, relationship is in tension with that which we have already encountered in 1 Cor. and Rom. where (and contrary to our contention), the body of the church (head and all) is made mystically one with the once crucified but now risen and exalted body of Christ. And those who resist this mystical argument still insist that the two σώματα must be made to interface in some metaphorical way.[50]

It means, in a word, that insofar as our thesis is concerned, κεφαλή is really the *crux interpretum* in our verse (v. 18) -- and in the entire epistle for that matter. Contrary to most, it is our conviction that the usual physiological understanding of the term is exegetically implausible, resting as it is on the questionable assumption that in some anatomical sense, κεφαλή constitutes the necessary complement to σῶμα as ecclesiological language in Col. To buttress our position, we will argue on three levels: (1) the theological

THE SOMATIC ECCLESIOLOGY OF COLOSSIANS

background of κεφαλή; (2) Paul's use of the term in other epistles; and (3) his use of it in Col. itself.

First, and *contra* those who search and re-search the Graeco-Roman, Hellenistic materials in an attempt to understand κεφαλή there and who also concede that σῶμα in such sources never refers to an acephalous entity,[51] we suggest that κεφαλή can best be understood against the backdrop of the Hebrew Scriptures -- that which is now generally regarded as the most likely background (theologically speaking) of vv. 15-20 as a whole.[52]

It is instructive to note in this regard that a comparative analysis of the *LXX*[53] and the *MT*[54] reveals that most often, κεφαλή is used to translate שׁ ‏ר ‏; and that either word can refer to the physical or anatomical head of persons or beast, for example, Jacob's head (Gen. 28:11), the head of the chief baker in Egypt (Gen. 40:16), the head of the passover lamb (Ex. 12:9), or the head of a bull killed as a sin offering (Ex. 20:19). When used of people in a metaphorical sense, however, it (κεφαλή or שׁ ‏ר ‏) means chief, leader, or one who occupies a position of primacy in relation to others (see Deut. 28:13; Jud. 10:18; Isa. 7:8f.).[55] In a more exhaustive manner, Caird writes: "*Rosh* can mean: (a) the anatomical head; (b) the top of anything; (c) a chief or ruling person; (d) the first in a series; (e) a source."[56]

This information is helpful in that, at least, it gives us some idea of the semantic range that κεφαλή may have had for Paul who overall, shows a familiarity with, and a fondness for, the Greek version of the Hebrew Scriptures.[57] In looking at his use of the term in his epistles (our second level of argument), it comes as no surprise to us, then, that for him, κεφαλή is no less flexible in meaning, covering head, source, and supremacy.[58]

Statistically speaking, κεφαλή appears eighteen times in the Pauline corpus: 1 Cor., ten times; Rom., once; Col., thrice; and Eph., four times. Setting aside the four in Eph. for the moment,[59] and reserving those three in Col. for our third level of argument, let us look at the remaining eleven briefly since it really does not require that much to convince us of the semantic stretch of the term as it appears there.

First of all, we do find an obvious anatomical use of κεφαλή in two places: one in 1 Cor. and the other in Rom.; specifically, 1 Cor. 12:21 and Rom. 12:20. In the former, the term appears within the context of Paul's use of the human body as a role model for the Corinthian church. In discussing the charisms which the Corinthians had each received, the apostle informs them that in the use of such gifts, they should both care for, and cooperate with, each other. For him, the head cannot (should not) say to the feet, "I don't need you".

The other anatomical use of the term (Rom. 12:20) is really based on a quotation from Prov. 25:21f. Paul quotes from the Wisdom literature in

THE CHURCH AS THE BODY OF CHRIST

order to remind the Roman brethren that, among other things, the ethic of *lex talionis* is not the most appropriate for the Christian. Instead, the Christian should respond positively to the needs of his/her enemies -- and in practical ways to boot. If s/he is hungry or thirsty, food or drink should be provided. By so doing, according to the apostle, burning coals will then be heaped upon the enemy's head.

In terms of the other nine occurrences of κεφαλή outside of Col. and Eph., we find that they are all bunched in 1 Cor. 11:2-16, a pericope in which Paul discusses the issue of women praying and prophesying at church with uncovered heads.[60] In this passage, κεφαλή sometimes refers to the anatomical head of both men (vv. 4,7) and women (vv. 5,10). However, in v. 3, the apostle establishes what appears to be a hierarchy by referring to God as the head of Christ, to Christ as the head of men, and to men as the head of women. With regard to the last in the series (men *vis-à-vis* women), it is not entirely clear what the apostle means by it, suggesting as it does the subordination of women to men (cf. vv. 11f.; 7:1-4; Gal. 3:27f.); a subordination which the apostle seeks to justify by appealing to God's design as reflected in His created order (vv. 7-9).

As a whole, the pericope bristles with exegetical difficulties that need not detain us here; for example, the real nature of the problem that is being addressed, a subordinationistic Christology (v. 3), the contextual meaning of κατακαλύπτῳ (covered -- vv. 6f.), ἀκατακαλύπτῳ (uncovered -- vv. 5,13), ἐξουσία (authority -- v. 10) and περιβολαίον (covering -- v. 15); and of course, the rather enigmatic reference to angels who, at worship, seemingly prefer to linger around women with covered heads.[61]

This notwithstanding, it must be pointed out that Paul leaves us with no doubt that in this passage (1 Cor. 11:2-16), κεφαλή does not only mean head in the strict anatomical sense of the word. In referring to God as head of Christ, to Christ as head of men, and to men as head of women, the apostle obviously is not speaking anatomically at all since he is not suggesting that Christ, men, and women are all headless. In fact, this *reductio ad absurdum* would push us to say that both Christ and men are headless heads. In using κεφαλή in v. 3, Paul most likely is speaking of the primacy, supremacy, or perhaps, even the source of the one in relation to the other; a meaning that is in keeping with the metaphorical use of the term in the *LXX*.[62]

That having been said, let us now turn to the third level of our argument, namely, the use of κεφαλή in Col. itself. We consider this most important since so far we have dealt only with what Paul may have known about κεφαλή based on the *LXX* and how he has used it elsewhere in 1 Cor. and Rom. We are yet to determine how he uses the word in communicating with the Colossians themselves.

As we have already mentioned, the word appears three times in the epistle. In addition to its appearance in Col. 1:18, our first E σῶμα text, κεφαλή appears twice more in 2:10 and 19. In the former (v. 10), it is important to note, first of all, that Paul makes mention of Christ as κεφαλή of all rule and authority but with no reference to the church as σῶμα at all.[63] This should at least discourage us from assuming that σῶμα and κεφαλή are necessary anatomical complements in Col. In 1:18, for example, both terms appear; in 1:24, only σῶμα does; here in 2:10, it is only κεφαλή; in 2:19, it is both; and in 3:15, again only σῶμα does. Further, the church is imaged as *the whole body* (πᾶν τὸ σῶμα) in 2:19, thus removing any lingering doubt that Paul may have decapitated the church in 1:18. In addition, Paul makes mention of Christ as κεφαλή from whom (ἐξ οὗ) the church as a whole body grows via its limbs, ligaments and linkages (2:19).

If Paul considers κεφαλή and σῶμα as anatomical complements here in 2:19, it is rather peculiar that he does not use an ablative feminine relative pronoun to correspond with the feminine, κεφαλή. His decision to use ἐξ οὗ (masculine -- pointing to Χριστός) in lieu of ἐξ ἧς (feminine -- pointing to κεφαλή) strongly suggests to us, at least, as it did to Meuzelaar earlier,[64] that in Paul's mind, κεφαλή and σῶμα are not considered physiological partners at all. That is, the metaphor of the church as σῶμα does not require exegetically the metaphor of Christ as κεφαλή.

In 2:19, Paul really has his attention fixed and focussed on the false teachers at Colossae when he speaks of Christ as κεφαλή. He is accusing *them* of not holding on to Christ, the κεφαλή; the One who is pre-eminent in all things (see 1:15-20; 2:9f. again). And in doing so, Paul is not implying that these trouble-makers constitute an acephalous aberration in need of a κεφαλή in the person of Christ. Instead, the apostle also makes mention of the church as σῶμα which stands apart from Christ as κεφαλή (exegetically) and he does so in order to emphasize the primacy of position that Christ occupies *vis-à-vis* not only the aberrants but also the church as a whole.

Following Caird and a few others, therefore, we affirm that in Col.: "The metaphor of Christ as head is thus quite independent in origin of the metaphor of the church as body, though the two have been brought together."[65] In saying this, we find ourselves both in agreement and disagreement with Wright. In commenting on 2:10, he states: "The word 'head' was as flexible and evocative in Hebrew or Greek as it is in English, and it would be ridiculous to squeeze all Paul's uses of it into exactly the same mould."[66] We do agree that κεφαλή was flexible but disagree that in Col., Paul uses it in one way in 2:10 (non-anatomically) and in another in 1:18 and 2:19 (anatomically) -- as Wright would have it. There is really no reason that is exegetically compelling to accept this view.

For Paul, σῶμα in Col. still points to the human body (with its head included). It is for this reason also that in speaking about the church as a body for the last time in the epistle (3:15), the apostle could declare that in Christ, everyone has been called into the local church as one body (one whole human body);[67] be they Jew or Greek, circumcised or not; barbarian, Scythian, slave, or free.

In addition to speaking about the church as σῶμα, however, the apostle also lifts up Christ to the Colossians as the κεφαλή of both church (1:18; 2:19) and cosmos (2:10). For him, Christ is first and foremost the unrivalled Lord of both. He is the creator and redeemer and the One to whom primacy of position has now been accorded (1:15-20).

D. Summary

To summarize, then, let us simply re-affirm what by now may have become quite predictable: that in Col., and as was true of 1 Cor. and Rom. earlier, Paul likens the churches at both Colossae and Laodicea in the Lycus Valley of Asia Minor to a human body, a whole human body (πᾶν τὸ σῶμα - - 2:19) and one for which he joyfully suffers the afflictions of Christ as he daily executes his gift of apostleship among the Gentiles (1:24-29). For Paul, the human body acts as an important role model for the church because it suggests interconnectedness, interdependence, life and growth (2:19). As a multi-membered and integrated whole, it also says something about the possibility of, and the necessity for, those in a multi-cultural and multi-racial church to be at peace among themselves, to empathize with each other, and to love without dissimulation (3:11-17).

In speaking about Christ as κεφαλή of the church, His σῶμα (1:18; 2:19), the apostle does not make use of Christ's personal body in a direct way; that is, the two σῶματα are neither made one mystically nor related to each other metaphorically. In addition, κεφαλή should not be interpreted as head in an anatomical sense. This means, in essence, that κεφαλή and σῶμα, though brought together at times, are not to be considered necessary complements of each other. For us, and according to Gibbs, "the essential point is that κεφαλή (in Col.) provides not a biological but a juridical analogy."[68] The term denotes sovereignty, supremacy and lordship; and in the case of Christ, it applies to Him not only in relation to the church but also in relation to the cosmos (1:18; 2:10,19).

ENDNOTES

Chapter Five

1. N.T. Wright, *The Epistles of Paul to the Colossians and to Philemon* (Unpublished MS in the library of the Faculty of Religious Studies, McGill University, 1984), p. 8. This has since been published in the *TNTC* series (1988).

2. See Brown, *The Churches*, pp. 47-53. For a contrary position, see Ridderbos, *Paul*, pp. 376-387.

3. See the format we have already followed in dealing with 1 Cor. and Rom.; in particular, the Introductions for both Chapters Three and Four.

4. The others, of course, are 1 Cor., Rom., and Eph. See succeeding chapter for a discussion of the last epistle mentioned.

5. For example, see D. Schmidt, "The Authenticity of 2 Thessalonians." For Schmidt, both 1 Cor. and Rom. are among "the Pauline pillars". See pp. 291f.

6. Brown, *op. cit.,* p. 47. For a helpful historical overview of the discussion, see Raymond Collins, *Letters That Paul Did Not Write: The Epistle to the Hebrews and the Pauline Pseudepigrapha* (Delaware: Michael Glazier, 1988), pp. 171-208.

7. E. Lohse, *Colossians and Philemon,* translated by W.R. Poehlmann, in *Herm.* (Philadelphia: Fortress Press, 1971); and E. Schweizer, *The Letter to the Colossians: A Commentary,* translated by A. Chester (Minneapolis: Augsburg, 1976).

8. One theological issue that is usually raised in this regard is the $\sigma\tilde{\omega}\mu\alpha$ ecclesiology (with its conspicuous $\kappa\epsilon\phi\alpha\lambda\dot{\eta}$ Christology) of the epistle as compared and contrasted with 1 Cor. and Rom. More on that to follow.

9. Wright, *op. cit.,* p. 59. Gibbs, however, is illustrative of those who are so unsure about the issue as to be inconsistent. In a footnote, he declares concerning himself: "This writer agrees with the position that Col. was written by Paul...." Nevertheless, Gibbs discusses Col. as a post-Pauline epistle alongside Eph. and never once ascribes authorship to Paul in the discussion itself. Consistently, he makes mention of "the author of Col." See John G. Gibbs, *Creation and Redemption*, p. 97, n. 2 and 94-114 *passim.*

10. P.T. O'Brien, *Colossians and Philemon* (Waco, Texas: Word, 1982), pp. xli - xlix. Roy Yates, among others, is also a proponent of Pauline authorship (1978). See his article in *Studia Biblica, vol. III. Papers on Paul and Other New Testament Authors*, p. 464.

11. Wright, *op. cit.,* pp. 59f. (See n. 6, *supra.*) Bruce also subscribes to Pauline authorship. See his commentary, *Colossians, Philemon, and Ephesians* (Grand Rapids: Wm. B. Eerdmans, 1984), pp. 30-32.

12. We reserve judgment on Eph. for the succeeding chapter.

13. Bruce, *op. cit.,* p. 32.

14. E.g., Wright, *op. cit.,* pp. 52-55; and p. 325, n. 29 where, among others, he refers to the writings of G.S. Duncan, one of the earlier pioneers of such a view (the 1950's).

15. E.g., B. Reicke, "Caesarea, Rome, and the Captivity Epistles", in *Apostolic History and the Gospel*, edited by W.W. Gasque *et al.* (Grand Rapids: Wm. B. Erdmans, 1970), pp. 277-286; and J.A.T. Robinson, *Redating the New Testament*, p. 352.

16. This is the majority view with Lightfoot usually cited as one who exerted a dominant influence here. See J.B. Lightfoot, *Saint Paul's Epistles to Colossians and to Philemon* (London: Macmillan, 1875); G.B. Caird, *Paul's Letters from Prison* (Oxford: Oxford University Press, 1976), pp. 2-6. A more recent proposal re: the Roman hypothesis would have us date Colossians in the mid-to-late 60's during Paul's second Roman imprisonment after, supposedly, he had already visited Spain further west. For this novel and highly conjectural proposal, see Steve Mason and Tom Robinson, *An Early Christian Reader* (Toronto: Canadian Scholars' Press, 1990), pp. 364-366.

17. Wright, *op. cit.,* p. 53.

18. E.g., see J.M. Robinson and H. Koester, *Trajectories Through Early Christianity* (Philadelphia: Fortress Press, 1971). Brown, for example, uses the word (trajectory) within the context of his discussion of N.T. ecclesiology. See, *The Churches*, p. 50, n. 73.

19. See the Introduction to Chapters Three and Four.

20. For that, see H. Koester, *Introduction to the New Testament: Volume One -- History, Culture, and Religion of the Hellenistic Age* (Philadelphia: Fortress Press, 1982), pp. 164-203; O'Brien, *op. cit.,* pp. xxx-xli; and G. La Piana, "Foreign Groups in Rome during the First Centuries of the Empire," *HTR* 20 (1927): 183-203.

21. For a fairly competent discussion of the Rabbinic (and therefore Jewish) background to the references to elemental spirits, angels, principalities and powers in Col., see Cathy Hird, *Principalities and Powers in Pauline Theology* (Unpublished M.A. Thesis, McGill

University, 1986), and the works cited there.

22. For an informative overview of such positions, see F.O. Francis and W.A. Meeks, *Conflict at Colossae: A Problem in the Interpretation of Early Christianity Illustrated by Selected Modern Studies*, rev. edn. (Montana: Scholars Press, 1975); O'Brien, *op. cit.*, pp. xxx-xli; and Schweizer, *op. cit.*, pp. 125-134.

23. In addition to n. 21 *supra*, see E. Lohse, *Colossians and Philemon, ad loc.*

24. Wright, *op. cit.*, pp. 31-44.

25. Formerly in 1 Cor. and Rom. By third time, we are not referring to the specific statistical use of σῶμα as E in those epistles; rather, that the Corinthians and Romans as Christian communities were so addressed.

26. For the meaning of these sigla, see the List of Abbreviations, p. ix.

27. See A. Q. Morton *et al.*, *A Critical Concordance to the Letter of Paul to the Colossians, The Computer Bible*, vol. XXIV, edited by J. Arthur Baird *et al.* (Biblical Research Associates Inc., 1981), p. 46.

28. See discussion to follow.

29. According to Schweizer, Benoit, among a few others, has argued unconvincingly for σῶμα as C here, meaning that the casting away of the body of flesh in the circumcision of Christ refers to Christ's own death and impalement on the cross rather than to the Christian's baptismal passage from death to life and the faith, faithfulness, and fellowship that go along with it. See Schweizer, *op. cit., ad loc.* Bruce, a more recent proponent of the C view, is somewhat confusing. In his commentary, he translates the verse so as to yield a C understanding of σῶμα. He does so by inserting an epexegetic καί into the verse. For him, v. 11b reads: "... by stripping off the body of flesh, -- that is to say, with the circumcision of Christ." However, he subsequently comments on the verse by simply juxtaposing a C interpretation with an E without telling us which one he favours since evidently, he does not believe that Paul intends both concurrently. See his *Colossians, ad loc.*

30. See Lk. 3:22 and 1 Tim. 4:8, the only other two appearances of the adverbial form in the N.T.

31. Moule, *Col., ad loc.* Two ancient commentators to whom Moule refers are Chrysostom (345-407) and Augustine (354-430).

32. *Ibid.*

95

33. See his *Col., ad loc.*, where he also makes mention of Caird as another proponent of C but for whom σωματικῶς means solid reality.

34. Lohse does not subscribe to Pauline authorship. See n. 7, *supra.*

35. Lohse, *Col., ad loc.*

36. Schweizer, *op. cit., ad loc., n. 11.*

37. E.g., see Schweizer, *op. cit., ad loc.;* and Bruce, *op. cit., ad loc.,* plus the works cited there in n. 50.

38. E.g., Plato's famous image of the cave in his *Republic* 514a - 518b (as cited in Lohse, *op. cit., ad loc., n. 16).*

39. See Bruce, *op. cit., ad loc.*

40. Of the other 143 appearances of σῶμα in the N.T., Rev. 18:13 should also be isolated since σῶμα there does not mean body either. Rather, it means slave. See p. 24, n. 7 again for the break-down of all 51 extra-Pauline references.

41. R.P. Martin, *Colossians., ad loc.;* Bruce, *op. cit., ad loc.,* n. 110; also see Best *op. cit.,* p. 12, for a view similar to Bruce's.

42. See M. Hengel, "Hymns and Christology", in *Studia Biblica*, pp. 185ff. This article is reproduced as a chapter in his, *Between Jesus and Paul: Studies in the Earliest History of Christianity* (Philadelphia: Fortress Press, 1983), pp. 78-96; also see Wright, *op. cit.,* pp. 101f. and 110f. Wright is of the opinion that Paul may well have composed the poem (hymn) himself. For a similar view, see M.D. Hooker, "Were There False Teachers in Colossae?" in *Christ and Spirit in the New Testament*, edited by B. Lindars *et al.* (Cambridge: At the University Press, 1973), pp. 316f., 329.

43. E.g., Käsemann, "Eine urchristliche Taufliturgie", in *Festschrift Rudolf Bultmann zum 65 Geburtstag Uberreicht*, edited by E. Wolf (Stuttgart: W. Kohlhammer Verlag, 1949), pp. 139f.; Lohse, *op. cit., ad loc.;* and N. Kehl, *Der Christushymnus im Kolösserbrief* (Stuttgart: Katholisches Bibelwerk, 1967), p. 93-98.

44. See C.F. Burney, "Christ as the Ἀρχή of Creation", *JTS* 27 (1925-26): 160-177; also W.D. Davies, *Paul and Rabbinic Judaism*, pp. 147-176. Davies builds much of his case on the Rabbinic speculations concerning Adam's body. He does so because he is of the opinion that the apostle Paul is articulating an Adamic Christology in 1:15-20.

45. Wright, *op. cit., ad loc.*

46. See Caird, *Paul's Letters*, pp. 160-164; and Wright, *op. cit., ad loc.*

47. R. P. Martin, *op. cit.*, p. 39. For an elaboration of these two themes within the context of the hymn, see, for example, Gibbs, *Creation and Redemption*, pp. 94-114.

48. According to Bruce, for example, "when head and body are used as correlative terms, the physiological relation is in the foreground...." See *Col., ad loc.*

49. For this, see the discussion by Ridderbos in *Paul,* pp. 376-387.

50. It is this perceived tension (regarding κεφαλή-σῶμα) between 1 Cor./Rom. and Col. that tempts some scholars to doubt the Pauline authorship of Col.; e.g., Lohse. See nn. 7f., *supra.*

51. See the full discussion of H. Schlier, s.v. "Κεφαλή" in *TDNT,* vol. III, pp. 673-681; and Ridderbos, *Paul,* pp. 385ff.

52. See n. 48, *supra* and the accompanying text.

53. A. Rahlfs, ed., *Septuaginta,* 2 vols., 4th edn. (Stuttgart: 1949).

54. R. Kittel, *Biblia Hebraica Stuttgartensia* (Stuttgart: 1977).

55. See Schlier, *op. cit.*

56. Caird, *Paul's Epistles,* p. 78. In addition to n. 55 *supra,* also see R. Scroggs, "Paul and the Eschatological Woman" *JAAR* 40 (1972): 281-303, esp. 298f. Κεφαλή is also used to refer to capital cities such as Damascus of Syria and Samaria of the Northern Kingdom of Israel. See Isa. 7:8f. In addition, the term is sometimes used interchangeably with ἀρχή and even πρωτότοκος. See Gibbs, *Creation and Redemption*, pp. 102ff.; also see, Best, *op. cit.,* pp. 124f., and Minear, *Images,* pp. 205ff.

57. For that, see E.E. Ellis, "A Note on Pauline Hermeneutics", *NTS* 2 (1955-56), pp. 131ff.; and *idem, Paul's Use of the Old Testament* (Edinburgh: T. & T. Clark, 1957). In addition, see A.T. Hanson, *Studies in Paul's Technique and Theology* (London: SPCK, 1974), pp. 136-168.

58. See Stephen Bedale, "The Meaning of *Kephalē* in the Pauline Epistles", *JTS* 5 (1954): 211-215. Also relevant here is my unpublished M.A. thesis, *Paul's Counsel Regarding the Head Covering in 1 Cor. 11:2-16* (Michigan: Andrews University, 1977), pp. 44f., and the works cited there. Also see Caird, *Paul's Epistles*, p. 78.

59. Since we are yet to discuss the authorship of Eph., we will not, at this time, allow it to inform the discussion. See Chapter Six. In terms of the overall statistics, κεφαλή appears 75 times in the N.T.: 18 in the *corpus Paulinum* and 57 elsewhere, namely, Matt. -- 12; Mk. -- 8; Lk. -- 7; Jn. -- 5; Acts -- 5; 2 Pt. -- 1; and Rev. -- 19. See Morgenthaler, *Statistik,*

ad loc.

60. V. 2 (thrice); vv. 4f. (twice each); vv. 7,10 (once each).

61. A detailed discussion of this passage is found in my unpublished M.A. thesis referred to in n. 58 *supra*, and the works cited there. In addition, see J. Murphy-O'Connor, "Sex and Logic in 1 Corinthians 11:2-16", *CBQ* 42 (1980): 482-500; and more recently, Brendan Byrne, *Paul and the Christian Woman* (Minnesota: The Liturgical Press, 1988), pp. 31-58.

62. Also in agreement are: Barrett, *1 Cor., ad loc.;* and Caird, *op. cit.,* pp. 77f.

63. By placing Col. on a Gnostic grid, Lohse and Loymeyer, among others, have argued unconvincingly that originally, the cosmos was considered a $\sigma\hat{\omega}\mu\alpha$ with the so-called redeemed-Redeemer functioning as $\kappa\epsilon\phi\alpha\lambda\dot{\eta}$ in relation to it but that the author of Col. has Christologized the entire concept here. It is for this same reason that they consider the mention of $\dot{\epsilon}\kappa\kappa\lambda\eta\sigma\acute{\iota}\alpha$ in 1:18 as a Pauline intrusion into what, supposedly, was originally a hymn about the cosmos as $\sigma\hat{\omega}\mu\alpha$. See Lohse, *op. cit., ad loc.* And for an adequate refutation of such a view, see Best, *op. cit.* pp. 115-126.

64. See Meuzelaar, *Der Leib des Messias*, pp. 105ff.

65. Caird, *op. cit.,* p. 78. According to Ridderbos, "'head' and 'body' form two separate figurative categories and retain this independence even when they are linked together". See, *Paul,* pp. 376ff., esp. 383. Also see Moule, *Origin*, p. 75 who agrees with this view, as does Meuzelaar. See *ibid.*

66. Wright, *op. cit., ad loc.*

67. Wright concedes that $\sigma\hat{\omega}\mu\alpha$ in 3:15 is "a simple metaphor, in which the church is understood as a single living organism whose 'members'...must act in harmony with each other". However, he considers it, "hard to imagine that Paul is not also alluding to the Church as *Christ's* own body" (emphasis his), based on his interpretation of 1:18 and 2:19. We find this approach exegetically unacceptable. For us, nowhere in Col. does the apostle refer to the church as Christ's own body if by that is meant Christ's physical body. See *op. cit., ad loc.*

68. Gibbs, *Creation and Redemption*, p. 105.

CHAPTER SIX

THE SOMATIC ECCLESIOLOGY OF EPHESIANS

A. Introduction

The epistle to the Ephesians acts as a most fitting terminus for our discussion of the church as σῶμα Χριστοῦ within the Pauline corpus. It is Best's considered opinion, for example, that the epistle "is a thoroughly 'ecclesiastical' document -- in the best sense of the word 'ecclesiastical'."[1]

Not only is it true that the epistle is 'ecclesiastical' through and through but it is also true that it employs σῶμα as ecclesiological language much more often than the other three which, together, constitute our team of four, namely, 1 Cor., Rom., and Col. As we have already determined, σῶμα as E appears four times in 1 Cor. (10:17; 11:29; 12:13,27)[2]; once in Rom. (12:5)[3]; and four times in Col. (1:18,24; 2:19; 3:15).[4] In the case of Eph., however, there is now solid scholarly consensus (and in our judgment, rightly so) that σῶμα is made to function in an E way on nine separate occasions -- thus equalling the other three combined.[5] Without exegetical effort, we can identify them quite easily. They are: 1:23; 2:16; 3:6; 4:4,12,16, (bis); and 5:23,29.[6]

In keeping with our thesis which, up to this point, has run like an Ariadne's thread throughout our discussion, we will look at the σῶμα texts in Eph. to see if the thread of our thesis runs through that epistle as well; to see if, as in the case of 1 Cor., Rom., and Col., the church there has the human σῶμα as its metaphorical referent. More than that, we will also need to deal with the conspicuous κεφαλή Christological concept that we first encountered in Col. In doing so, we will attempt to determine which interpretation of the term is most faithful to, and consistent with, the σῶμα ecclesiology of the epistle as a whole.

But before we do that, we will address ourselves, though briefly, to some critical introductory issues. It is against this backdrop that we will then be able to discuss, with some sense of the who, when, why, and where, those ecclesiological concerns that are of relevance to us.

1. Authorship and Authenticity of Ephesians

For most scholars today, what Origen once said about Heb. is very applicable to Eph. as well: Who wrote it? Only God knows.[7] Markus Barth once referred to the epistle as "a stranger at the door of the Pauline corpus"[8] and Kirby writes: "Of all the letters in the New Testament which are attributed to Saint Paul, none produces such a sharp division of opinion as the letter to the Ephesians."[9]

THE CHURCH AS THE BODY OF CHRIST

Up until the late eighteenth century (1792), when E. Evanson, the British deist and Unitarian, first seriously questioned the authorship and authenticity of Eph., Paul was generally considered to be its author (see Eph. 1:1; 3:1).[10] However, and according to Brown's 'broad approximation', about 80% of scholars today judge that the apostle did not write the epistle.[11] Instead, they insist that it was written long after his time.[12] Some of the names that scholars have suggested over the years as possible candidates include Luke, Tychicus, Timothy and Onesimus, each of whom was either among Paul's co-workers (Luke, Tychicus and Timothy), his converts (Tychicus and Onesimus), or both (Tychicus) (see, e.g., 1 Cor. 16:10f.; Col. 4:7ff.; Phil. 1:1; and Phlm. 1:8-22). Those scholars who refuse to attempt to identify the *auctor ad Ephesios* simply ascribe the epistle to an unknown soldier of the cross.

Markus Barth is right in observing that, in essence, the main arguments against Pauline authorship fall into four main groups. They are: "(1) Vocabulary and Style; (2) Similarity to, perhaps literary dependence upon, Colossians; (3) Historical and literary relationships; and (4) Theological distinctions."[13]

Admittedly, the cumulative impact of the arguments of those who oppose Pauline authorship and the strength of conviction with which they present them cannot be denied.[14] But as was true of the integrity of 1 Cor. [15] and the authorship and authenticity of Col.[16], some arguments tend to be most persuasive when they are kept in isolation from those which supposedly, are intended to prove the same point--in this case, that Eph. is deutero-Pauline. When isolation gives way to interaction, however, the case sometimes becomes less cogent. Then, there are some arguments which seem compelling only to those who, on other grounds, have already made up their minds one way or the other--either for or against Pauline authorship.[17]

Granted that all of this sounds rather general, abstract and perhaps, impressionistic, we do suggest that it is entirely consonant with Cadbury's very perceptive comment on the issue made over thirty years ago. It is a comment which still has a ring of contemporaneity to it. He wrote then:

> Persons who otherwise agree on critical questions often differ sharply here. They may feel the strength of the arguments on each side, but are ashamed to make no choice. So they answer the question one way or the other, more because of their unwillingness to admit indecision than out of clear conviction. The same arguments are quite differently appraised by advocates of the same side. In the pressure to arrive at some decision, now one, now another, minor matter is given

undeserved weight. Perhaps the individual scholar vacillates in his opinion, or over the years shifts from one side to another. The book on the question he has read most recently may move him, but not always as the author intended.[18]

Two of the books which we have read "most recently", that have moved us, and, in this case, as the authors intended, are Caird's and M. Barth's commentaries on Eph.[19] An examination of the evidence usually marshalled against Pauline authorship has led both of them to the following carefully worded conclusions which at this time, reflect our conviction as well.[20] In Caird's words:

> When all...has been said, the problem of Ephesians remains. It is curiously unlike the other Pauline letters. There are difficulties in attributing it to Paul. But these are insignificant in comparison with the difficulties of attributing it to an imitator. We shall therefore provisionally accept the traditional ascription.[21]

And according to Barth:

> If the maxim "innocent until proven guilty", *in dubio pro reo,* is applied here, then the tradition which accepts Paul as the author of Ephesians is more recommendable than the suggestion of an unknown author. The burden of proof lies with those questioning the tradition. The evidence produced by them is neither strong nor harmonious enough to invalidate the judgment of tradition. Although it cannot be definitely proven that Ephesians is genuinely Pauline, nevertheless it is still possible to uphold its authenticity.[22]

This being the case, permit us to end here with Best who puts it rather well. In his view, if Eph. "is not written by Paul it was written by someone sufficiently close to him as to continue his thought; we believe the evidence to tilt slightly in favour of Pauline authorship."[23]

2. Chronology of Ephesians

The chronological implications of our pro-Pauline position regarding authorship are reasonably clear. Those who date the epistle in the 70's,[24] the 80's,[25] or the 90's[26] of the first century C.E., i.e., after Paul's death in the mid-60's in Rome, are obviously at variance with the position to which we have just tentatively committed ourselves. Our pro-Pauline position means, at least, that we consider the mid-60's as our *terminus ad quem*. However, what is less clear is our *terminus a quo*.

The informed guesses that have been hazarded so far range from the mid-50's to the early 60's. Like Col., the epistle's date is tied to its place of origin and both of them are located either in Ephesus, Caesarea, or Rome.[27] The rationale for choosing these locations is that those who subscribe to Pauline authorship generally consider the epistle to have been written, if not at the same time as, then shortly after Col. For one thing, approximately three-fifths of Col. seems to be reproduced and redacted in Eph.;[28] also (and perhaps more important), Paul, the prisoner, uses Tychicus as the courrier for both epistles (see Col. 4:2-9; Eph. 3:1; 6:21f.).

Having already located Col. in Rome and having already dated it in the early-to-mid-60's, it means that, for us, Eph. is best located in Rome as well and dated in the 60's. In addition, we consider the un-provable hypothesis which J.B. Lightfoot and others have advanced to be fairly plausible; and that is: Eph. may well have been the epistle which Tychicus originally carried to the Laodiceans (among others) and which was to have been shared with the Colossians who themselves, were to share theirs with them (see Col. 4:15f.). At least, this may well have been Marcion's view who, in his *Apostolikon*, has the epistle addressed to the Laodiceans.[29]

Bruce's comments on this Laodicean hypothesis are sufficiently clear and cautious to allow us to end with him. He states:

> It is conceivable that, when a special letter was sent to the church of Colossae, one in more general terms was sent by the same messenger to the other churches in the district, including those at Hierapolis and Laodicea, and that this might be our Ephesians. More than this cannot be said.[30]

3. The Church in Ephesians: A General Description

Based on the tone and tenor of the epistle, it may be best to treat it as an encyclical sent to Christians perhaps in Ephesus and most likely to those at Laodicea, Hierapolis, and Colossae in the Lycus Valley of Asia Minor. This, at least, accounts for the fact that in comparison with the three others already examined, Eph. is written in "much more general terms".[31]

The church there is portrayed as a Christ-created and Spirit-supervised phenomenon in the world (e.g., 1:3-8; 2:1-9; 3:1-6; 4:1-6). Among other things, it is to be one (2:14-16; 4:1-3,10-13), holy (1:3-8; 4:17-22; 5:3-5,25-27), catholic (2:16; 3:1-6), and apostolic (2:19-22). In addition, it should be worshipful (2:1-3; 4:17-20; 5:6-17) and not worldly (5:18-20) in its orientation.[32]

In addition to σῶμα, there are other ecclesiological metaphors like temple (2:20), house (2:20f.), household (2:19), family (3:15; cf. 5:1,8) and perhaps, bride (5:21-33). However, no special congregation is ever mentioned and, for the most part, the addressees are simply identified as 'you' (e.g., 1:1b,2; 2:1,2; 3:1-5; 4:1-3; 5:3ff.; 6:10). The closest that we ever get to an identification of its recipients is the apostle's reference to Gentiles; those who, in his words, "were (once) separated from Christ, alienated from the commonwealth of Israel, and strangers to the covenants of promise; having no hope and without God in the world" (2:11f. -- RSV; cf. 3:1-6).

From this, we can draw the inference that the apostle not only sent the epistle to a number of churches in Asia Minor but also that he had the Gentile Christians chiefly in view. And if in fact the Colossians were recipients of it as Bruce, inter alios, has tentatively suggested,[33] then it becomes quite tempting to think that as an epistle, Eph. must have sounded to them as if it were written to complement and counterbalance some of what they were told in Col.; in particular, Paul's firm stand against Jewish theological and ethical aberrations in the church (see Col. 2).[34]

If Paul, the apostle to the Gentiles (3:1-3), left himself open to the charge of being anti-Jewish in Col., here in Eph., he puts things in their proper redemptive-historical and eschatological perspective (see Eph. 2f.). The apostle declares that through Christ, the Messiah, the uncircumcised but faithful Gentiles have now become an integral part of the bona fide and end-time people of God. They have now become sharers in Israel's privilege, as it were. In a word and in a way, then, Col. and Eph. together constitute at least an argument which is analogous to that which we find in Rom. 9-11. However, all of this is but a suggestion; perhaps even tantalizing, but more than that will not now be said.[35]

Instead, we will now endeavor to ascertain what the apostle chooses to tell and teach the Gentiles in the Lycus Valley and perhaps, Ephesus, about the church as the σῶμα of Christ and Christ as κεφαλή of it. We will seek to determine if Paul uses his κεφαλή-σῶμα language as he does in Col.; or, if in Eph., he uses it in a manner that is so inconsistent with it that it disfigures the thesis which has guided us to this point, namely, that the church as σῶμα has the human σῶμα, the whole human σῶμα, as its tertium comparationis and that therefore, Christ as κεφαλή stands clearly apart from, and is not in an anatomical relationship with it, the church.

THE CHURCH AS THE BODY OF CHRIST

C. Σῶμα as E in Ephesians

Σῶμα and its cognates appear ten times in the epistle. Judging from the *Critical Concordance,* we have σῶματος four times (4:12,16; 5:23,30); σῶμα, thrice (1:23; 4:4,16); σύσσωμα, once (3:6);[36] σῶματι, once (2:16); and σῶματα, also once (5:28).[37]

It is only in 5:28 that Paul uses σῶμα in an unambiguously A way. Appearing in the "nuptial" pericope of 5:21-33, itself a part of the *Haustafeln* (5:21 - 6:9), σῶματα there refers to Christian husbands whose bodies should be made the objects of no greater love than that which they themselves bestow on their wives. To illustrate the point, the apostle makes mention of the undying and self-denying love which Christ, the κεφαλή, has for the church, His σῶμα (5:23-28).

The other nine ocurrences of σῶμα and its cognates are particularly relevant to us since in those cases, and in accordance with the prevailing *communis opinio*, we find σῶμα used in at least, an E way.[38] That is, in Eph., and unlike 1 Cor., Rom. and Col., σῶμα may not be functioning as C alone--if at all. However, this is taking us ahead of ourselves somewhat. Such a claim must await further confirmation or disconfirmation.

Another presupposition with which we approach the whole κεφαλή-σῶμα question in Eph. is this: We are in full agreement with the general consensus which suggests that Eph. is best regarded as a competent reflection and echo of much of what we do see and hear in the other authentic epistles of Paul: 1 and 2 Cor. and Romans, for example, and Col. especially. With regard to Col. *vis-à-vis* Eph., Wright correctly observes that: "To read the two letters side by side is to be struck over and over again by close similarities of argument and wording...."[39]

In terms of the relationship between the epistle and the corpus as a whole, Johnston has this to say: "Eph. may be given the status of an inspired exposition of the Pauline message."[40] This is no more true than in the area of ecclesiology although it may be argued that there is greater stress on "the cosmic significance of the church and its mission."[41]

In spite of Paul's penchant for piling one ecclesiological metaphor upon another (e.g., Eph. 3:6) and at times, even to mix them (e.g., Eph. 4:12), he still presents us in Eph. with an ecclesiological statement that is recognizable elsewhere in his corpus; at least, in those epistles which we have already identified: 1 and 2 Cor., Rom., and Col.

At the risk of being accused here of *petitio principii,* let us also go on to affirm that insofar as the σῶμα-σῶμα and κεφαλή-σῶμα debate is concerned, all nine σῶμα texts in Eph. have clear exegetical connections with those other epistles; and they are as follows: Eph. 1:22f. derives its bearings from Col. 1:24; 2:10; Eph. 2:16 from Col. 3:15; Eph. 3:6 from Rom. 12:5; Eph. 4:4,12,15 from 1 Cor. 12:12-27; Col. 1:18; 2:19; and finally, Eph. 5:23,30 from 1 Cor. 6:12-20; 11:2-16; 2 Cor. 11:1-6; Rom. 12:5; and Col. 1:18. The implication here should be clear: We are suggesting that in Eph. we find essentially the same statement being made regarding Christ as κεφαλή and the church as σῶμα--that the church has the human body, the whole human body, as its metaphorical signifier and that Christ as κεφαλή has primacy or supremacy, headship or lordship accorded him. But then, all of this should occasion no surprise since, as is generally assumed, Eph. was at least sent to some of the same Christians to which Col. was sent--at Colossae and Laodicea; unless, of course, we also assume and can then prove that these Christians were told and taught something radically different about σῶμα and κεφαλή.

In our view, scholars such as Caird, Gibbs, Ridderbos, and a host of others are correct in interpreting κεφαλή and the E use of σῶμα in Eph. not only within the context of Col. but also against the backdrop of the other epistles in which such ecclesiological issues appear, namely, 1 Cor. and Rom.[42] In fact, we know of no scholar who ever isolates Eph. on the basis of its σῶμα ecclesiology and its κεφαλή Christology. Instead, they tend to yoke the epistle to Col. and then place them both over against 1 Cor. and Rom. In addition, and with reference to σῶμα as E, scholars generally (and rightly so) regard Rom. as riding "piggy back" on 1 Cor.; and Eph., on Col. The reason for this is quite simple: Rom. 12:4ff. is an obvious re-use of the body analogy of 1 Cor.--especially 12:12-27; and Eph., with its κεφαλή Christology alongside a σῶμα ecclesiology is a re-deployment of that which we encounter in Col.

To repeat, then, all of this means, in a word, that what we do find in Eph. in terms of the κεφαλή-σῶμα question essentially is no different from what we have already found to be true in Col., Rom., and 1 Cor., namely, κεφαλή there does not place Christ in an organic or anatomical relationship with an acephalous σῶμα, the church, and that σῶμα there does not point to Christ's personal body but instead, to the human body, the whole human body, as metaphor for the church.

With this serving as a prospective summary, then, let us now examine the data before us. This is important if for no other reason than that it will help to keep us in step with one of our own methodological convictions mentioned earlier on: that an author should at least be allowed to interpret himself or herself within the context of the document in which s/he chooses to express himself or herself. And to do so, we now turn our attention to Eph. 1:22f. where, for the first time, both κεφαλή and σῶμα appear. The text reads as follows:

THE CHURCH AS THE BODY OF CHRIST

...πάντα ὑπέταξεν ὑπὸ τοὺς πόδας αὐτοῦ, καὶ αὐτὸν
ἔδωκεν κεφαλὴν ὑπὲρ πάντα τῇ ἐκκλησίᾳ, ἥτις ἐστὶν
τὸ σῶμα αὐτοῦ, τὸ πλήρωμα τοῦ τὰ πάντα ἐν πᾶσιν
πληρουμένου.[43]

...He (God) put all things under His (Christ's) feet, and gave
Him as head over all things to the church, which is *His body*,
the fullness of Him who fills all in all. (Translation and
emphasis mine)

These vv. come as a sequel to the two immediately preceding ones in
which Paul uses the language of both praise and prayer to inform the Asia
Minor Christians that Christ, having been raised by the power of God, now
sits exalted in heavenly places, at God's right hand, and above every name
that is named.[44] The apostle continues to radiate his joy by insisting that all
of this is true not only for this age but also for the age to come (vv. 20f.).
Earlier, we juxtaposed vv. 22f. with Col. 2:10 rather than with Col. 1:18
and we did so for very good reasons. It is true that the latter (1:18) may be
considered subsidiarily relevant with its mention of the church as σῶμα.
However, and unlike it (Col. 1:18), Paul in Eph. 1:22f. is not really imaging
the risen Christ as κεφαλή of the church, His σῶμα, per se. Instead, he is
portraying Him as κεφαλή over all things--all rule, authority, power and
dominion (1:21). Or, using the language of Ps. 8:6b which he cites, everything
has been put under His (Christ's) feet.
This passing metaphorical reference to Christ's feet based on Ps. 8:6b,
it should be pointed out, is particularly important for our present purposes
since it strongly suggests that for Paul, κεφαλή and σῶμα do not constitute
anatomical complements at all--at least, not on the basis of vv. 22f. If they
did, then σῶμα here would have to be defined not only as an acephalous
entity (with Christ as head), but also as an acephalous, footless amputee
(since Christ now has the feet as well).
Even bearing in mind Frye's observation that metaphors are inherently
illogical[45] (and mixed ones perhaps, more so), there is nothing in the verses
(vv. 22f.) which would make such a bizarre definition of ʾbody' as caricatured
above, exegetically compelling. For one thing, Paul will later do in Eph. what
he has already done in Col.--refer to the church(es) as one whole human body
(πᾶν τὸ σῶμα), any whole human body (which, we may add, is clearly distinct
from Christ's personal body) (see Col. 2:19; Eph. 4:16).
In short, and unlike πόδας and σῶμα, κεφαλή does not function as
an anatomical metaphor in Eph. 1:22f. at all. As Gibbs has already pointed
out, "κεφαλή provides not a biological but a juridical analogy."[46] We cannot

106

go along with Robinson, for example, when he says that:

> The word with which κεφαλή must be taken is σῶμα. The head and body are complementary terms, and every time the headship of Christ is mentioned in Ephesians or Colossians it is in the closest conjunction with His body, the church.... He (Christ) is head only of His own resurrection body, in which Christians are incorporate.[47]

Christ's own personal body cannot conceivably be relevant here in Paul's reference to Christ as κεφαλή (v. 22) and to the church as σῶμα (v. 23). The apostle is not suggesting that the church is or is like a decapitated Christ. In fact, the real anatomical metaphor with which κεφαλή is being associated exegetically is not σῶμα, pointing to the church, but πόδας, pointing to all things (including the church) that have now been subjected to Christ, the κεφαλή. Sampley and Caird, for example, put it rather well. The former comments on Eph. 1:22f. as follows:

> To speak of Christ as the κεφαλή in v. 22b is to speak of Christ as the one who exercises authority and power. The statement that opens 1:22 -- 'and He has put all things under His feet' -- is paralleled with καὶ αὐτὸν ἔδωκεν κεφαλὴν ὑπὲρ πάντα τῇ ἐκκλησίᾳ (v. 22b). Such an association of diverse images reinforces the picture of the absolute authority conveyed to Christ over all things, including the church.[48]

And for Caird:

> The idea of Christ as head is not in any way derived from the image of the church as His body, although the two ideas occur together in Eph. 4:15 and Col. 1:18. Paul developed it quite independently (1 Cor. 11:3), drawing no doubt on the metaphorical uses of 'head' in the Old Testament (e.g., Isa. 7:8,9; Hos. 1:11). That the two ideas of head and body were not inseparable in his mind is proved...by Col. 2:10, where, shortly after a reference to Christ as head of the body, the church, he speaks of Him as 'head of all rule and authority'. This last passage (Col. 2:10), rather than Col. 1:18, is the parallel that illuminates the present usage (Eph. 1:22f.). It is as head over the whole realm of spiritual power that Christ becomes God's gift to the church.[49]

107

THE CHURCH AS THE BODY OF CHRIST

Having determined, therefore, that Eph. 1:22f. has Col. 2:10 (and not 1:18) as its Christological equivalent and that σῶμα there (Eph. 1:22f.), with reference to the church, could not conceivably have Christ's personal body in view, let us now focus our attention on the other σῶμα and/or κεφαλή texts in the epistle, namely, 2:16; 3:6; 4:4,12,15f.; 5:23,30. As was true of Col., we do not need to look at these texts separately. Eph. 1:22f., with its mention of both κεφαλή and σῶμα, acts as a pace-setter for the rest of the epistle where the κεφαλή-σῶμα issue is concerned; that is, the pertinent Christological and ecclesiological elements are already incorporated in it.

In 2:14-16, Paul contends that Christ, the bringer of God's peace, has removed the wall of hostility that once kept Jews and Gentiles apart; in Christ and at the cross, traditional divisions and distinctions have been crossed out (v. 16). For Paul, Jews and Gentiles now constitute one new person (v. 15b); or, changing the metaphor, they have both been called into one body, the church (v. 16). In 3:6, the apostle's penchant for σύν compounds in the epistle and elsewhere is exhibited in his affirmation that in Christ Jesus through the gospel, the messianic mystery of long ago has now been made known in that Jews and Gentiles alike are now fellow heirs (συγλκηρονόμα), fellow members of the body (σύσσωμα) and fellow partakers of the promise (συμμέτοχα) (cf. 2:6; Rom. 6:4-8; 8:17,22; 1 Cor. 12:26). In 4:4-16, he again makes mention of the church as one body (v. 4) but this time, of the abundance of gifts with which it has been endowed by Christ through the Spirit (vv. 7-12) and of the need for all its limbs, ligaments and linkages to do their Spirit-inspired part.[50] For Paul, this is necessary if the body of the church is to grow and go from childhood to adulthood, from disunity to unity, always abounding in truth and love (vv. 13-16).

In 4:15, mention is again made of Christ, the κεφαλή, and according to the apostle, the church is to grow up in every way into Him (εἰς αὐτόν). Some scholars, undoubtedly convinced that κεφαλή and σῶμα are physiological partners, contend that Paul, in this verse, is encouraging the church as σῶμα to grow up into Christ, the κεφαλή. For Robinson, "the notion of 'growing up into the head', however crude physiologically, is obviously possible only to someone (Paul) whose thinking through and through is in organic categories."[51] Further, evidence is sometimes sought within the Greek and later Graeco-Roman physiological and especially, neurological traditions to show that the head was perceived not only as the organ and originator, but also as the direction and destination of the body's growth. The names usually mentioned as supposedly providing confirmation for such a view are Hippocrates (ca. 460-380 B.C.E.) and Galen (ca. 130-200 C.E.). Markus Barth, however, has rightly pointed out that the notion of growth into the head is not supported by physiological theories contemporary with Paul.[52]

In addition, such physiological arguments are inadequate if for no other reason than that their proponents either fail to recognize or refuse to give weight to the fact that like Col. 2:19, κεφαλή and σῶμα are not grammatically and exegetically conjoined in Eph. 4:15f. Paul does not portray Christ as κεφαλή from which (ἐξ ἧς) the body of the church grows. Rather than employ the feminine relative pronoun as κεφαλή requires, he uses ἐξ οὗ, the masculine--precisely what he had already done in Col. 2:19.[53] Granted that unlike Col. 2:19, the masculine, Χριστός, does come between κεφαλή and ἐξ οὗ in Eph. 4:15f. and that ἐξ οὗ is therefore grammatically permissible because of it, the argument still stands that Paul does not consider κεφαλή and σῶμα as anatomical complements. If he did, he could and most likely would still have used the feminine ἐξ ἧς to draw our attention back to κεφαλή, the feminine substantive. In addition, v. 16 makes it quite clear that it is the *whole* body and not an acephalous σῶμα which is used as signifier for the church; also, that proper bodily growth is made possible not by the head but rather when all the limbs, ligaments and linkages of the *whole* body function as they should; that is to say, it is the *whole* body itself which causes itself to grow. In the case of the body of the church, however, Godly growth is made possible when each charism(s)-endowed limb or ligament does his or her Spirit-inspired part.

It means, then, that growth εἰς αὐτόν (4:15) is best taken as growth towards Him rather than into Him. For Paul, Christ is the goal of the church's growth. In its march towards maturity, towards the stature of the fullness of Christ (v. 13), the church must forever regard Him as the norm of perfection by which to measure its feeble but faithful efforts. For us, it also means that the physiological interpretation of κεφαλή is unnecessary and unfaithful to the passage (4:15f.) -- as was the case in 1:22f. and further back in Col. 1:18 and 2:19.

Strong confirmation for our non-physiological interpretation of κεφαλή can readily be found in 5:21-33, the last pericope in which both κεφαλή and σῶμα appear in the epistle. According to Caird, for example, this pericope puts the non-physiological explanation of κεφαλή "beyond doubt".[54]

In 5:21-33, the analogy is drawn between the Christ-church relationship and that between husbands and wives. Both Christ and husbands are considered heads; the former *vis-à-vis* the church and the latter, their wives (vv. 23-30). Quite reminiscent of 1 Cor. 11:2-16, κεφαλή here cannot be taken physiologically since obviously, Paul is not suggesting that wives are without heads and that husbands are without bodies (cf. vv. 28f.); or that Christ is an asomatic κεφαλή and the church an acephalous σῶμα with both in need of each other in some anatomical sense. Rather, the apostle is using

109

THE CHURCH AS THE BODY OF CHRIST

κεφαλή in the passage to underscore the place of primacy that Christ occupies *vis-à-vis* the church, His σῶμα, as well as that which presumably, husbands occupy *vis-à-vis* their wives.

Also of importance here, is the view that the church as σῶμα is not a reference to Christ's personal body taken either mystically or metaphorically. This is clear from the husband-wife analogy since the inference cannot validly be drawn that the husband's body and that of his wife are one and the same or that one is a metaphorical referent for the other. The two bodies (husband's and wife's) remain separate even when figuratively, they are said to become one flesh (vv. 30f.).

It means, then, that as κεφαλή, Christ stands over His church as Lord, leader, and lover of it (see 5:25). And conversely, the church, likened to a whole human body rather than to Christ's personal body, ever remains in subjection to Him (5:1); to Him whose self-denying love is pure, holy and without blemish.

It is for this reason, therefore, that we are forced to express some discomfort with Kirby's view. For him, "Ephesians 5:29-30 and 1 Corinthians 12:12-14 express the same idea, for in both passages Christ Himself is the body and believers are members of that body."[55]

D. Summary

In Eph., and as was true of 1 Cor., Rom., and Col., Christ and the church are not one in body but one in Spirit (4:3f.; cf. 1 Cor. 6:15-20; 12:13). With the use of σῶμα, Paul repeats much of what he has already said to the Corinthians, Romans, Colossians, and Laodiceans, namely, that Christ fills the church with His diverse gifts of grace through the Spirit (Eph. 1:23; 4:4-16; cf. 1 Cor. 12:12-27; Rom. 12:4-8; Col. 1:24); and that such charisms are for both the church's growth (Eph. 4:4-16; Col. 2:19), and for a life of love (Eph. 4:4-16; 5:21-33; cf. 1 Cor. 12:31 - 13:13; Rom. 12:9; Col. 3:12-15). In Eph., Christ is not the church; rather, the church is His (Eph. 1:23; 3:6; 5:23,30; cf. 1 Cor. 12:27; Rom. 12:5; Col. 1:24); and as the church's Lord, He stands and reigns over it (Eph. 4:15f.; 5:23; cf. 1 Cor. 12:3; Col. 1:18; 2:19). In addition, special emphases associated with σῶμα in Eph. include unity and equality -- unity in the faith and equality among all. For the apostle, both Jews and Gentiles are now on equal footing in the church (2:16; 3:6; 4:4-16; cf. 1 Cor. 10:17; 11:29; 12:13; Rom. 12:5; Col. 3:11-15).

What cannot be said of Eph., however, is that it presents us with a σῶμα ecclesiology which has Christ's personal body at the heart of it. The truth is, σῶμα as C does not appear in the epistle at all (again see 1:23; 2:16; 3:6; 4:4,12,16 (*bis*); 5:23,28,30). Instead, and like 1 Cor., Rom., and Col., the

THE SOMATIC ECCLESIOLOGY OF EPHESIANS

E use of σῶμα there points to the human body, the *whole* human body, as a metaphorical signifier for the church. And like Col., κεφαλή there identifies the once crucified but now risen Christ as the One to whom primacy or supremacy, headship or lordship has now been accorded -- not only with respect to the church in particular, but also with respect to the cosmos in general (Eph. 1:22f.; 4:15f.; cf. Col. 1:18; 2:10).[56]

CHAPTER SIX

Endnotes

1. Best, *One Body In Christ,* p. 139. Neyrey is but one of many others who also regard Eph. as focusing on the community. See, *Christ is Community,* p. 249. For Johnston, ecclesiology is the primary topic in Eph. See, *Doctrine of the Church in the New Testament,* p. 91; and for Brown, the epistle presents us with "a massive emphasis on the Church." See, *The Churches,* pp. 49f.

2. See Chapter Three of this study.

3. See Chapter Four of this study.

4. See Chapter Five of this study.

5. Some commentators include the following: G.H.P. Thompson, in *CBC* (1967); G. Johnston, in *TCB* (1967); C. Leslie Mitton, *Ephesians,* in *NCB* (London: Oliphants, 1976); Norbert Hugedé, *L'Épître Aux Éphesiens (Génève: Labor et Fides, 1982);* and F.F. Bruce, in *NICNT* (1984). Other scholars include: Banks, *Paul's Idea of Community;* Best, *One Body In Christ;* Brown, *The Churches;* Gundry, *SŌMA;* J.C. Kirby, *Ephesians: Baptism and Pentecost* (Montreal: McGill University Press, 1968); Küng, *The Church;* Martin, *The Family and the Fellowship;* Minear, *Images;* Ridderbos, *Paul;* and Robinson, *The Body.*

6. For an English rendition of these (à la *RSV*), see pp. 19f. of this study again.

7. See W. G. Kümmel, *Introduction to the New Testament,* pp. 275f; and Collins, *Letters That Paul Did Not Write,* pp. 132-170; and esp. pp. 47f.

8. M. Barth, *The Broken Wall: A Study of the Epistle to the Ephesians* (Chicago: The Judson Press, 1959), p. 9.

9. Kirby, *op. cit.,* p. 3.

10. For brief historical sketches extending from the Apostolic Fathers to the present, see, for example, the commentaries of M. Barth in *AB,* pp. 36-41; Hugedé, *op. cit.,* pp. 9f.; and Caird, *Paul's Epistles,* pp. 9-11.

11. Brown, *op. cit.,* p. 47.

12. Chronology is to be discussed later.

13. Barth, *Ephesians*, p. 38. What makes some scholars suspicious about Pauline authorship is the omission from some *MSS* (e.g., P^{46} $\aleph$ and B) of ἐν 'Εφέσῳ in 1:1 and that Marcion knew the epistle as having been sent to Laodicea. However, the argument that the epistle may not have been sent to Ephesus originally has no logical relation to that which says that Paul never wrote it. In no *MS*, for instance, is Paul ever protrayed as not being the author of the epistle. This *non sequitur* seems all too common among those who attach much importance to the omission of ἐν 'Εφέσῳ in the verse. For one example in this regard, see Mitton, *op. cit.*, p. 3.

14. A good case in point is Johnston's Detached Notes, Part A, entitled, "The Authenticity of 'Ephesians'", found at the back of his published dissertation, *The Doctrine of the Church*, pp. 136-140. There, he basically builds on the influential work of Goodspeed but with some minor modifications. Along the way, he states quite clearly that, "Paul himself did not write 'Ephesians'". See p. 138.

15. See Introduction of Chapter Three again.

16. See Introduction of Chapter Five again.

17. It should be pointed out that those of the 'pro-Pauline party' also exhibit a strength of conviction of their own. However, neither side tends to consider passion and persuasion to be in direct proportion to each other -- at least, not when judging the other side. For a major work devoted exclusively to the 'pro-Pauline' hypothesis, see the fairly lengthy dissertation of A. Van Roon which was published as, *The Authenticity of Ephesians* (Leiden: E.J. Brill, 1974); an earlier but still substantial work is E. Percy, *Die Probleme der Kolösser- und Epheserbriefe* (Lund: Gleerup, 1946).

18. H.J. Cadbury, "The Dilemma of Ephesians", *NTS* 5 (1958-59): 93.

19. M. Barth, *op. cit.;* and G.B. Caird, *op. cit.*

20. We are using Pauline authorship here in a slightly extended sense. Whether the apostle wrote the epistle himself or he delegated the authority to one of his amanuenses whose work he then endorsed does not really matter to us. We are basically expressing our lack of conviction regarding the view that Eph. is a pseudonymous work written years after Paul's death. Also see G.H.P. Thompson, *op. cit.*, p. 29.

21. G.B. Caird, *op. cit.*, p. 29.

22. M. Barth, *op. cit.*, p. 41. Interestingly, Barth made this remark some fifteen years after having referred to the epistle as "a stranger at the door of the Pauline corpus." See n. 8 *supra*. Also, and in spite of his strong stand against Pauline authorship, it does appear that Johnston is still willing to leave the door of possibility open--at least ajar. At the very end of his detached note, for example, (see n. 14, *supra*) he writes concerning Eph. 1-3: "One

could well imagine Paul composing it himself, in a mood of exalted praise and prayer." See, *op. cit.,* p. 140. Also of interest in this regard is Kirby's observation. He writes: "The grammatical and syntactical construction is carried on through the whole letter, which would argue for common authorship." See Kirby, *op. cit.,* p. 128. Kirby, however, does not subscribe to Pauline authorship (see p. 165). Other proponents of Pauline authorship include Hugedé, *op. cit.* (1973); and Bruce, *op. cit.* (1984). Also see John P. Pritchard, *A Literary Approach to the New Testament* (Norman: University of Oklahoma Press, 1972). For Pritchard, "the objections to Pauline authorship merit the Scottish verdict of not proven." See p. 262.

23. Best, *op. cit.,* p. 139. Earlier, Dodd wrote: "Whether the Epistle is by Paul or not, certainly its thought is the crown of Paulinism." In fact, Dodd regarded this as the weightiest argument for Pauline authorship. See "Ephesians," in *ABC,* edited by F.C. Eiselen *et al.* (New York: 1929), pp. 1224f. For Bruce: "It (Eph.) may justifiably be described as an exposition of the quintessence of Paul's teachings." See, "The Epistles of Paul," in *PCB,* pp. 927-939; esp. p. 934; according to Goulder, there are literary indications that, "2 Thessalonians (as well as Ephesians and Colossians) is by Paul himself." See Michael Goulder, "The Pauline Epistles," in *The Literary Guide to the Bible,* edited by Robert Alter and Frank Kermode (Cambridge, MA: Harvard University Press, 1987), p. 481; and in Arnold's words: "...I believe that the apostle Paul himself surfaces as the most viable candidate for the role of author." See Clinton E. Arnold, *Ephesians: Power and Magic: The Concept of Power in Ephesians in Light of its Historical Setting,* in SNTSMS (Cambridge: At the University Press, 1989), p. 171.

24. E.g., J.C. Kirby, *op. cit.,* p. 169. He locates it "probably some time in the seventies."

25. E.g., G. Johnston, *op. cit.,* p. 140. Here, he dates it "ca. A.D. 80-85." However, some twenty-five years later, in his commentary on the epistle, he says that the date "may be about A.D. 90-95." See, *Ephesians, Philippians, Colossians and Philemon,* p. 7. The rationale for not going beyond 95 C.E. is that *1 Clem.,* dated ca. 96 C.E., seems to have been influenced by it.

26. E.g., R. Brown, *op. cit.,* p. 47. He states: "The period A.D. 90-100 is plausible." Barth informs us that in fact, for those who oppose Pauline authorship, the period can stretch from "ca. A.D. 70 to 170." See *op. cit.,* p. 50.

27. See Introduction of Chapter Five for earlier discussion.

28. Johnston, *op. cit.,* p. 137; Wright, *Colossians,* pp. 56ff.

29. See n. 13, *supra.* Evidently, Lightfoot was the first to advance this view in a serious and scholarly way. Among those who still see merit in it are Bruce, Caird and Wright.

30. Bruce, *op. cit.*, pp. 230f. Wright is also a proponent of the Laodicean hypothesis but unlike us, would date the epistle in the mid 50's from Ephesus as he does for Col. See his *Colossians*, pp. 269ff. It should also be pointed out that those who regard Eph. as a pseudonymous work would generally concede that both Col. and Eph. were eventually sent to some of the same addressees; in particular, those in the Lycus Valley.

31. Bruce, *ibid.* In addition to Laodicea and Hierapolis, Bruce perhaps, should have added Ephesus as well. (See n. 30, *supra*). As Kirby correctly pointed out, the fact that later church tradition came to associate the epistle with Ephesus must mean that the epistle was associated with the city and church(es) in some way and at some point. For him, however, Ephesus was the place of origin in the 70's, while for us, it was probably part of the circuit which Tychicus followed and therefore, one of the destinations of the epistle, back in the early-to-mid--60's. Of course, our position is a bit problematic in that Paul spent about three years working in Ephesus and therefore, would have known the Christians there so well as to be able to write to them in far more specific terms than he does in Eph. However, if the letter was meant to be a circular (see Wright, *op. cit.*, pp. 269ff.) and its addressees included those whom Paul did not know (e.g., the Laodiceans and the Colossians) then a general tone would be more appropriate. Those at Ephesus who knew him well would still be able to make sense out of the correspondence. Had he been too specific, on the other hand, those who did not know him in the flesh might have had far more difficulty making "heads or tails" out of the epistle; unless of course, the specific problems in the churches were so similar as to justify it; for example, as in the case perhaps, of the Colossians and the Laodiceans who had the same "epistle with specifics" (i.e., Col.) sent to them. We do acknowledge, of course, that this line of reasoning may not be the most compelling. Perhaps, it is best that we simply say that we do not know why the epistle is as it is. Paul must have had some reason (unknown to us at the present time) for writing it the way he did. Arnold has made a more recent suggestion that sounds rather attractive especially in view of the fact that there would have been a number of churches within the vicinity of Ephesus itself. See his *Ephesians: Power and Magic*, pp. 5f.

32. Kirby has shown that the epistle itself is liturgical through and through and that it may well have been written during the season of Pentecost--reflecting as it does so many themes that are reminiscent of the covenant renewal celebration at Pentecost. See Kirby, *op. cit.*, pp. 125-149.

33. See n. 30, *supra.*

34. See earlier discussion in Chapter Five and Wright's commentary, *ad loc.*

35. Also see Bruce, *op. cit.*, pp. 231f.; and Sampley, *"And the Two Shall Become One Flesh,"* pp. 158-162. Cf. M. Rese, "Church and Israel in the Deutero-Pauline Letters," *SJT* 43 (1990): 19-32.

36. This σύν construction is *hapax legomenal* within the context of the New Testament as a whole. See Morgenthaler, *Statistik, ad loc.*

37. A.Q. Morton *et al., A Critical Concordance to the Letter of Paul to the Ephesians: The Computer Bible,* vol. XXII (Biblical Research Associates Inc., 1980), p. 62.

38. See n. 5, *supra.*

39. Wright, *Colossians, op. cit.,* p. 56.

40. G. Johnston, *Ephesians,* p. 6. See n. 23, *supra* for the similar views of Dodd and Bruce. Also see Caird, *op. cit.,* pp. 20-29, who makes mention of Goodspeed and Mitton; and Kirby, *op cit.,* p. 169. The implication of this consensus is that Eph. should be seen as sharing an essentially Jewish background with the other epistles, not Gnostic as some would have it. See M. Barth, *Ephesians,* pp. 182-210, for an excellent discussion and critique of the once popular Gnostic hypotheses.

41. Johnston, *op. cit.,* p. 6; Also see n. 1 *supra.*

42. For a sample of a relatively long list of scholars and commentators, see n. 5, *supra.*

43. Πληρουμένου is especially problematic here. As a participle, should it be taken as passive or middle? And should we interpret the verse to the effect that the church is the bearer of Christ's fullness and therefore completes Him? For a refutation of such "an incomplete view" of Christ and the plausible suggestion that the verse is in fact portraying Christ as the embodiment of God's fullness, see Caird, *op. cit.,* pp. 48f. Also cf. Eph. 3:19; 4:10; and Col. 1:19; 2:9.

44. This is a passing reference to Ps. 110. See D.M. Hay, *Glory at the Right Hand,* for an informative discussion of the importance of Ps. 110 in early Christian thought. Also see, T.G. Allen, "God the Namer: A Note on Ephesians 1:21b," *NTS* 32 (1986): 470-475.

45. See N. Frye, "The Expanding World of Metaphor," *JAAR* 53 (1985): 585-598, esp. 588.

46. J.G. Gibbs, *Creation and Redemption,* p. 105. Also see p. 98, n. 68 of this study.

47. Robinson, *The Body,* p. 66. We find it rather strange for Robinson to argue that Christ as κεφαλή and the church as σῶμα are always discussed together in Col. His own citation of Col. 2:9f. should have dissuaded him of that. There, only κεφαλή appears--and in relation to the cosmos to boot.

48. Sampley, '*And The Two Shall Become One Flesh,*' pp. 123f.

49. Caird, *Paul's Prison Epistles,* pp. 48f.

50. With regard to 2:14-16 and the possible influence, among others, of Isa. 57 (a mere echo), see Michael S. Moore, "Ephesians 2:14-16: A History of Recent Interpretation," *EvQ* 54 (1982): 163-168. For a discussion of the influence of Ps. 68 and of the theme of Pentecost (as covenant renewal) which permeate Eph. 4, see Kirby, *op. cit.,* pp. 125ff. Also, mention should be made of Ridderbos. He is somewhat inconsistent in that he seems to argue for C in 2:16 on the basis of Col. 1:22 but then treats it (2:16) as E throughout -- in the actual discussion of the text and on the basis of Eph. 4:4. See, *Paul*, pp. 377f. As a *hapax legomenon* in both the Pauline corpus and the N.T. as a whole, σύσσωμα may well be one of Paul's neologisms. No evidence contemporary to, or antedating him has yet been found to show that the word did exist. Also, those scholars who exhibit some difficulty here in determining whether σύσσωμα is E alone, C alone, or a combination thereof, perhaps fail to recognize that σύσσωμα, along with συγκληρονόμα and συμμέτοκα, is tied to ἐν Χριστῷ Ἰησοῦ and, therefore, would make C or C/E exegetically difficult. The thought pattern is quite similar to that of Rom. 12:5; οἱ πολλοὶ ἓν σῶμα ἐσμεν ἐν Χριστῷ, where σῶμα here is clearly E alone. See earlier discussion of this passage in Chapter Four. Also see Abbott, *Ephesians,* in *ICC, ad loc.,* for essentially the same argument.

51. Robinson, *The Body,* p. 66.

52. For the views of J.B. Lightfoot *inter alios,* see M. Barth, *Eph.,* pp. 186ff. As far as we know, Galen summed up the accumulated progress of knowledge attained between 300 B.C.E. and 100 C.E.

53. See earlier discussion of Col. 2:19 in Chapter Five of this study; and Caird, *op., ad loc.*

54. Caird, *op. cit.,* p. 78. Sampley has provided us with a detailed discussion of this passage and, among other things, he argues that Gen. 2:24 exerts a pervasive influence on the entire pericope (not just vv. 30-33) and that the whole is patterned after the ἱερὸς γάμος, the holy but figurative marriage between God and Israel (e.g., Hos. 1-3; Isa. 54:5-8; Jer. 2:2). See Sampley, *op. cit.*

55. Kirby, *op. cit.,* p. 28. See our discussion of 1 Cor. 12:13,27 in Chapter Three. There, we argued that Christ's personal body is not in view but that σῶμα functions as E (and that alone) throughout.

56. Like Caird earlier (see n. 49 *supra*), Ridderbos sums up our conviction very well. For him: "The ground for this conjunction (κεφαλή and σῶμα) does not lie in that 'head' and 'body' in Paul's thought may be said gradually to have merged into one composite metaphor, but that both concepts, each in its own way, and each from 'its own side', materially give expression to the same idea, namely, that of the church's belonging to Christ.... The conjunction of both points of view (κεφαλή and σῶμα)...is sometimes so close as to give the impression that both representations run over into each other, as in Eph. 4:15ff. and Col. 2:19. This is no more than appearance, however. A fading of the boundaries does not take place.... 'Head' and 'body' form two separate figurative

117

categories and retain this independence even when they are linked together." See *Paul*, pp. 382f.

CHAPTER SEVEN

SUMMARY AND CONCLUSION

It is seldom (if ever) easy to prove that that which many thoughtful others have long considered difficult is in fact quite simple. And perhaps, this is no truer than in our attempt to re-examine the way in which σῶμα is handled ecclesiologically in the Pauline corpus.

The fundamental question which has driven the 'modern' grammatico-historical and exegetical discussion since its inception in 1919 with the publication of Traugott Schmidt's *Der Leib Christi*[1] is this: What is the nature of the relationship between Christ Himself via His once crucified but now risen σῶμα and the church as σῶμα? The answers given, informed as they are by this basic question (and presupposition), tend to oscillate between one of an ill-defined mystical unity and a mysterious metaphorical identity.[2]

Undoubtedly, this hermeneutical assumption which places Christ Himself, via His σῶμα, in some sort of direct relationship with the church as σῶμα may have contributed most to the elevation and emphasis which the motif has enjoyed over the years--in fact, over the centuries.[3] And this is understandable. If the assumption is made that Christ and the church are brought together in virtue of His once crucified but now risen body, that the church is an extension of that body,[4] or that Christians are members of it,[5] then it becomes quite logical that not only will the church be made to share in Christ's glory, in the type of adoration and adulation of which He is most worthy, but also that the body metaphor itself will be given pride of place over all the other Pauline ecclesiological metaphors which do not suggest such an intimate Christ-church relationship in the first place; or which do not lend themselves readily to what may be termed a triumphalistic, Christological ecclesiology. Branick, for example, is quite right in pointing out the harmful effects, particularly on Roman Catholic ecclesiology, that a C/E interpretation of σῶμα has had. In his words:

> The human reality of the church tended to be lost from view. It was not easy, for example, to call the church the body of Christ and to think of it as sinful. Nor was it immediately evident why it might need reform and renewal.[6]

Unlike the others, the σῶμα metaphor is most vulnerable to dogmatic manipulation and may well account for the apparent reluctance with which some scholars, be they Roman Catholic, Episcopalian (Anglican) or Protestant, and allegedly on exegetical grounds, refuse to disabuse their minds of the basic assumption to which we have just referred, namely, that Christ's personal body is in some direct relationship with the church as body. Instead, attempts are sometimes made to doctor up this assumption by conceding that Christ Himself via His body and the church itself may not be directly related but that Christians, as limbs of His, together constitute the "corporate Christ" - - still a nebulous concept at best.[7]

In this study, we have argued that the basic question regarding the nature of the relationship between the two bodies is ill-posed. We have attempted to explore more fully than has been done heretofore, the possibility and probability that when used with reference to the church, $\sigma\hat{\omega}\mu\alpha$ in the Pauline corpus does not point to Christ's personal body at all but rather, to the human body (any human body). And, in a subsidiary way, we have also insisted that $\kappa\epsilon\phi\alpha\lambda\acute{\eta}$, in relation to Christ, performs a non-physiological function vis-à-vis the church, His $\sigma\hat{\omega}\mu\alpha$. For us, $\kappa\epsilon\phi\alpha\lambda\acute{\eta}$ is performing juridical duties in both Col. and Eph. and it is used to identify the crucified but risen Christ as the One to whom primacy or supremacy, headship or lordship has now been accorded -- not only in relation to the church(es) but also in relation to all rule, authority, power and dominion (see Col. 2:10; Eph. 1:22).

In pressing these positions, we have placed ourselves in the company of a mere handful of scholars[8] but at variance with the vast majority for whom Christ Himself, via His personal body, is either mystically one with, or metaphorically related to, the church, His $\sigma\hat{\omega}\mu\alpha$. Further, we have disagreed with all those (and many there are) for whom $\kappa\epsilon\phi\alpha\lambda\acute{\eta}$ in Col. and Eph. carries an anatomical definition for Christ when mention is made of Him in relation to the church, His $\sigma\hat{\omega}\mu\alpha$.[9]

On an earlier occasion during our discussion of the basic hermeneutical assumption others make in interpreting $\sigma\hat{\omega}\mu\alpha$ as E in the Pauline corpus, we chose to make passing reference to the proverbial Ariadne's thread.[10] This time, we do so in our attempt to signify the exegetical consistency with which $\sigma\hat{\omega}\mu\alpha$ as ecclesiological language is employed in the corpus--in particular, 1 Cor., Rom., Col., and Eph.[11] It is a consistency which, we have argued, is entirely in keeping with our thesis and because of this, we believe that the thesis, as we have advanced it, hangs by more than "just a thread". By this, we mean to suggest that the thesis is not tied only to a tiny part of the Pauline data but instead, to all of it.

The eighteen references to $\sigma\hat{\omega}\mu\alpha$ as E which we have found in the corpus have convinced us that the human body and not Christ's personal body is in view. Also, we are satisfied that the four references to Christ as $\kappa\epsilon\phi\alpha\lambda\acute{\eta}$ vis-à-vis the church, His $\sigma\hat{\omega}\mu\alpha$, provide us with no exegetical warrant for the prevailing assumption that Christ and the church are to be anatomically

SUMMARY AND CONCLUSION

conjoined in some inexplicably mystical or even metaphorical manner. Rather, we have determined that Paul, the apostle to the Gentiles (Col. 1:24-29; Eph. 3:1-3), chose to lay hold of the human σῶμα, the *whole* human σῶμα, as one of the many metaphors for the church; as one of the many metaphors with which to describe whose who had gone from death to life; to describe those who had now come to experience the communal joy of spiritual fellowship with their risen Lord.

Speaking of metaphors, Frye's reminder is perhaps most appropriate here. He writes:

> ...metaphors are curiously self-contradictory. First, they assert, or appear to assert, that A is B. But they also imply that A is quite obviously not B, and nobody could be fool enough to imagine that it was. The metaphor is totally illogical, for logic preserves the common-sense principle that A is always A, never B.[12]

With this before us, then, let us now summarize what Paul, in four of his epistles that span about a decade,[13] sought to tell and teach Christians at Corinth, Rome, Colossae, Laodicea, and perhaps, Hierapolis and Ephesus, about σῶμα as E in relation to the mystery of the gospel (see Col. 1:21-29; Eph. 3:1-3). For Paul, the human σῶμα provides a rather useful metaphorical backdrop against which to discuss the kind of relationships that should prevail not only among Christians but also between them and Christ Himself.

When we merge all the contexts within which σῶμα as E appears in the corpus, we gain some insight into Paul's concept of the church; of those to whom God in Christ has now given the benefits and the blessings of the new age -- whether they be Jew or Gentile (1 Cor. 12:12-27; Col. 1:24ff.; Eph. 2:11-16; 3:1-6), male or female (1 Cor. 11:2-16; 12:12-27), affluent or indigent (1 Cor. 11:17-34), slave or free (Col. 3:11-15). For Paul, the church, both local and universal, has been endowed with diverse gifts each of which, like the body's limbs, must be considered necessary but insufficient for both life and growth (see 1 Cor. 12-14; Rom. 12; Col. 1:24ff.; Eph. 4:4ff.); for him, the church, both local and universal, is owned by Christ and operated through His Spirit (see 1 Cor. 12:13,27; Rom. 12:5; Col. 1:18,24ff.; Eph. 3:6); and for him, the church, both local and universal, is the place where love, unity, equality, purity, peace and truth are ever to abound (1 Cor. 10:17; 11:29; 12:31; Col. 3:11-15; Eph. 4:11-16; 5:21-33).

As we promised at the beginning of our study, we will, in conclusion, also briefly address ourselves to three specific issues. They are: (1) the question of ecclesiological developments and/or deviations that may have

THE CHURCH AS THE BODY OF CHRIST

arisen on the basis of σῶμα; (2) the implications of this study for Pauline ecclesiology as a whole; and (3) a reconsideration of the source hypotheses in light of our investigation and findings.

Concerning the first, we found no reason to believe that Paul may have moved from a relatively undeveloped to a more profound σῶμα ecclesiology, going from 1 Cor. to Eph.; or, that he deviated substantially from his earlier usage(s). Two examples should suffice: (1) It is not true to say that σῶμα in 1 Cor. and Rom. refers to the body *in toto* whereas in Col. and Eph., it is headless. We have argued that this distinction is exegetically implausible;[14] and (2) It is not entirely true to say that whereas σῶμα refers only to the local church in 1 Cor. and Rom., it refers to the universal or catholic church in Col. and Eph.[15] Such a distinction is too neat for the evidence. Granted, the church is described consistently in more universal terms in Eph. (see 1:23; 2:16; 3:6; 4:4-16). But then, this may be due, more than anything else, to the possibility that originally, Eph. was written as a circular letter or encyclical to Christians in different communities in Asia Minor.

When we consider the other three epistles, however, we find that Paul is able to slip from one level (the local) to the other (the universal) quite readily. In writing to the Corinthians, he likens the church to a human body of which he, and presumably others not at Corinth, are a part (see 1 Cor. 10:16f.); and later, in his mention of charisms such as apostleship and prophecy, it is rather doubtful that he has only the local church at Corinth in mind (see 1 Cor. 12:12-30). In Rom., he makes mention of the fact that it is we (presumably himself and others) who, with the Roman Christians, constitute the body (12:5). And in Col., he seems to speak universally of the church as σῶμα in 1:18 and 2:19 but less obviously so in 1:24 and 3:15.[16] In other words, Paul, from the beginning, was able to liken both the local and the universal church to σῶμα -- a human σῶμα.[17]

Instead of developments and deviations, what we do find is that Paul is able to emphasize different aspects of the σῶμα metaphor in accordance with the specific pastoral issue(s) with which he is grappling. He is able to do so because of what Caird aptly refers to as "a high degree of correspondence,"[18] between the church and the attributes and activities of the human body. To the Corinthians, for instance, he can stress unity (1 Cor. 10:16f.), inter-relationships (11:29), and inter-dependence (12:12-27); to the Romans, it is unity and reciprocity (12:4-8); to the Colossians (and Laodiceans), it is submission (1:18), suffering (1:24; cf. 1 Cor. 12:26), growth and harmony (2:19; 3:11-15); and in Eph., it is all of the above (see 1:22f.; 2:16; 3:6; 4:4-16; 5:21-33).

In terms of our second promise, namely, a statement on the implications of our study for Pauline ecclesiology as a whole, let us make three observations: First, σῶμα as ecclesiological language should no longer be used as a basis upon which to build what may be regarded as a triumphalistic ecclesiology in which Christ via His body and the church as body are treated as one and the same -- however that oneness is understood; second, σῶμα as an ecclesiological metaphor is not to be allowed to say so much that it renders almost inaudible the voice of other Pauline metaphors for the church. Clowney, for example, has put his finger on the abiding problem caused by our over-elevating any ecclesiological metaphor at the expense of others within the N.T. as a whole. In his words: "So long as one metaphor is isolated and made a model, men [sic] are free to tailor the church to their errors and prejudices."[19]   One inference that can and should be drawn from our study is that overall, σῶμα is no closer to the divine than the others.

Our third observation, notwithstanding Clowney's warning, is that we should resist the temptation to swing with the proverbial pendulum. That is to say, by exegetically exposing σῶμα as the human body, the *whole* human body, and not Christ's personal body in any sense, does not mean that σῶμα should now be discarded as "just another metaphor" which perhaps, has long outlived its usefulness. The idea of dynamism and development -- of σῶμα -- imparts to the church a "flesh-and-blood" character. The language of living and loving, of co-ordination and co-operation, is entirely compatible with, and therefore, is usually yoked to it.[20]

And finally, the source hypotheses about which we can and will be rather brief as well: As we demonstrated at the beginning of our study, much thoughtful energy has been expended in an abortive attempt to account for the provenance of this distinctive Pauline use of σῶμα. So much so that it could almost be said: *quot homines, tot sententiae.*[21]   The fact is, we really do not and perhaps, will never know where Paul got this creative idea of speaking about the church as a human body. Besides, it is not inconceivable that he may well have given it birth himself.[22]   In the end, however, it is neither important for, nor determinative to, our understanding of how he actually uses it in his epistles; and for that reason, we have chosen not to join the hunt. We need not and therefore, will not scour land and sea in search of the source(s) of it. The most we can say is that our thesis gives 'thumbs down' to any hypothesis which keeps alive the assumption that in the Pauline corpus identity of bodies is being advocated, i.e., Christ's and the church's; or any hypothesis which moves us in that direction without having the two bodies actually meet and merge. We take this position, of course, because our study of σῶμα as E in 1 Cor., Rom., Col., and Eph., has led us to conclude that:

THE CHURCH AS THE BODY OF CHRIST

In the Pauline corpus, the human σῶμα, and not Christ's personal σῶμα, is used consistently as the *tertium comparationis* for the church as σῶμα and that any 'solution' which suggests a mystical or metaphorical relationship between Christ's personal σῶμα and the church as σῶμα or by extension, any 'solution' which implies a physiological understanding of κεφαλή in relation to Christ and the church, His σῶμα, will not do.[23]

ENDNOTES

Chapter Seven

1. See p. 11, n. 3.

2. See Best, *One Body,* pp. 192ff.; Jewett, *Paul's Anthropological Terms,* pp. 203ff; and Schmidt, *Der Leib Christi,* pp. 249f.

3. See p. 11, n. 3.

4. See p. 15, n. 33.

5. See p. xix, n. 16.

6. See Branick, *The Church as Idea and Fact,* p. 47. Other ecclesiological metaphors include field, building, and temple (1 Cor. 3); the resurrected people (Rom. 6); the olive tree (Rom. 9-11); and the family (Eph. 3). See Minear, *Images.*

7. E.g., Moule, *The Origin of Christology;* and Ziesler, *Pauline Christianity.*

8. E.g., Gundry, *SŌMA,* pp. 223ff. However, we could not endorse everything Gundry and others had to say about σῶμα as E either; e.g., the assumption that a detailed discussion of σῶμα as A is necessary for an understanding of σῶμα as E (see p. 59, n. 80 of this study).

9. Here, we are in basic agreement with scholars like Caird, *Paul's Prison Epistles;* Gibbs, *Creation and Redemption;* and Ridderbos, *Paul.*

10. See pp. 7ff.

11. For σῶμα as E, again see 1 Cor. 10:17; 11:29; 12:13,27; Rom. 12:5; Col. 1:18,24; 2:19; 3:15; Eph. 1:23; 2:16; 3:6; 4:4,12,16; 5:23,30 (18 times); and for κεφαλή, see Col. 1:18; 2:19; Eph. 4:15; 5:23 (4 times).

12. N. Frye, "The Expanding World of Metaphor," p. 588.

13. This, of course, presupposes Pauline authorship for Eph. -- a position to which we tentatively committed ourselves in this study. For those who do not subscribe to Pauline authorship, the period can stretch to as much as forty years.

14. See Chapters Five and Six, section C, for details; and Ziesler, *op. cit.,* pp. 54f. for whom there is significant development.

15. E.g., Küng, *The Church,* p. 299.

16. Also see Bruce, *Col.* pp. 237ff., for a similar view.

17. Incidentally, the Christological conundrum that this obviously creates has not been addressed by those who regard the personal body of Christ and the body of the church as being one and the same. In practical terms, how many personal bodies of Christ will there be if *each* Christian community, be it the house church or the local church (see Branick, *House Church),* and all together are considered His very body? For an allusive reference to such a Christological problem, see Ziesler, *op. cit.,* pp. 62f.

18. Caird, *The Language and Imagery of the Bible*, p. 153.

19. Clowney, "Interpreting the Biblical Models of the Church," p. 105.

20. We do concur with Ridderbos. Concerning both metaphors of 'head' and 'body', and the profound pneumatic unity between Christ and the church, he writes: "They ('head' and 'body')...do not occupy a monopolistic position in Paul's ecclesiology. But we may surely be permitted to say that they give expression to that unity (between Christ and the Church) in a fashion that in the richness of its possibilities for application is nowhere surpassed or even has its equal in all of Paul's preaching and in the whole of the New Testament." See, *Paul*, p. 383.

21. See pp. 2-7, for the list of nine hypotheses again.

22. E.g., *à la* Ziesler, *op. cit.,* p. 56.

23. See Chapter One, Section B.

SELECTED BIBLIOGRAPHY

1. Primary Sources

Aland, K. *et al.,* ed. *The Greek New Testament,* 3rd. edn. Munster, 1975.

Elliger, K. *et al. Biblia Hebraica Stuttgartensia.* Stuttgart, 1968-76.

Nestle, E. and A. *et al. Novum Testamentum Graece.* 26th edn., revised. Stuttgart, 1981.

The Bible. *Authorized (King James) Version.* 1611.

-----. *Revised Standard Version.* New York: Thomas Nelson and Sons, 1952.

Rahlfs, A. ed. *Septuaginta.* 2 vols. Stuttgart, 1961.

2. Reference Works

Bauer, W., *et al. A Greek-English Lexicon of the New Testament and Other Early Christian Literature.* Chicago: Chicago University Press, 1959.

Blass, F., Debrunner, A., and Funk, R. *A Greek Grammar of the New Testament and Other Early Christian Literature.* Chicago: Chicago University Press, 1962.

Brown, F., Driver, S.R. and Briggs, C.A. *A Hebrew and English Lexicon of the Old Testament.* Oxford: Clarendon Press, 1952.

Danby, H. *The Mishnah.* Oxford: Oxford University Press, 1933.

Hatch, E. and Redpath, H.A. *A Concordance to the Septuagint and Other Greek Versions of the Old Testament.* Oxford: Clarendon Press, 1897.

Metzger, B.M. *Index to Periodical Literature on the Apostle Paul.* Leiden: E.J. Brill, 1966.

-----. *Textual Commentary on the Greek New Testament.* New York: United Bible Societies, 1971.

Morgenthaler, R. *Statistik Des Neutestamentlichen Wortschatzes.* Zurich, 1958.

Morton, A.Q. *et al. A Critical Concordance to the Letter of Paul to the Ephesians: The Computer Bible.* Vol. XXII. Biblical Research Associates, 1980.

-----. *A Critical Concordance to the Letter of Paul To The Colossians. The Computer Bible.* Vol. XXIV. Biblical Research Associates, 1981.

3. Secondary Sources

(a) Articles

Agnew, F.H. "The Origin of the N.T. Apostle-Concept: A Review of Research," *JBL* 105 (1986): 75-96.

Ahern, B.M. "The Christian's Union With the Body of Christ in Corinthians, Galatians, and Romans," *CBQ* 23 (1961): 199-209.

Allan, J.A. "The 'In Christ' Formula in Ephesians," *NTS* 5 (1958-59):54-62.

Barth, M. "A Chapter On The Church: The Body of Christ," *Int.* 12 (1958): 133-136.

Barton, S.C. "Paul's Sense of Place: An Anthropological Approach to Community Formation in Corinth," *NTS* 105 (1986): 225-246.

Batey, R. "The *MIA SARX* Union of Christ and the Church," *NTS* 13 (1966-67): 270-281.

Bedale, S. "The Meaning of *Kephalē* in the Pauline Epistles," *JTS* 5 (1954): 211-215.

Benoit, P. "Corps, tête et plerôme dans les épîtres de la captivité," *RB* 63 (1956): 7ff.

Bonnard, P. "L'Église corps du Christ dans le Paulinisme," *RThPh* 3 (1958): 268-82.

Bouyer, L. "Ou en est la Théologie du Corps Mystique?" *RSR* 22 (1948): 313-333.

Boyd, D.G. "Spirit and Church in 1 Corinthians 12-14 and the Acts of the

Apostles," in *Spirit Within Structure: Essays in Honor of George Johnston on the Occasion of His Seventieth Birthday.* Edited by E.J. Furcha. Pennsylvania: Pickwick Publications, 1983.

Brooks, O.S. "A Contextual Interpretation of Galatians 3:27," in *Studia Biblica: Papers on Paul and Other New Testament Authors (Sixth International Congress on Biblical Studies).* Edited by E.A. Livingstone. Sheffield: JSOT Press, 1980.

Brown, R.E. "The Unity and Diversity in New Testament Ecclesiology," in *New Testament Essays.* New York: Doubleday, 1965.

Brunt, J. "Rejected, Ignored, or Misunderstood? The Fate of Paul's Approach to the Problem of Food Offered to Idols in Early Christianity," *NTS* 31 (1985): 113-124.

Burney, C.F. "Christ as the *Archē* of Creation," *JTS* 27 (1925-26): 160-177.

Callan, T. "Prophecy and Ecstasy in Graeco-Roman Religion and in 1 Corinthians," *Nov. T.* 27 (1985): 125-140.

Cadbury, H.J. "The Dilemma of Ephesians," *NTS* 5 (1958-59): 91-102.

Culliton, J. "Lucien Cerfaux's Contribution Concerning 'The Body of Christ'," *CBQ* 29 (1967): 41-59.

Cuming, G.J. "EPOTISTHĒMEN (1 Corinthians 12:13)," *NTS* 27 (1981): 283-285.

Daines, B. "Paul's Use of the Analogy of the Body of Christ, with Special Reference to 1 Corinthians 12," *EvQ* 54 (1982): 71-78.

Davis, P.G. "The Mythic Enoch: New Light on Christology," *SR* 13 (1984): 335-343.

Denton, D.R. "Inheritance in Paul and Ephesians," *EvQ* 54 (1982): 157-162.

Dianich, S. "The Current State of Ecclesiology," in *Where Does The Church Stand?* Edited by G. Alberigo *et al., Con.,* vol. 146. New York: The Seabury Press, 1981.

Dillistone, F.W. "How is the Church Christ's Body?" *TT* 1 (1945-46): 62ff.

129

Dodd, C.H. "Ephesians," in *ABC*. Edited by F.C. Eiselen *et al.* New York: Abingdon, 1929.

Ellis, E.E. "A Note on Pauline Hermeneutics," *JTS* 5 (1954): 211-215.

-----. "Paul and His Co-workers," *NTS* 17 (1971): 437-452.

-----. "*Sōma* in First Corinthians," *Int.* 44 (1990): 132-144.

Fenton, J. "Mystici Corporis and the Definition of the Church," *AER* 128 (1953): 448-459.

Furnish, V.P. "Belonging to Christ: A Paradigm for Ethics in First Corinthians," *Int.* 44 (1990): 145-157.

Havet, J. "Christ collectif ou Christ individuelle - 1 Cor. 12:12?" *EThL* 23 (1947): 499-520.

Hick, R.I. "Aesop and the Organic Body: The Body Political and the Body Ecclesiastical," *JBR* 31 (1980): 29-35.

Hill, A.E. "The Temple of Asclepius: An Alternative Source for Paul's Body Theology," *JBL* 99 (1980): 287-309.

Hooker, M.D. "Were There False Teachers in Colossae?" in *Christ and Spirit in the New Testament.* Edited by B. Linders *et al.* Cambridge: At the University Press, 1973.

Johnston, G. "The Constitution of the Church in the New Testament," in *PCB*. Edited by M. Black. Edinburgh:Thomas Nelson and Sons, 1962.

-----. "The Doctrine of the Church in the New Testament," in *PCB*. Edited by M. Black. Edinburgh: Thomas Nelson and Sons, 1962.

Judge, E.A. "Demythologizing the Church," *Int.* 11 (1972): 155-167.

Käsemann, E. "Eine urchristliche Taufliturgie" in *Festschrift Rudolf Bultmann zum 65 Geburstag.* Edited by E. Wolf. Stuttgart, 1949.

Kearns, C. "The Church as the Body of Christ According to St. Paul," *IER* 90 (1958): 1-11; 145-157; and *IER* 91 (1959): 1-15; 313-327.

Keck, L.E. "Toward the Renewal of New Testament Christology," *NTS* 32

(1986): 362-377.

Kemphorne, R. "Incest and the Body of Christ: A Study of 1 Corinthians vi. 12-20," *NTS* 14 (1968): 568-574.

Kesich, V. "Unity and Diversity in New Testament Ecclesiology," *SVTQ* 19 (1975): 109-127.

Kilpatrick, G.S. "A Parallel to the New Testament Use of *Sōma*," *JTS* 13 (1962): 17ff.

Knox, W.L. "Parallels to the N.T. Use of *Sōma*," *JTS* 39 (1938): 243-246.

Koenig, J. "From Mystery to Ministry: Paul as Interpreter of Charismatic Gifts," *USQR* 33 (1978): 167-174.

Kress, R. "The Church as *Communio:* Trinity and Incarnation as the Foundation of Ecclesiology," *Jur.* 36 (1976): 127-58.

La Piana, G. "Foreign Groups in Rome during the First Centuries of the Empire," *HTR* 20 (1927): 183-203.

Lawlor, F.X. s.v. "Mystical Body of Christ," in *NCE* 10 (1967): 166-170.

Leon-Dufour, X., s.v. "Corps," in *Vocabulaire de Théologie Biblique.* Edited by X. Leon-Dufour *et al.* Paris: Cerf, 1962.

Luzzi, J. "Solidaridad del *sōma tou Cristou*," *CyF* 16 (1960): 3045.

Macdonald, M. "Women Holy in Body and Spirit: The Social Setting of 1 Corinthians," *NTS* 36 (1990): 161-181.

Malina, B. "Religion in the World of Paul," *BTB* 16 (1986): 92-101.

Martelet, G. "Le Mystère du Corps de l'Ésprit dans le Christ resuscité dans l'Église," *VC* 12 (1958): 39ff.

May, M.A. "The Ordination of Women: The Churches' Responses to *Baptism, Eucharist, and Ministry*," *JES* 26 (1989): 251-269.

McNamara, K. "The Idea of Church: Modern Developments in Ecclesiology," *IQR* 33 (1966): 99-113.

Moo, J. "Israel and Paul in Romans 7:7-12," *NTS* 32 (1986): 122-135.

Moore, M.S. "Ephesians 2:14-16: A History of Interpretation," *EvQ* 54 (1982): 163-168.

Murphy-O'Connor, J. "Sex and Logic in 1 Corinthians 11:2-16," *CBQ* 42 (1980): 482-500.

O'Day, G. "Jeremiah 9:22-23 and 1 Corinthians 1:26-31: A Study in Intertextuality," *JBL* 109 (1990): 259-267.

Patterson, J.M. "House Churches in Rome," *V.C.* 23 (1969): 264-272.

Perriman, A. "'His Body, Which is the Church...': Coming to Terms with Metaphor," *EvQ* 62 (1990): 123-142.

Porter, J.R. "The Legal Aspects of the Concept of 'Corporate Personality' in the Old Testament," *VT* 15 (1965): 361-380.

Ramoroson, L. "L'Église, Corps Du Christ dans les Écrits Pauliniens: Simple Esquisses," *Sc. et Es.* 30 (1978): 129ff.

Rawlinson, A.E.J. "Corpus Christi," in *Mysterium Christi*. Edited by G.K.A. Bell *et al.* London: Longmans, 1930.

Reicke, B. "Caesarea, Rome, and the Captivity Epistles," in *Apostolic History and the Gospel*. Edited by W.W. Gasque. Grand Rapids: Wm. B. Eerdmans, 1970.

Reid, J.K.S. "Article Review: Baptism, Eucharist, and Ministry," *SJT* 37 (1984): 519-527.

Rese, M. "Church and Israel in the Deutero-Pauline Letters," *SJT* 43 (1990): 19-32.

Reuss, J. "Die Kirche als 'Leib Christi' und die Herkunft dieser Vorstellung bei dem Apostel Paulus," *BZ* (1958): 103-127.

Richards, J.R. "Romans and 1 Corinthians: Their Chronological Relationship and Comparative Dates," *NTS* 13 (1966): 14-30.

Richardson, W. "Liturgical Order and Glossalalia in 1 Corinthians 14:26c-33a," *NTS* 32 (1986): 144-151.

Rogerson, J.W. "The Hebrew Conception of Corporate Personality: A Reexamination," *JTS* 21 (1970): 1-16.

Schmidt, D. "The Authenticity of 2 Thessalonians: Linguistic Arguments," in *SBLSP*. Chico, CA: Scholars Press, 1983.

Schlier, H., s.v. "Κεφαλή," in TDNT, Vol. III. Grand Rapids: Wm. B. Eerdmans, 1971.

Schweizer, E. "Die Kirche als Leib Christi in den Paulinischen Homologumena," *TLZ* 86 (1961): 161-174.

-----., "Σōma," in *TDNT*, vol. VII. Grand Rapids: Wm. B. Eerdmans, 1971.

-----., "The Church as the Missionary Body of Christ," *NTS* 8 (1961): 1-11.

Scroggs, R. "Paul and the Eschatological Woman," *JAAR* 40 (1972):281-303.

Taylor, T.M. "Kingdom, Family, Temple, and Body: Implications from the Biblical Doctrine of the Church for the Christian Attitude Amid Cultural and Racial Tensions," *Int.* 12 (1958): 174-193.

Thornton, L.S. "The Body of Christ," in *The Apostolic Ministry*. Edited by K.E. Kirk. London: Hodder and Stoughton, 1946.

Via, D.O., Jr. "The Church as the Body of Christ in the Gospel of Matthew," *SJT* 11 (1958): 271-286.

Watson, D.F. "1 Corinthians 10:23 - 11:1 in the Light of Greco-Roman Rhetoric," *JBL* 108 (1989): 301-318.

Wedderburn, A.J.M. "The Body of Christ and Related Concepts in 1 Corinthians," *SJT* 24 (1971): 74-96.

-----., "A New Testament Church Today?" *SJT* 31 (1978): 517-532.

-----., "Some Observations of Paul's Use of the Phrases ‛in Christ' and ‛with Christ'," *JSNT* 25 (1985): 83-97.

Worgul, G.S., Jr. "People of God, Body of Christ: Pauline Ecclesiological Contrasts," *BTB* 12 (1982): 24-28.

Yates, R. "A Re-examination of Eph. 1:23," *E.T.* 83 (1971-72): 146-151.

Zapalena, T. "Vos Estis Corpus Christi (1 Cor. 12:27)," *VD* 37 (1959): 78-95; 162-170.

Ziesler, J.A. *"Sōma* in the *LXX,"* *Nov. T.* 25 (1983): 133-145.

(b) Books

Abbott, W. ed. *The Documents of Vatican II.* New York: Guild Press, 1966.

Adair, John. *The Becoming Church.* London: S.P.C.K., 1977.

Alter, Robert and Frank Kermode, eds. *The Literary Guide to the Bible.* Cambridge, MA: Harvard University Press, 1987.

Arnold, Clinton E. *Ephesians: Power and Magic: The Concept of Power in Ephesians in Light of its Historical Setting,* in SNTSMS. Cambridge: At the University Press, 1989.

Aubert, R. *Prophets in the Church: Theology in the Age of Renewal,* in *Con.* vol 37. New York: Paulist Press, 1968.

Balch, D. *Let Wives Be Submissive: The Domestic Code in 1 Peter.* Chico: Scholars Press, 1981.

Banks, R. *Paul's Idea of Community.* Exeter: Paternoster Press, 1981.

Barr, J. *The Semantics of Biblical Language.* London: Oxford University Press, 1961.

Barrett, C.K. *Essays on Paul.* Philadelphia: Westminster Press, 1982.

Barth, M. *The Broken Wall: A Study of the Epistle to the Ephesians.* Chicago: The Judson Press, 1959.

Batey, R. *New Testament Nuptial Imagery.* Leiden: E.J. Brill, 1971.

Beker, J.C. *Paul The Apostle.* Philadelphia: Fortress Press, 1980.

Best, E. *One Body in Christ: A Study in the Relationship of the Church to Christ in the Epistles of the Apostle Paul.* London: S.P.C.K., 1955.

Boff, L. *Ecclesiogenesis: The Base Communities Re-invent the Church.* Maryknoll: Orbis, 1986.

Bouyer, L. *L'Église de Dieu: Corps de Christ et Temple de L'Ésprit*. Paris: Cerf, 1970.

Bowe, B.E. *A Church in Crisis: Ecclesiology and Paranaesis in Clement of Rome*, in HDR. Minneapolis, MN: Fortress, 1988.

Branick, V.P. *The House Church in the Writings of Paul*. Delaware: Michael Glazier, 1989.

Brown, R.E. *et al. Antioch and Rome: New Testament Cradles of Catholic Christianity*. New York: Paulist Press, 1983.

Bultmann, R. *Theology of the New Testament*. Vol. 1. New York: Scribner and Sons, 1951.

Burnham, F.B. *Postmodern Theology: Christian Faith in a Pluralist World*. San Francisco: Harper and Row, 1989.

Byrne, B. *Paul and the Christian Woman*. Minnesota: The Liturgical Press, 1988.

Caird, F.B. *The Language and Imagery of the Bible*. Philadelphia: The Westminster Press, 1980.

Carson, D.A. ed. *Biblical Interpretation and the Church: The Problem of Contextualization*. Nashville: Thomas Nelson Publishers, 1984.

Cerfaux, L. *The Church in the Theology of St. Paul*. New York: Herder and Herder, 1959.

Chestnut, G.F. *Images of Christ: An Introduction to Christology*. Minneapolis: Seabury Press, 1984.

Chevasse, C. *The Bride of Christ*. London: The Religious Book Club, n.d.

Childs, B.S. *The New Testament as Canon: An Introduction*. Philadelphia: Fortress Press, 1984.

Cobble, J.F. *The Church and the Powers: A Theology of Church Structure*. Peabody, MA: Hendrickson Publishers, 1988.

Collins, R.F. *Letters That Paul Did Not Write: The Epistle to the Hebrews and Pauline Pseudepigrapha*. Delaware: Michael Glazier, 1988.

Colpe, C. *Die religionsgeschichtliche Schule: Darstellung und Kritik ihres Bildes vom gnostischen Erlösermythus.* Göttingen, 1961.

Corley, B.C. ed. *Colloquy on New Testament Studies: A Time for Reappraisal and Fresh Approaches.* Georgia: Mercer Press, 1983.

Court, J. and K. *The New Testament World.* Englewood Cliffs, NJ: Prentice-Hall, 1990.

Davies, W.D. *Paul and Rabbinic Judaism.* London: S.P.C.K., 1948.

-----. *Jewish and Pauline Studies.* Philadelphia: Fortress Press, 1984.

Deimel, L. *Leib Christi: Sinn und Grenzen einer Deutung des inner kirchlichen Lebens.* Freiburg, 1940.

De Lorenzi, L. ed. *Freedom and Love: The Guide for Christian Life (1 Cor. 8-10; Rm. 14-15).* Rome: St. Paul's Abbey, 1981.

Donovan, D. *The Church as Idea and Fact.* Delaware: Michael Glazier, 1988.

Doohan, H. *Paul's Vision of Church.* Delaware: Michael Glazier, 1989.

Dudley, C.S. and Hilgert, E. *New Testament Tensions and the Contemporary Church.* Philadelphia: Fortress Press, 1987.

Dulles, A. *Models of the Church.* New York: Doubleday, 1974.

Dulles, A. and Granfield, P. *The Church: A Bibliography.* Delaware: Michael Glazier, 1985.

Dungan, D.G. *The Sayings of Jesus in the Teachings of Paul.* Philadelphia: Fortress Press, 1971.

Dunn, J.D.G. *Baptism in the Holy Spirit: A Re-examination of the New Testament Teaching on the Gift of the Spirit in Relation to Pentecostalism Today,* in *SBT.* London: SCM Press, 1970.

Elliott, J.H. *A Home for the Homeless: A Sociological Exegesis of 1 Peter -- Its Situation and Strategy.* Philadelphia: Fortress Press, 1981.

Ellis, E.E. *Paul's Use of the Old Testament.* Edinburgh: T. & T. Clark, 1957.

-----. *Pauline Theology: Ministry and Society.* Grand Rapids: Wm. B. Eerdmans, 1989.

Flew, R.N. *The Nature of the Church.* New York: Harper and Row, 1952.

Francis, F.O. *et al.* *Conflict at Colossae: A Problem in The Interpretation of Early Christianity Illustrated by Selected Modern Studies.* Montana: Scholars Press, 1975.

George, T. ed. *John Calvin and the Church.* Louisville: Westminster/John Knox Press, 1989.

Gibbs, J.G. *Creation and Redemption: A Study in Pauline Theology.* Leiden: E.J. Brill, 1971.

Goosens, W. *L'Église Corps Du Christ D'Après Saint Paul: Étude de Théologie Biblique.* Paris: J. Gabala, 1949.

Grudem, W. *The Gift of Prophecy in 1 Corinthians.* Washington, D.C.: University Press of America, 1982.

Guénel, V. ed. *Le Corps et Le Corps Du Christ dans la Prémière Épître aux Corinthiens.* Paris: Cerf, 1983.

Gundry, R. *SÕMA in Biblical Theology: With Emphasis on Pauline Anthropology.* Cambridge: At the University Press, 1976.

Hall, D.J. *Has the Church a Future?* Philadelphia: The Westminster Press, 1980.

-----. *Thinking the Faith: Christian Theology in a North American Context.* Minneapolis: Augsburg, 1989.

Halton, T. *The Church: Message of the Fathers of the Church.* Delaware: Michael Glazier, 1985.

Hamer, J. *The Church is a Communion.* London: Geoffrey Chapman, 1964.

Hanson, A.T. *Studies in Paul's Theology and Technique.* London: S.P.C.K., 1974.

Hanson, S. *The Unity of the Church in the New Testament.* Uppsala, 1946.

Harrington, D.J. *God's People in Christ: New Testament Perspectives on the Church and Judaism.* Philadelphia: Fortress Press, 1980.

-----. *Light of All Nations: Essays on the Church in New Testament Research.* Delaware: Michael Glazier, 1982.

Hay, D.M. *Glory at the Right Hand: Ps. 110 in Early Christianity.* Nashville: Abingdon, 1973.

Hays, R.B. *Echoes of Scripture in the Letters of Paul.* New Haven: Yale University Press, 1989.

Hengel, M. *Between Jesus and Paul: Studies in the Earliest History of Christianity.* Philadelphia: Fortress Press, 1983.

Hinson, E.G. ed. *Understandings of the Church in Sources of Early Christian Thought.* Philadelphia: Fortress Press, 1985.

Holmberg, B. *Paul and Power: The Structure of Authority in the Primitive Church as Reflected in the Pauline Epistles.* Lund: Studentlitteratur, 1978.

Hooker, M.D. *A Preface to Paul.* New York: Oxford University Press, 1980.

Hurst, L.D. and Wright, N.T. eds. *The Glory of Christ in the New Testament: Studies in Memory of George Bradford Caird.* Oxford: Oxford University Press, 1987.

Jay, E. *The Church: Its Changing Image Through Twenty Centuries.* 2 vols. London: S.P.C.K., 1978.

Jewett, P. *Paul's Anthropological Terms: A Study of Their Use in Conflict Settings.* Leiden: E.J. Brill, 1971.

Johnston, G. *The Doctrine of the Church in the New Testament.* Cambridge: At the University Press, 1943.

Jones, A.M. *Paul's Message of Freedom: What Does It Mean for the Black Church?* Chicago: The Judson Press, 1984.

Judge, E.A. *The Social Pattern of Christian Groups in the First Century.* London: Tyndale, 1960.

Käsemann, E. *Essays On New Testament Themes.* London: SCM Press, 1964.

-----. *Leib und Leib Christi.* Tübingen: Mohr, 1933.

-----. *Exegetische Versüche und Besinnungen.* Göttingen, 1960.

-----. *Perspectives on Paul.* Philadelphia: Fortress Press, 1971.

Kehl, N. *Der Christushymnus im Kolösserbrief.* Stuttgart, 1967.

Kilpatrick, G.D. *The Eucharist in Bible and Liturgy: The Moorhouse Lectures, 1975.* Cambridge: At the University Press, 1983.

Kim, S. *The Origin of Paul's Gospel.* Tübingen: Mohr, 1981.

Kirby, J.C. *Ephesians: Baptism and Pentecost.* Montreal: McGill University Press, 1968.

Knox, W.L. *St. Paul and the Church of the Gentiles.* Cambridge: At the University Press, 1939.

Koenig, J. *Charismata: God's Gifts for God's People.* Philadelphia: The Westminster Press, 1978.

Koester, H. *Introduction to the New Testament: Volume One -- History Culture, and Religion of the Hellenistic Age.* Philadelphia: Fortress Press, 1982.

Kümmel, W.G. *Introduction to the New Testament.* Trans. by A.J. Mattill, Jr. New York: Abingdon, 1966.

Küng, H. *The Church.* New York: Image Books, 1976.

-----. *The Church Maintained in Truth: A Theological Meditation.* New York: The Seabury Press, 1980.

-----. *Theology for the Third Millennium: An Ecumenical View.* New York: Doubleday, 1988.

Lang, Mabel. *Cure and Cult in Ancient Corinth: A Guide to The Asklepieion.* New Jersey: Princeton University Press, 1977.

Lesser, R.H. *The Church Indeed is His Body.* Bombay: St. Paul Publications,

1970.

Lewis, W. *Idol Meat in Corinth: The Pauline Argument in 1 Corinthians 8 and 10.* Chico: Scholars Press, 1985.

Longenecker, R. *Paul: Apostle of Liberty.* New York: Harper and Row, 1964.

Lyons, G. *Pauline Autobiography: Toward a New Understanding.* Atlanta, Georgia: Scholars Press, 1985.

MacDonald, M.Y. *The Pauline Churches: A Socio-Historical Study of Institutionalization in the Pauline and Deutero-Pauline Writings.* Cambridge: At the University Press, 1988.

Mack, B.L. *Rhetoric and the New Testament.* Minneapolis, MN: Frotress, 1990.

Malherbe, A.J. *Social Aspects of Early Christianity.* Baton Rouge: Louisiana State University Press, 1977.

-----. *Paul and the Popular Philosophers.* Minneapolis: Fortress Press, 1989.

Malina, B. *Christian Origins and Cultural Anthropology: Practical Models for Biblical Interpretation.* Atlanta: John Knox Press, 1986.

Martin, D.B. *Slavery as Salvation: The Metaphor of Slavery in Pauline Theology.* New Haven, CT: Yale University Press, 1990.

Martin, R. P. *Worship in the Early Church.* Grand Rapids: Wm. B. Eerdmans, 1964.

-----. *The Family and the Fellowship: New Testament Images of the Church.* Grand Rapids: Wm. B. Eerdmans, 1979.

-----. *The Spirit and the Congregation: Studies in 1 Corinthians 12-15.* Grand Rapids: Wm. B. Eerdmans, 1984.

Mascall, E.L. *Christ, the Christian, and the Church.* London: Longmans, 1946.

Mason, S. *et al.* *An Early Christian Reader.* Toronto: Canadian Scholars' Press, 1990.

Meeks, W. *The First Urban Christians: The Social World of the Apostle Paul.*

140

New Haven: Yale University Press, 1983.

Meier, J.P. *The Mission of Christ and His Church: Studies in Christology and Ecclesiology.* Delaware: Michael Glazier, 1990.

Mersch, E. *Le Corps Mystique du Christ.* Louvain: Museum Lessianum, 1933.

-----. *The Whole Christ: The Historical Development of the Doctrine of the Mystical Body.* Durham: Dobson Books, 1949.

-----. *The Theology of the Mystical Body.* St. Louis: B. Herden, 1958.

Meuzelaar, J.J. *Der Leib des Messias: Eine exegetische Studie über den Gedanken vom Leib Christi in den Paulusbriefen.* Assen, 1961.

Michel, O. *Das Zeugnis des Neuen Testaments von der Gemeinde.* Göttingen, 1941.

Minear, P.S. *Images of the Church in the New Testament.* Philadelphia: The Westminster Press, 1960.

-----. *Obedience of Faith: The Purposes of Paul in the Epistle to the Romans.* London: SCM Press, 1971.

Moltmann, J. *The Church in the Power of the Spirit: A Contribution to Messianic Ecclesiology.* New York: Harper and Row, 1977.

-----. *On Human Dignity: Political Theology and Ethics.* Philadelphia: Fortress Press, 1984.

Moule, C.F.D. *The Origin of Christology.* Cambridge: At the University Press, 1977.

Mura, E. *The Mystical Body of Christ.* St. Louis: B. Gerder, 1963.

Murphy-O'Connor, J. *Becoming Human Together: The Pastoral Anthropology of St. Paul.* Delaware: Michael Glazier, 1982.

Murray, R. *Symbols of Church: A Study in Early Syriac Tradition.* Cambridge: At the University Press, 1975.

Mussner, F. *Christus, das All und die Kirche im Epheserbrief.* Trier, 1955.

141

Nehrey, J.H. *Christ is Community: The Christologies of the New Testament.* Delaware: Michael Glazier, 1985.

O'Grady, J.F. *Models of Jesus.* New York: Doubleday, 1980.

Osiek, C. *What Are They Saying About the Social Setting of the New Testament?* New York: Paulist Press, 1984.

O'Toole, R. F. *Who is a Christian? A Study in Pauline Ethics.* Collegeville, MN: The Liturgical Press, 1990.

Panikulam, G. *Koinōnia in the New Testament.* Rome: Biblical Institute, 1979.

Pelton, R.S. ed. *The Church as the Body of Christ.* Indiana: University Of Notre Dame, 1963.

Percy, E. *Der Leib Christi in den paulinischen Homologumena und Antilogumena.* Lund, 1942.

-----. *Die Probleme der Kolösser-und Epheserbriefe.* Lund: Gleerup, 1946.

Petersen, N.R. *Rediscovering Paul: Philemon and the Sociology of Paul's Narrative World.* Philadelphia: Fortress Press, 1985.

Pfitzner, V.C. *Paul and the Agōn Motif.* Leiden: E.J. Brill, 1967.

Pritchard, J.P. *A Literary Approach to the New Testament.* Norman: University of Oklahoma Press, 1972.

Puskas, C.B. *An Introduction to the New Testament.* Peabody, MA: Hendrickson Publishers, 1989.

Rader, W. *The Church and Racial Hostility: A History of Interpretation of Ephesians 2:11-12.* Tübingen, 1978.

Rahner, Karl. *The Shape of the Church to Come.* London: S.P.C.K., 1974.

Richardson, P. *Paul's Ethic of Freedom.* Philadelphia: The Westminster Press, 1979.

Ridderbos, P. *Paul: An Outline of His Theology.* Grand Rapids: Wm. B. Eerdmans, 1975.

Rikhof, H. *The Concept of Church: A Methodological Inquiry into the Use of Metaphors in Ecclesiology.* London: Sheed and Ward, 1981.

Robinson, H.W. *The Christian Doctrine of Man.* Edinburgh: T. & T. Clark, 1913.

Robinson, J.A.T. *The Body: A Study in Pauline Theology.* London: SCM, 1952.

-----. *Redating the New Testament.* Philadelphia: The Westminster Press, 1976.

Roetzel, C.J. *Judgment in the Community: A Study of the Relationship Between Eschatology and Ecclesiology.* Leiden: E.J. Brill, 1972.

Sampley, J.P. *'And the Two Shall Become One Flesh': A Study of Traditions in Ephesians 5:21-33.* Cambridge: At the University Press, 1971.

-----. *Pauline Partnership in Christ: Christian Community and Commitment in Light of Roman Law.* Philadelphia: Fortress Press, 1983.

Sanders, E.P. *Paul, the Law, and the Jewish People.* Philadelphia: Fortress Press, 1983.

Schatzmann, A. *Pauline Theology of Charismata.* Peabody, MA: Hendrickson Publishers, 1987.

Schenke, H.M. *Der Gott 'Mensch' in der Gnosis: Ein religionsgeschichtlicher Beitrag zur Diskussion über die paulinische Anschauung von der Kirche als Leib Christi.* Göttingen, 1962.

Schmidt, K. *The Church.* London: Adam and Charles Black, 1950.

Schmidt, T. *Der Leib Christi. Eine Untersuchung zum Urchristlichen Gemeindegedanken.* Leipzig, 1919.

Schmithals, W. *Gnosticism in Corinth.* Nashville: Abingdon, 1971.

Schnackenburg, R. *The Church in the New Testament.* New York: Seabury Press, 1965.

Scholem, G. *Jewish Gnosticism, Merkabah Mysticism, and Talmudic Tradition.* New York: Schocken, 1960.

Schweitzer, A. *The Mysticism of Paul the Apostle*. London: A. and C. Clark, 1931.

Soiron, T. *Die Kirche als der Leib Christi*. Düsseldorf, 1951.

Stevens, R.J. *Community Beyond Division: Christian Life Under South Africa's Apartheid System*. New York: Vantage Press, 1984.

Thiessen, G. *The Social Setting of Pauline Christianity: Essays on Corinth*. Philadelphia: Fortress Press, 1982.

Thiselton, A.C. *The Two Horizons: New Testament Hermeneutics and Philosophical Description with Special Reference to Heidegger, Bultmann, Gadamer, and Wittgenstein*. Grand Rapids: Wm. B. Eerdmans, 1980.

Thornton, L.S. *The Common Life in the Body of Christ*. London: Dacre Press, 1944.

Thurian, M. ed. *Ecumenical Perspectives on Baptism, Eucharist, and Ministry*. Geneva: World Council of Churches, 1983.

Thuruthumaly, J. *Blessing in Paul*. India: Kerala, 1981.

Torrance, T.F. *Royal Priesthood*. Edinburgh: T. & T. Clark, 1955.

Tromp, S. *Corpus Christi Quod Est Ecclesia*. New York: Vantage Press, 1960.

Usami, K. *Somatic Comprehension of Unity: The Church in Ephesians*. Rome: Biblical Institute Press, 1983.

Verner, D.C. *The Household of God: The Social World of the Pastoral Epistles*. Chico: Scholars Press, 1981.

Welch, J.W. ed. *Chiasmus in Antiquity*. Hildesheim: Gerstenberg, 1981.

Weiss, H. *Paul of Tarsus: His Gospel and Life*. Rev. edn. Michigan: Andrews University Press, 1989.

Whiteley, D.E.H. *The Theology of St. Paul*. Philadelphia: Fortress Press, 1964.

Wikenhauser, A. *Die Kirche als der mystische Leib Christi nach dem Apostel Paulus*. Munster, 1949.

Yarbrough, O.L. *Not Like the Gentiles: Marriage Rules in the Letters of Paul.* Atlanta, Georgia: Scholars Press, 1985.

Ziesler, J. *Pauline Christianity,* in *OBS.* Oxford: Oxford University Press, 1983.

(c) Commentaries

Abbott, T.K. *A Critical and Exegetical Commentary on the Epistles to the Ephesians and to the Colossians.* Edinburgh: T. and T. Clark, 1897.

Barrett, C.K. *A Commentary on the First Epistle to the Corinthians,* in *HNTC.* New York: Harper and Row, 1968.

Barth, M. *Ephesians.* 2 vols. in *AB.* New York: Doubleday, 1974.

Best, E. *A Commentary on Romans,* in *CBC.* Cambridge: At the University Press, 1967.

Betz, H.D. *Galatians: A Commentary on Paul's Letter to the Church in Galatia,* in *Herm.* Philadelphia: Fortress Press, 1979.

Bruce, F.F. *1 and 2 Corinthians,* in *NCBC.* London: Oliphants, 1971.

-----. *Colossians, Philemon, and Ephesians,* in *NICNT.* Grand Rapids: Wm. B. Eerdmans, 1984.

Caird, G.B. *Paul's Letters from Prison.* Oxford: Oxford University Press, 1976.

Conzelmann, H. *A Commentary on the First Epistle to the Corinthians,* in *Herm.* Philadelphia: Fortress Press, 1975.

Cranfield, C.B. *A Commentary on Romans,* in *ICC.* Edinburgh: T. and T. Clark, 1979.

Dodd, C.H. *The Epistle of Paul to the Romans,* in *MNTC.* London: Collins Fontana Books, 1961.

Grosheide, F.W. *The First Epistle to the Corinthians,* in *NICNT.* Grand Rapids: Wm. R. Eerdmans, 1953.

Héring, J. *The First Epistle of St. Paul to the Corinthians.* London: The

Epworth Press, 1962.

Hugedé, N. *L'Épître Aux Ephésiens.* Génève: Labor et Fides, 1982.

Hurd, J.C. *The Origin of 1 Corinthians.* London: S.P.C.K., 1976.

Johnston, G. *Ephesians, Philippians, Colossians, and Philemon.* London: Thomas Nelson and Sons, 1967.

Käsemann, E. *Commentary on Romans.* Grand Rapids: Wm. B. Eerdmans, 1980.

Leenhardt, F.J. *The Epistle to the Romans: A Commentary.* London: 1961.

Lightfoot, J.B. *Saint Paul's Epistles to Colossians and to Philemon.* London: Macmillan, 1875.

Lohse, E. *Colossians and Philemon,* in *Herm.* Philadelphia: Fortress Press, 1971.

Martin, R.P. *Colossians: The Church's Lord and the Christian's Responsibility.* Grand Rapids: Zondervan, 1972.

-----. *Commentary on 1 and 2 Corinthians.* Waco, TX: Word, 1988.

Mitton, C.L. *Ephesians,* in *NCB.* London: Oliphants, 1976.

Murphy-O'Connor, J. *1 Corinthians.* Delaware: Michael Glazier, 1979.

O'Brien, P.T. *Colossians and Philemon.* Waco, Texas: Word, 1982.

Orr, W.F. *et al.* *A Commentary on 1 Corinthians,* in *AB.* New York: Doubleday, 1976.

Robertson, A. *et al.* *A Critical and Exegetical Commentary on the First Epistle of Paul to the Corinthians,* in *ICC.* Edinburgh: T. and T. Clark, 1967.

Robinson, J.A.T. *Wrestling With Romans.* Philadelphia: The Westminster Press, 1979.

Schweizer, E. *The Letter to the Colossians: A Commentary.* Minneapolis: Augsburg, 1976.

Synge, F.C. *St. Paul's Epistle to the Ephesians: A Theological Commentary.* London: S.P.C.K., 1941.

Talbert, C.H. *Reading Corinthians: A Literary and Theological Commentary on 1 and 2 Corinthians.* New York: Crossroad, 1989.

Thompson, G.H.P. *The Letters of Paul to the Ephesians, to the Colossians, and to Philemon.* Cambridge: At the University Press, 1967.

Weiss, J. *Der Erste Korintherbrief.* Göttingen, 1897.

Wilckens, U. *Der Brief An Die Römer (Rom. 6-11),* in *EKKNT.* Zurich, 1980.

Wright, N.T. *The Epistles of Paul to the Colossians and Philemon,* in *TNTC.* Grand Rapids: Wm. B. Eerdmans, 1987.

4. Unpublished Materials

Crutchley, D.E. *Tarsus, Jerusalem, or Rome: Understanding Paul's Use of Legal Metaphors in the Hauptbriefe.* Ph.D. Thesis, Southwestern Baptist Theological Seminary, 1985.

Lewis, L.A., Jr. *'As a Beloved Brother': The Function of Family Language in the Epistles of Paul.* Ph.D. Thesis, Yale University, 1985.

Smith, D. *Social Obligation in the Context of Communal Meals: A Study of the Christian Meal in 1 Corinthians in Comparison with Graeco-Roman Meals.* Th.D. Thesis, Harvard University, 1980.

Wright, N.T. *The Messiah and The People of God: A Study in Pauline Theology with Particular Reference to the Argument of the Epistle to the Romans.* D. Phil. Thesis, Oxford University, 1980.

Yorke, G.L.O.R. *Paul's Counsel Regarding the Head-Covering in 1 Cor. 11:2-16.* M.A. Thesis, Andrews University, 1977.

-----. "The Ecclesiological Handling of Σῶμα in 1 Corinthians: The Problem and a Proposal." Paper read at the New England Regional *SBL* Meetings held at Andover Newton Theological School, Massachusetts, U.S.A., March, 1985.

AUTHOR INDEX

152

SUBJECT INDEX

153